D1571210

CORPORATE COMEBACK

CORPORATE COMEBACK

Managing Turnarounds and Troubled Companies

Arnold S. Goldstein

WILEY

JOHN WILEY & SONS
New York • Chichester • Brisbane • Toronto • Singapore

Copyright © 1988 by Arnold S. Goldstein.
Published by John Wiley & Sons, Inc.

All rights reserved. Published simultaneously in Canada.

Reproduction or translation of any part of this work
beyond that permitted by Section 107 or 108 of the
1976 United States Copyright Act without the permission
of the copyright owner is unlawful. Requests for
permission or further information should be addressed to
the Permissions Department, John Wiley & Sons, Inc.

This publication is designed to provide accurate and
authoritative information in regard to the subject
matter covered. It is sold with the understanding that
the publisher is not engaged in rendering legal, accounting,
or other professional service. If legal advice or other
expert assistance is required, the services of a competent
professional person should be sought. *From a Declaration
of Principles jointly adopted by a Committee of the
American Bar Association and a Committee of Publishers.*

Library of Congress Cataloging-in-Publication Data:
Goldstein, Arnold S.
   Corporate Comeback: Managing turnarounds and troubled companies.
   Bibliography: p.
   1. Small business—United States—Management.
2. Small business—United States—Finance.   3. Indus-
trial management—United States.   4. Business
failures—United States.   I. Title.
HD62.7.G643   1988   658.1'55   87-27413
ISBN 0-471-84488-8

Printed in the United States of America
10 9 8 7 6 5 4 3 2 1

To the countless men and women
whose courage to turn failure into triumph
provided the inspiration for this book

And to my wife Marlene
for her tireless efforts
in helping me
create it

Preface

THERE'S a seemingly endless genre of books that glow with the tales of entrepreneurs waxing rich in their own successful businesses. It's the recurring theme on which we build the great American dream and best-selling book.

But this is not the world of business I know or write about. Instead, this is a book for the countless companies struggling to survive day by day. It's a book for beleaguered owners and managers who know too well what it's like to grope through a twilight of no cash, no credit, dwindling sales, and mounting losses. Most of all, this is a book for those who eagerly reach out for help in the face of impending failure. I write this book for these people.

Very few books have been written on the important subject of business turnarounds. The topic is extremely difficult to write about because it is so broad in scope. The existing turnaround books approach the subject from a widely different perspective, and, notwithstanding their valuable contributions, I sensed the need for a very different kind of book.

Corporate Comeback is the first widely available book to focus on the small and mid-sized firm. While there are valuable lessons to be learned from the exploits of companies such as Chrysler, Texaco, and Penn Central, the problems, options, opportunities, and resources of the corporate giants have little in common with those of smaller companies, which account for nine out of ten business failures. This book is intended to respond to their very special needs.

A turnaround is a far from simple task. Neither a "quick-fix" nor a magical formula for renewed success is offered here, for no such formula exists. Instead this book is designed to provide practical answers to "nuts and bolts" questions. The long, complex, and tedious process of a turnaround becomes more manageable as you discover how to define objectives, set goals, design a workable plan for total corporate recovery and then implement it step by step. Each chapter will guide you through an important phase of the turnaround, underscoring the successful strategies. Of more importance than doing things right, you will find advice on the right things to do.

Comprehensive in scope, *Corporate Comeback* goes beyond the strategies needed to save the failing business and fully explores alternate goals—from selling and liquidating the company to protecting yourself from personal liabilities arising from business failure.

Corporate Comeback will prove equally useful to managers who want to avoid financial difficulties, since much of its advice is as effective in preventing business ailments as it is in curing corporate ills.

Accountants, attorneys, and consultants who advise and counsel the problem business will gain new insights as will other constituent groups—lenders, creditors, employees, customers, and suppliers—who are inevitably affected by the stricken firm.

Every book is the sum and substance of the author's own experience and background. I bring to this book a rewarding and challenging career as a bankruptcy attorney with a leading Boston law firm. More recently I founded Galahow & Company which is today one of the nation's largest consulting firms to smaller companies in financial difficulty. During my 25-year career I have had the good fortune to help over 2000 troubled companies, a good many of which went on to achieve spectacular success and make valuable contributions in the marketplace. Yet I learned equally valuable lessons from those who failed. By sharing the experiences of my many clients who have traveled the same bumpy road, you will learn what it takes to put a financially troubled business together again. I remain indebted to my clients for all that they have taught me. They are the true architects of this book.

ARNOLD S. GOLDSTEIN

Chestnut Hill, Massachusetts
January 1988

ARNOLD S. GOLDSTEIN

Arnold S. Goldstein brings to this book an extensive background in turnaround management, as President of Galahow & Company, a leading national consulting firm in the field. He is also a senior partner in the Boston law firm of Meyers, Goldstein & Kosberg where he specializes in insolvency law. Over his 25-year career he has helped rescue nearly 2000 financially troubled companies.

Dr. Goldstein has authored 24 books on small business management, including *Turnaround Strategies* and *How to Save Your Business*.

Having lectured at several law schools and graduate schools of business, Dr. Goldstein also holds a full professorship at Northeastern University.

Contents

CORPORATE COMEBACK

1

Measuring the Corporate Half-Life

BUSINESS stands right up there alongside apple pie and base-ball as a fundamental part of the American way of life. We can trace this entrepreneurial heritage all the way back to the year 1606, when shares of stock were sold for $62 in the Jamestown venture to establish the first permanent settlement in America. Within a decade the young Jamestown venture was belly-up, leaving behind hordes of angry British investors, one Indian tribe reportedly still awaiting payment for corn and turkey, and a ragtag colony of entrepreneurs.

Thus is the underpinning of American business—on a stage since populated with countless other pioneers, adventurers, rogues, and just plain hard-working folks hoping for a better way of life. Some find it, others do not. However, they all soon learn that enthusiasm, energy, and euphoria are not always enough to steer them safely through the treach-erous rapids we call modern enterprise.

To most businesspeople, failure is anathema, a lurking demon ready to grab someone else but unable to touch them. But the grim reaper of business is, unfortunately, alive and well today. In fact, the grim reaper may be working overtime as the number of business failures reaches a new high with each passing year, enveloping a far broader range of or-ganizations, even companies that appeared indestructible only a few short years ago. Clearly the corporate half-life is becoming shorter.

1

The question is not whether a business will fail, but when. The commonly bantered statistic is that 80 percent of all start-ups fail within the first five years. Few companies survive more than a few decades, and when they do they are usually so significantly altered as to be unrecognizable. Tom Watson of IBM reminded us several years ago that

> Of the top 25 industrial corporations in the United States in 1900, only two remain in that select company today. One retains its original identity; the other is a merger of seven corporations on that original list. Two of those 25 failed. Three others merged and dropped behind. The remaining 12 have continued in business, but each has fallen substantially in its standing.

And two of those have folded since Tom Watson's observation.

Wherever we look we are reminded that success and failure are terms distanced only by time—often a very short time. Seventeen years ago *Forbes* magazine selected the 10 most "profitable" U.S. companies, focusing on net worth, profitability, and growth. By 1985 three of them no longer existed as independent companies and four others were floundering after years of dismal earnings.

Success can be fleeting. In a *Business Week* cover story entitled "Oops!" Thomas Peters and Robert Waterman's *In Search of Excellence* (Harper & Row, 1982) was given a dose of hindsight: in just two years 14 of the 43 companies cited for their excellence had hit the skids. Not one of these companies regained its former luster.

Corporate casualties can often be found in stunning numbers within certain industries. All 11 new professional basketball leagues founded in the past eight years have gone belly-up. But hopes die hard; others are now being formed. Over 90 auto manufacturers failed before the three major automakers emerged victors. We now see the same shakeout in the computer field. Of 75 computer companies founded in the late 1960s only 10 still survive. A fresh bumper crop appears on the scene every year and disappears shortly thereafter like wheat scythed in a freshly harvested field.

No industry or type of business seems safe from the devastating statistics. Franchised businesses, boasting to be the safest of all entrepreneurial activities, had unprecedented casualties in 1986, as 112 major franchise companies vanished.

Nor is corporate failure the exclusive province of the small, undercapitalized business—it occurs increasingly among large industrial and financial corporations. The past decade was a watershed in this respect with such colossal failures as Wickes Corporation, Itel, Braniff Airlines, Manville Corporation, and Texaco creating a broad cross-section of giants who succumbed to various misfortunes.

What is perhaps the major revelation of this decade is the swiftness with which the healthiest corporations can be transformed into debt-ridden cripples. Many once considered in the citadel of capitalism have become battered by the vagaries of the marketplace or that one big product disaster.

For example, A.H. Robins, once ranked among the top 10 pharmaceutical firms until 1985 when difficulties arising from its defective Dalkon Shield, an intrauterine contraceptive device, caused hundreds of thousands of product liability claims to descend upon the company, cascading Robins into Bankruptcy Code Chapter 11 reorganization, where it hopefully will begin to work its way out of trouble.

Manville Corporation suffered a similar fate to Robins, but with asbestos claims; and Manville too hopes to regain solvency through Chapter 11. Both A.H. Robins and Manville show how one faulty product can quickly and without warning undermine even the strongest company.

Another of the country's more spectacular sudden collapses was GEICO (Government Employees Insurance Company) which, in 1975, went from the country's fifth-largest auto insurer to the brink of insolvency after posting an eye-popping $126 million loss on income of $603 million.

Even companies that are known to be in trouble can surprise us with the speed with which they disappear. The most dramatic example was W.T. Grant and Company, the vast retail chain, which abruptly liquidated its 360 stores employing over 35,000 employees, much to the surprise of everyone but top management. It was perhaps the Grant case more than any other that drove home the point that "the bigger they are only means the harder they fall."

Yet it was Texaco that showed just how very thin the veneer between corporate success and failure can really be. In 1986 Texaco ranked as one of the world's wealthiest corporations, and one logically able to ignore as anything but a nuisance the claim of Pennzoil that Texaco wrongfully interfered with Pennzoil's agreement to take over Getty Oil. After a few short moments of deliberation a feisty Texas state court jury handed Pennzoil a $10.5 billion victory, adding Texaco to the roster of proud companies which awake one morning to find themselves in bankruptcy.

The experiences of companies like Robins, Grant, and Texaco shatter the image of large corporations as being indestructible. But even when we come to terms with their vulnerability, we seldom think of them as having "glass jaws."

The truth of the matter is that there are many more businesses with "glass jaws" than we can possibly know about. Whether they are small businesses or larger corporations we have no idea of how many businesses actually fail each year.

What is clear is that the statistics are woefully understated. The Small Business Administration reports approximately 25,000 business failures a year—a ridiculously conservative estimate when we consider there are over 650,000 start-ups each year joining nearly 15 million existing businesses.

A closer estimate may be 500,000 failures every year. Few of these companies go through the formal ritual of bankruptcy (where the statistics are measurable) but instead fade away through lender foreclosure, receivership, or other state insolvency proceeding. Nor can we discount the large number of smaller enterprises that quietly close their doors as their disillusioned owners walk away.

THE MANY MEANINGS OF FAILURE

The difficulty in discussing the failed company is that no two people think of "failure" in precisely the same terms. A firm can be characterized as a managerial failure, financial failure, or legal failure. Although these terms are sometimes used interchangeably, they have distinctively different meanings.

A company can be a managerial failure long before it is a financial failure. And it can linger as a financial failure without ever becoming a legal failure.

Managerial Failure

Countless companies can be declared managerial failures because they do not live up to their potential. The great myth of management is that management is successful by its own sheer ability to turn a profit. The size of the profit somehow seems irrelevant. Conversely, we tend to condemn management which incurs losses despite the fact that the company side-stepped far greater losses only due to the skilled navigation of management. But which is the managerial failure—the manager who earns a $1 million profit when the company in more capable hands could have earned $5 million, or the manager who confines losses to $1 million when the company was ordained to lose $5 million? Often we give the failure label to the wrong manager.

It is not enough for a business merely to be profitable. It must be as profitable as it has the potential to be. Anything less is managerial failure.

The wrong yardstick is often used when we talk about success and failure. Too many companies are preoccupied with sales instead of profits. Managers have become so accustomed to chasing sales, they often forget there is a bottom line to the income statement. According to *Computer and Software News*, "The stock market is getting tired of computer chains who double sales only to double losses." And taking another shot at managerial failure is Raymond Rose of Oliver Rose Securities who is quick to remind us, "The P/E ratio doesn't mean anything when there is no E."

Penn Central was a managerial failure long before it was a financial one. In its more recent years it either incurred losses or earned so little that stockholders would have done appreciably better stuffing their investment under the mattress. Although this would be of secondary importance to Will Rogers who liked to quip, "I'm more concerned about the return *of* my investment than I am the return *on* investment," less tolerant stockholders cling to the belief that something productive should be done with their money to earn more money, an objective too few managers can achieve. Yet this too may not matter much, according to Will Rogers: "Executives who do not produce successful results hold on to their jobs only about five years. Those who produce results hang on about half a decade."

Stagnation is a form of managerial failure. There are an untold number of companies that grope along for years at or near break-even, producing unsatisfactory returns for their stockholders. A company may not move off dead center for years and when it does it almost always goes into a downturn rather than an upturn. Chrysler, for example, was a dead-center company from 1960 until 1968, when its performance plummeted. All we need do is study the earning records of many corporations to discover the managerial failures of today who will become the financial failures of tomorrow.

For every firm that drowns in a sea of red ink there are hundreds that are merely doused. In 1985, nearly one-half of the nation's 1,723,828 corporations registered a loss. These are the firms that are striving to be average. Of the approximate 50 percent that showed a profit, two-thirds earned for their stockholders no more than could be earned in a secure, liquid savings account. Only one corporation in seven performed better.

Even operations which appear to be successful may have a less-than-glowing financial statement. For example, according to *The Washington Post*, W. Clement Stone of Combined International Corporation never managed to wring a profit from *Success* magazine. And Chase Revel, Inc., the former publisher of *Entrepreneur* magazine, was itself forced into Chapter 11 reorganization.

Larger corporations are not the only ones plagued by managerial failure. Small, family-owned businesses can also slumber along, generating less than a week's pay for their owners. However, it is often difficult to assess the true economic performance of the smaller, family-owned businesses which comprise two-thirds of the 15 million existing companies. Owners of these enterprises have so many opportunities to distort the profit picture that they alone know whether their company is making or losing money.

Managerial failure, then, occurs either when the company fails to live up to its own potential or when the realized rate of return on invested capital is significantly and continually lower than prevailing rates on similar investments.

Financial Failure

Financial failure occurs either when the enterprise has chronic and serious losses or when the organization becomes insolvent with liabilities disproportionate to the assets. Frequently, a financially troubled company will suffer problems with both profitability and solvency as sustained losses necessarily weaken the overall financial strength of the organization.

There is no precise definition of "financial failure" and the term as a general reflection of economic condition can overlap managerial failure and legal failure. To an extent, financial failure is a bridge between the company that is merely subperforming (managerial failure) and the company formally declared a legal failure.

Legal Failure

Even a legal failure may defy precise definition. For example, the Bankruptcy Code uses a two-part test: The first is to declare a company legally bankrupt when its liabilities exceed its assets. There are, however, a number of companies that manage to operate for years with debts far in excess of assets. These firms continue in business only due to creditor leniency and patience. We have observed many companies with debts considerably higher than assets eventually turn the corner, produce a profit, and gradually straighten out their balance sheets, much to the relief of patient creditors. But these debt-ridden firms, to survive, must depend on the twin factors of creditor patience and rapidly improved profits.

A company can also be declared bankrupt when it is unable to pay its debts when they fall due. This rather archaic test would, of course, suggest that 90 percent of the companies in America are bankrupt, undoubtedly a legislative throwback to more Victorian times when businesspeople actually paid their bills on time.

Of course, the fact that a business closes its doors does not in itself mean it is a legal failure. An entrepreneur may discontinue operations for a number of reasons, such as loss of capital, illness, retirement, or other personal reasons. Even when a business is closed due to nonexistent or inadequate profits it is not declared a legal failure provided it pays its debts in full.

There are a sizable number of companies that are financial failures, but for one reason or another they continue to linger on a long plateau without becoming legal failures.

Conversely, a substantial number of companies declare Chapter 11 bankruptcy—an admission of legal failure—but emerge from bankruptcy with a new balance sheet, a new lease on life, and, although they may no longer be a legal failure, they may well continue on as financial failures until they become profitable.

"Failure," of course, is a very relative term, and does not exist in the abstract. A company's performance can be measured against all other businesses, comparable companies within the same industry, or its own prior performance. How the company stacks up will largely depend on the individual making the assessment.

Managers, as can be expected, are always tolerant of their own managerial performance, and even when the organization does poorly they are likely to see it as caused by external factors beyond their control. Managers apparently are quite successful in convincing stockholders to reach the same conclusion, which helps explain why stockholders can show such great patience with their poorly performing managers. Survey after survey discloses that those within the organization—management and stockholders alike—are far less critical of corporate performance than those outside the organization who see matters more objectively.

Companies do become particularly tolerant of their own dismal performance because they have become acclimated to poor performance. Penn Central and W.T. Grant were two examples of perennially poor performers whose stockholders and managers accepted such performance as the normal corporate condition, deferring any real turnaround attempt until the deteriorating financial condition could no longer be ignored.

Conversely, it may not be enough for a company merely to be successful. It must be *more* successful than its stockholders and the financial community expects it to be. On December 27, 1984 Toys 'R' Us announced that its sales over the Christmas season had grown a spectacular 17 percent. There was only one problem. The brokerage firms had been telling everyone the growth would be 30 percent. The day following the announcement, Toys 'R' Us stock dropped seven points—from 47 to 40—and continued to spiral downward in the months to follow. Had Wall Street predicted a 10 percent increase, the news of 17 percent would undoubtedly have sent the stock soaring. Success, like failure, is all too often a matter of our own expectations.

PROFILES OF CORPORATE COLLAPSE

Just as companies survive and thrive in many different ways, like living objects they also die in many different ways. While it is impossible to classify the various cycles with precision, certain patterns of corporate decline do emerge.

Nearly a decade ago, insolvency expert John Argenti authored *Corporate Collapse* (Wiley, 1976) in which he constructed a model of the three prevailing types of corporate failure.

Type 1 companies were described as small companies that never rose above a poor or marginal level of performance. In 1976, for example, 55 percent of all business failures occurred in firms less than five years old. These were not "entrepreneurial firms" in the strict sense of the word because they were never destined to be fast-growth ventures. More typically they were the run-of-the-mill and garden-variety type businesses: luncheonettes, retail shops, small service businesses, and the host of other operations that dot Main Street and form the backbone of our free enterprise system.

Type 2 companies are the high-rollers: firms that not only get off the ground but quickly reach spectacular heights before crashing down again. National Student Marketing Services, which reached meteoric heights in the mid-1950s before cascading to oblivion several years later, was a prime example. Osborne Computer was another Type 2 candidate as was Bernie Cornfeld's controversial Investors Overseas Services, Ltd. (IOS).

While Type 1 companies are headed by storekeepers, welders, machinists, printers, and other steady but less visible people whose personalities are in rhythm with their business, the characters who head Type 2 companies are as colorful as the companies they head. Type 2 owners are the flamboyant, restless dreamers whose ambitions reach to the sky. These are the firms built on blind ambition if not an absurd concept. And these are the enterprises that can capture the imagination of the investing public, fueling the company to fantastic heights where even more money can be attracted. While firms in this category may be perfectly legitimate (such as Osborne) they may also operate with shades of fraud (Equity Funding).

Type 2 companies make the most interesting casualties because people have a curious fascination with any company that can appear and disappear in such short order, like a starburst. When these same companies are headed by luminaries whose names become household names, the intrigue deepens. And who can resist snickering at the long list of celebrities who as investors inevitably get suckered in? Type 2 failures remain fairly rare only because so few companies fall into this category. According to Argenti, "Fewer than 10 percent of all companies are type 2 firms."

The Type 3 company, in contrast to the other two types, is the larger, more established firm, usually professionally managed and publicly owned. These firms have been around for a while and through their longevity they may have become sluggish, or lost touch with their markets, or developed hardening of the corporate arteries. Some of these companies—Chrysler, Braniff, Massey-Ferguson, and Wickes—have enjoyed years of profitable operation before going into decline. Texaco, Robins, and Manville typify the Type 3 size company but do not typify how Type 3 companies get into trouble.

As one digs deeper into the barrel one finds companies that do not fit the narrow profiles of good companies that have turned bad as contained in the Argenti study and it may not matter. More important than who the troubled company is, is the question of how the company is likely to respond to its problems.

The Type 1 companies—the small firms—are the least likely to survive a significant downturn. The small company by reason of its limited size has limited resources with which to rebuild. Because the company's failure has equally limited impact on lenders, suppliers, creditors, and labor unions, it is unlikely to receive the support afforded the larger company. Few small business owners who have lost their companies ask with more than idle curiosity why Chrysler and Lockheed were saved by governmental guarantees when hundreds of thousands of smaller companies vanish without a helping hand from Uncle Sam. Ultimately the small company survives because its owners remortgage the house, work double duty, and are blessed with a few cooperative creditors. However it happens, there are too few people who care to help.

The smaller company will also be hampered in its turnaround efforts by its own shallow management capabilities. A baker has few qualifications to turn around a bakery and a pharmacist has never studied how to turn around a drugstore. When trouble strikes, the small business owner may have little idea of where to turn just as he or she has little idea of what to do. The net result is that the company may fade away with no attempt to achieve a turnaround. Even when these small firms reach out for professional help, too few turnaround consultants or qualified insolvency lawyers are available. Further, the smaller company is no stronger than its owner because the owner is the company. When the owner gets sick or runs into other personal problems there is no management backup and liquidation therefore becomes the only alternative.

The most disturbing reality is that a great number of small companies fail when, with proper professional attention, they could be saved. James Rice, a Boston bankruptcy lawyer, says:

> The owner of the small business often doesn't realize the alternatives to liquidation, so he accepts bankruptcy as the path of least resistance. We see small companies auctioned every day that could

be successfully reorganized. Usually the owner is just so sick of the headaches he throws in the sponge.

However, the smaller firms also have considerable, often overlooked strengths that can be decisive in a workout. First, the company has great flexibility in its options, and is free of the constraints and complexities of the large corporations. The small firm can change form and shape with remarkable simplicity. Second, the small company, being less visible, will often have more indulgent creditors than its larger counterparts. Finally, owners of small businesses usually bring to a turnaround a far greater determination to succeed than do managers of large corporations, if only because they may have more at stake in a personal sense.

We often think of businesses as objects whose misfortunes can be measured in statistical and economic terms alone, but when we profile small business failures it in reality becomes a very human drama as beleagured owners fight to salvage their investment, livelihood, security, and possibly even their personal assets. More importantly, they fight to save their hopes, dreams, and aspirations, with far greater stubborness than is ordinarily observed in a corporate penthouse. This dogged determination and rugged individuality surely account for the surprisingly large percentage of successful small business turnaround—when a turnaround is attempted.

And there are signs the smaller companies are beginning to emulate their big brothers and fight back with increased vigor and frequency to stay in business. The New York bankruptcy courts, for example, report a tremendous upsurge in the number of small companies filing Chapter 11. Small companies that were once willing to give up gracefully now realize they do not have to give up the business when they can just as easily give up the creditors.

Of the three business types, the Type 2 company has the most dismal turnaround record. These companies lack turnaround success for two reasons: First, the company was typically built on a "sensational" concept (IOS, Equity Funding, National Student Marketing) rather than a sound one. Second, as a "high-roller" company, it may be plagued by bad press or poor reputation, creating a climate where too few people continue to support the organization.

While the Type 2 organization may not survive, its founders typically move on to greener pastures, starting new and often similarly spectacular enterprises. As Argenti reminds us, you can never quite kill a Type 2 company because the people who create them—flamboyant, loquacious, and bubbling with ideas—just refuse to stay down.

The mature, professionally managed Type 3 company has the best chance for corporate renewal because it is so visible. The greater the size of the troubled company the more profound the effect of failure and the greater the support for survival. Chrysler's demise would have cost nearly 300,000 jobs—no small consideration for politicians constantly on the prowl for votes. The larger corporation also has a greater reservoir of assets with which to rebuild. Mature companies generally go through three stages on the way to failure: initial downturn, plateau, and final collapse. A company with a reasonably strong balance sheet can plateau for years without coming to grips with its problems, but if it does act soon enough it invariably has sufficient assets to create a "viable core" business with which to go forward. This is not necessarily true with Type 1 and 2 companies who are usually not asset-rich to begin with. And while the mature, larger organization may lack managers with the dogged determination of more entrepreneurial companies, the mature organization has greater management strength and the ability to attract an effective turnaround team.

For all the differences between companies, their survival depends on remarkably similar strategies:

1. The company must recognize its problems and face the moment of truth so that a serious turnaround can begin.

2. The company must stem losses, marshal resources, and stabilize itself for the workout.

3. The company must understand the causes of decline, evaluate its present position, and design a long-term turnaround program.

4. The company must restructure its debt, regain profitability, and position itself so it can go forward as a stable, healthy enterprise.

Even when a company goes through the turnaround process its success may be short-lived. Turnarounds are a way of life for plenty of companies whose existence is nothing more than a roller coaster ride. Chrysler had turnarounds before, plenty of them, only to be followed by hair-raising reversals. The Great Atlantic and Pacific Tea Company (A&P) also had plenty of buoyant years following a turnaround effort, only to run awash again in red ink.

These, of course, are not successful turnarounds, when they merely give the company a short lease on life. Many managers think they achieved a lasting turnaround when their efforts were cosmetic. Sometimes the best decision management can make is to accept the reality that the company cannot be turned around as a viable organization and the interests of its employees, stockholders, and creditors are best served through a sale or liquidation. But it takes guts and rare objectivity for management to sit back and declare that the business is not a "good company" turned bad, but a "bad company" that can never be made good.

2

The Seeds of Destruction

WHAT do Braniff International, Osborne Computer, AM International, Dome Petroleum, Laker Airways, and Singer have in common? These once-proud organizations are either adrift in a sea of red ink and dependent on government for a death-cheating bailout, or they have recently vanished altogether. How do such corporations manage to plummet from heady success to spectacular failure? Often, these disasters are caused by a curious corporate paradox: corporate success seems to carry the seeds of failure along with it.

Every company has within it the seeds of its own destruction—the existing or potential Achilles heel destined to doom the company but for the expert maneuvering of management.

Why is it that some companies succeed while others with equal or greater resources and opportunities fail? This one question is the sum and substance of what management is all about, but the right answer can be illusive for four reasons.

1. Organizational failure in many companies can be traced to a multitude of factors. Generally, no single mistake or weakness is the sole culprit. Managers and turnaround consultants often oversimplify when interpreting the causes of corporate decline. The tendency is to pinpoint the problem so that it becomes narrowly defined and appears

14

amenable to a simple solution, the "quick-fix." Unfortunately, most companies suffer organizational problems with many roots and their successful turnaround requires a complex, multipronged attack to resolve the many different problems.

2. The symptoms of failure cannot be distinguished from the causes. Organizational failure resembles organic illness. The symptoms cannot always easily be distinguished from the disease. Often tactical errors are confused with the more fundamental weaknesses which gave rise to such errors. In most instances, failure is described and categorized as a clustering of symptoms, when in reality it may be caused by any one of a number of underlying reasons that remain buried.

3. The causes of failure are related to the general nature of the firm. Conglomerates do not have the same problems as simple, functionally organized companies. High-technology firms seldom face the same threats as those in stable industries. For example, high-technology firms have encountered most of their problems in the form of ill-conceived products—market innovations. Companies in stable industries may suffer from lack of innovation, diversification, and growth. Large, highly diversified firms often incur problems in controlling their divisions, profitably absorbing new acquisitions, or putting together the resources to support their growth. The causes of failure are as diverse as the firms.

4. The causes of failure can be a function of corporate maturity. Firms in the start-up stage face a different set of problems than the growth or mature organization. Our experiences with troubled firms disclose that many companies have difficulty in making the transition from one stage to another. And their problems are different. For example, the start-up company is likely to fail because of a poor business concept, poor financial planning, undercapitalization, or, more commonly, the sheer inability of management. On the other hand, the mature organization may suffer from too much corporate flab, archaic management policies, and general hardening of the corporate arteries, making the company vulnerable to changes in the marketplace.

Therefore, no simplistic approach can be taken toward defining the causes of corporate failure, any more than there are any simplistic formulas for success. Organizations are complex, and what may be a weakness in one company may be a strength in another. Even Tom Peters was forced to admit in *In Search of Excellence* that "Managers in every field are re-thinking the tried and, as it turns out, not so true management principles that have so often served their institutions poorly." Perhaps the most important principle of all for avoiding failure is to be true to the strategies that work best for your own organization.

THE CRISIS OF CHANGE

In today's fast-changing world, companies—indeed entire industries—become quickly vulnerable. The external changes I refer to are not the many minor changes of everyday business life but the dramatic and often unexpected events that strike at the core of a company's business.

Government regulations, court decisions, trade tariffs, raw material shortages, and changes in technology are only a few of the many external factors that can send even the strongest company on a sharp downturn.

Of course, it is far easier for managers to blame external events for their corporate ailments than it is to blame their own managerial inadequacy, and in some cases their claim is justified when events occur with such suddenness and severity that they could not have been predicted or protected against. But when examined closely, the inability to foresee the events is in itself a form of mismanagement as is the failure to calculate their consequences and impact on the business. Just as change creates opportunity, those who stagnate fall victim to one of four types of change: competitive, technological, market, or economic change.

Competitive Change

Competition is constantly shifting. Foreign, low-cost producers, the appearance of an entirely new competitor, or dramatic advances by an existing competitor can have a rapid and profound effect on any company.

We come across many firms in trouble because they stagnated while young upstart companies swept their markets away with new, innovative products, attractive services, or perhaps just a fresh and aggressive way of doing business. These troubled firms just did not have their ear to the ground and took their customers for granted. They shifted from the role of a leader to that of a follower who is inevitably forced to react. Companies on the cutting edge of their field may encounter other problems as a result of their adventures but they seldom feel the sting of someone puncturing their soft underbelly, as did W.T. Grant which saw its leadership position as a retail discounter slip away to more aggressive and dynamic chains such as K-Mart, Wol-Mart, and Woolco.

Technological Change

Alvin Toffler warned us of the effects of technological change in his best-selling blockbuster *Future Shock* (Bantam, 1970). The world as he sees it is indeed changing at an accelerated pace and too many companies cannot keep up.

The rapid technological progress of the past decade has spawned hundreds of new industries and the demise of others unable to adapt to turbulent change. Consider one industry: computers. Within this fast-moving industry there are no fewer than 20,000 shakeout companies a year, giving rise to the standing joke in Silicon Valley that new computer companies should hang up their signs with Velcro.

But even traditionally stable industries are falling victim to this new-age technology. The printing industry, for example, is in the throes of its own shakeout—battered by the rise of desktop publishing and larger plants featuring more technologically advanced equipment. American automakers who have long felt the pinch of foreign competition are expected to fall even further behind the Japanese who are a decade ahead of us in robotic automation. The list of pipestack industries that mistakenly believe they can compete in the 1980s with the techniques of the 1950s is endless.

Companies that are victims of technological change are typically victims of their own lack of foresight. All too often these companies can readily see the approaching change but neglect to reinvest in their own future, losing to cutting-edge companies by default.

Market Change

A great number of companies lose touch with their markets. The importance of market sensitivity will, of course, vary among industries. The garment industry, for example, shows how firms without a strong market sense frequently fail. As an annual ritual, hundreds of New York fashion houses go under after betting on the newest fashions.

Unlike those within the garment industry, most companies serve a less fickle consumer and must only adapt to gradual changes within their market. But the marketplace nevertheless changes for every company. Changes in life-style, demographics, social attitudes, and consumer preferences must be carefully exploited if the company is to succeed. As elementary as this may seem, many of the largest and most sophisticated companies ignore the lesson. American automakers' slowness to recognize consumers' growing preference for smaller cars lost a significant share of the domestic auto market to the responsive Japanese. Similarly, fast-growth companies such as Reebok Running Shoes achieve phenomenal success because they have an exquisite sense of an untapped market niche and aggressively tap it. But for every Reebok with its fingers on the market pulse, there's another that fails to keep up with even the most fundamental trends within its industry.

Economic Change

A sluggish economy and other economic woes are most commonly cited by management as the cause of failure but the excuse is invariably a cover-up for the sins of management.

A company can get away with a great deal when times are good and sales are strong, despite managerial inadequacies. Conversely, a tight economy uncovers corporate weaknesses, forcing many of the marginal companies out of existence.

Economics can, of course, play havoc with a company in many ways. Inflationary interest rates are a common cause of corporate bankruptcy as was seen in 1980–1981 when interest skyrocketed to 18–20 percent. Companies programmed to pay 10 percent and no longer able to service their debt folded by the thousands.

Sometimes a particular industry suffers a downturn and slackened demand notwithstanding a strong overall economy. The American farming industry remains on the ropes and the impact of its decline can be felt throughout the South and Midwest. Companies such as John Deere, International-Harvester, and Caterpillar, unable to sell equipment to the cash-poor farmer, have been forced to close factories and lay off thousands of workers. With a predictable domino effect, communities such as Davenport, Iowa and Rock Island, Illinois—towns dependent on these industries—have suffered the loss of hundreds of smaller businesses, creating a depression in mid-America.

Professor Edward Altman of New York University, who has written extensively on the causes of corporate decline, reports that a credit squeeze is one of the most important reasons for business collapse. A credit squeeze can certainly be anticipated during inflationary times when suppliers restrict credit to avoid borrowing at high rates. Credit is also tightened when sales are strong and suppliers are more willing to lose marginal credit customers.

Economic conditions cannot always be predicted, and management can hardly be blamed for guessing incorrectly. However, companies programmed to survive position themselves to function in bad times as well as good. They do so by planning for the worst, confident they can sustain the worst should it come, never gambling the corporate jewels on factors beyond their control.

THE TEN MOST COMMON ERRORS OF MANAGEMENT

Just as companies share common risks, they share common managerial snafus which may lead to business failure. There are errors of omission—the failure to act when action is needed—and errors of commission—problems created by actions the company takes.

Of course, the number of mistakes a company can make even when it is well managed is staggering. A very well-managed company may make fewer mistakes but lack the resources or ability to correct its mistakes. In reality such companies fail not because of the problems that are created but because of the problems that cannot be solved.

With few exceptions the failure of the company is the failure of management. Most turnaround consultants share my view that the overwhelming number of business failures are caused by internal factors—the errors of management. The Small Business Administration cites 87 percent of all bankruptcies to be directly attributable to poor management and Donald Bibeault, in *Corporate Turnaround* (McGraw Hill, 1982), says that in seven out of 10 cases decline is internally generated and at least partially at fault in two out of three remaining cases, an assessment that may be overly generous to today's manager.

What then are the most common errors of management? From a seemingly endless list, ten stand out as the most serious and reoccurring causes of failure: (1) overleverage, (2) overexpansion, (3) overdiversification, (4) overemphasis on sales, (5) inadequate control systems, (6) overdependence, (7) poor location, (8) improper pricing, (9) government constraints, and (10) poor planning.

Overleverage

Far too many companies begin with inadequate capital and/or excessive borrowed debt. We have all heard the success stories of how Apple Computer was started in a garage with $500 or how W. Clement Stone parlayed $100 into a $2 billion insurance conglomerate, and while these success stories fuel the American dream, there would be fewer failures if entrepreneurs started with the capital to match their enthusiasm.

Excess leverage is almost always the result of nonexistent or naive financial planning. Start-up entrepreneurs often do not understand the many hidden costs every new company encounters. Moreover, they are usually too optimistic, expecting profits far earlier and far greater than they can ever materialize.

This does not suggest the new venture should be funded with an abundance of capital for too great an investment can be no less a mistake than too little. The overfinanced company lends itself to slipshod spending and the possibility of losing more than necessary. So the well-planned and well-managed company strikes a careful balance between invested funds (equity) and borrowed funds (debt).

Overexpansion

Closely related to overleverage is the even more chronic problem of overexpansion.

Overexpansion can create overleverage as the company borrows heavily to finance its growth. Typically the company cannot generate the cash flow to cover the additional borrowing and like the thinly capitalized start-up firm falls victim to its own rosy projections of future profits. When the earnings fail to materialize we have one more company in serious trouble forced to either reverse direction and retrench or fail. Braniff Airlines, which now prospers as a shadow of its former self, is a prime example. So too within the discount field are chains such as J.M. Fields and Mammoth Mart, which quickly grew from single-store operations to retailing giants only to fall under the weight of their own rapid growth.

Although overexpansion can outrun the company's ability to finance itself, it may also outrun its ability to manage itself. It takes far different talent to run a large, sprawling operation than one that is small and highly centralized. Entrepreneurs accustomed to calling all the shots suddenly find they must learn to build management pyramids beneath them and learn how to delegate. Not all entrepreneurs comfortably make this transition and few do it successfully.

The company that neglects to build management to support the growing enterprise will in all probability also neglect other key operational areas: planning, finance, marketing, personnel, inventory control, and merchandising. While the core concept for the business is good, the company stumbles because it is running before learning how to walk.

Overdiversification

Overexpansion can be a dangerous exercise when moving rapidly through familiar territory. More problems, however, stem from strategic moves into unfamiliar territory. Companies have a hard enough time within familiar territory without journeying into someone else's territory.

Yet diversification remains a corporate buzzword with more and more companies—large and small—moving into unrelated areas, either through expansion or acquisition—a throwback to the 1960s when conglomerates discovered pyramiding companies was the quickest way to build stock values. The conglomerate, never designed for its intrinsic strength, offered unique opportunities for earnings/stock value manipulations.

Businesses often diversify in order to reduce risk. Overdependence on one industry is a common cause of failure so we can hardly be too critical of companies that decide to put their eggs in more than one basket. Yet management gurus such as Peter Drucker disagree with diversification as a sound strategy: "Complex businesses (conglomerates) have repeatedly evidenced their vulnerability to small but highly concentrated single market or single technology businesses. If anything goes wrong, there is a premium for knowing your business."

Managers usually attempt to justify their diversification on several grounds: inability to expand in existing industries, synergy between the existing and expanded operations, and highly advantageous acquisition opportunities being three common reasons. And each can be a logical reason for diversification—but only if the company has the resources to properly manage its diversification program.

Overemphasis on Sales

Managers who are more sales-oriented than profit-oriented are prime candidates for failure. Many companies plow ahead blindly building sales while the bottom line looks increasingly dismal.

This same mania for sales growth fuels overexpansion and over-diversification. Sales are seen as the panacea for all problems. Sometimes it is only an attempt to maintain a successful image in the face of a worsening financial picture, or increased sales produce cash flow which can be even more important over the short term than profits. Most often, however, management simply and mistakenly believes higher sales must inevitably lead to higher profits.

Many of our client companies got into trouble with precisely this faulty thinking. Our task then is to shrink the organization to the point where profits, not sales, control corporate planning. Often the restructured company has less than one-half its former sales but generate twice the profits.

Inadequate Control Systems

Another nearly universal feature of troubled companies is the absence of a basic control system. Very few of these companies really know where they have been and hence never have the information needed to tell them where they should be going, or how to get there.

The adequacy of financial controls as early-warning indicators is vital, but information must go beyond financial and accounting statements and delve into the heart of the business. Even when financial controls are in place the company may lack necessary operational controls. Surprisingly few companies—even those in the $10 million sales range—can accurately provide such basic information as pending orders, product costs and margins, customer sales analysis, or operational break-even point. This lack of information not only gets companies into trouble but it also keeps them there.

Too much information can be just as bad. Fascinated by their computers, comptrollers and middle managers are increasingly swamped with piles of data much of which is worthless and obscures the few important controls that are buried under the pile.

Deciding upon a management information system cannot be left to the accountants alone. Instead the management must decide on the needed information to accurately and continuously measure the corporate pulse. As important as having the right information may be, the corporate wastelands are blighted with the remains of those who had the information but never quite understood what to do with it.

Overdependence

Companies that rely on one key customer or supplier are particularly vulnerable as their health depends on its continued business dealings.

Companies often downplay their total dependency on another business or blindly believe the business relationship will last forever. Many of today's highly successful small and mid-sized companies that depend on one customer may well be out of business tomorrow. When W.T. Grant collapsed, the giant retailer took with it scores of small suppliers. There are undoubtedly thousands of defense contractors and subcontractors whose survival depends on their ability to win the bid on the next round of contracts. But what happens if they lose the bid or the government cuts back on its defense spending?

Companies can be equally dependent on a supplier or other support organization. Franchising, for example, is based on a constant flow of support from franchisor to franchisee. For example, when the Boston-based Women's World Health Spa System went under it forced a score of franchisees under with it. Kevin Harrington, the host of television's "Franchise America" show, reports, "Hundreds of people are buying rights to a franchise name and system that will no longer be around in a few years. The death of the franchisor inevitably means the death of the franchisee—which may well number in the hundreds."

If a franchisee has its own brand of vulnerability, so too does the company dependent on one source of supply. When that source dries up, or refuses to sell at reasonable prices, the company without a backup supplier quickly finds itself out of business. The United States discovered just how treacherous it can be to depend on one source of supply during the Middle-East oil embargo. Hundreds of Chrysler dealers suffered the same pangs of concern during the pre-Iacocca era. The message is clear: No company can afford to ignore the problem of dependency.

Poor Location

Retail businesses often fall on hard times because their physical location—suitable at the time the business opened—has gone through changes due to urban decay, redevelopment, or population shifts. For the retailer the corporate fortunes are directly tied to the ability of the organization to capture high-traffic sites.

The Liggett Drug chain, for example, once the nation's largest drug retailer, showed just how vulnerable a retailing organization can be to aggressive competitors who move in on the best locations. As Liggett confined itself to decaying downtown locations, young start-up chains such as Rite-Aid, Revco, and Gray Drug nimbly moved to suburban shopping centers with their growing populations, as Liggett shriveled to a handful of tired outlets.

Location is seldom mentioned as a cause of business decline, but considering the enormous number of retailing operations it can hardly be ignored as a significant factor. As more and more shopping becomes concentrated in enclosed malls—predominantly tenanted by chains—independent retailers will increasingly be left to only marginal or secondary locations.

Approximately 70 percent of our clients in the retail trades cite poor location as their primary problem. They may have simply chosen a bad location to begin with or sat by while the location gradually turned bad. Eventually sales drop to unacceptable levels or rents are no longer in line with income, eroding once-existing profits.

Rents are another factor to consider. For example, Boston with its skyrocketing real estate market can now command up to $30 a square foot for prime retail space. A decade ago comparable space rented for under $6. Only high-volume operators can survive in this inflationary rental market and as rents continue to spiral upward more marginal operators will fall by the wayside.

As a practical matter business owners either have to upgrade their operations so they can compete for desirable locations, stagnate in marginal locations, or close. This is often the key decision in retail turnaround strategy.

Improper Pricing

"When was the last time you compared your cost of doing business to the operating costs of the prior year? When was the last time you calculated your break-even point?" These questions were asked of over 300 furniture manufacturers at a recent convention. Fewer than 30 had the answers.

Many companies are in trouble today because they do not understand their cost structure and therefore operate with an unrealistic pricing strategy. As the old joke goes, "We lose $2 on every widget but make it up on volume." Nearly 50 percent of our manufacturing clients seem to operate with this same self-destructing philosophy, which helps explain why there are so many manufacturing firms that go down the tube.

The problem of identifying increased expenses, labor, and material costs is far easier than controlling these costs. Poor productivity and buying at noncompetitive prices will put a stranglehold on profits unless these inefficiencies can somehow be passed on to the customer in the form of higher prices—which is seldom the case in today's competitive world. Nevertheless, many companies do sell their products at too low a price when the market will readily accommodate a higher price. And far too many businesspeople—particularly small operators—choose to compete on the basis of price alone when they could gain a stronger competitive edge by selling service and upgraded quality.

The importance on proper pricing to the overall economics of the firm cannot be overstated. More than one company has discovered that the difference between a healthy profit and whopping loss is nothing more than a few pennies added to each widget.

Government Constraints

Government constraints on business are visible within every industry and are very relevant to business problems whether at the local level, where politicians may change zoning or traffic flows, or at the national or international level, where they can affect entire markets, distribution, and raw materials. Government agencies daily churn out hundreds of new laws and regulations which indelibly leave their mark on how business is to be done. More often than not, it means less business will be done, or it will be done less efficiently. The insidious encroachment by government is found in every aspect of corporate life: taxation, employment, pollution control, product safety, and consumer rights, to name but a few. We have gone well beyond George Orwell's 1984.

We recently helped to liquidate a nursing home that could no longer afford to wait for long-overdue Medicaid payments (180 days) and bailed out a construction firm whose projects have been long delayed by environmentalists (14 months). Wherever we travel in counseling businesses we find a government too anxious to impose its bureaucratic ways on companies that can neither function nor flourish in a strangling bureaucratic climate.

Whether one holds the view that governmental constraints are necessary or a needless obstruction is, of course, secondary. We must deal with the world as it is. But, increasingly, companies long frustrated by governmental red tape are throwing in the sponge voluntarily if they are not among the less fortunate forced out of business involuntarily.

Poor Planning

Any of the previously mentioned causes of failure can come under the broader heading of improper planning. Yet too many businesses start, operate, and even expand with faulty or inadequate strategic planning.

Proper planning is, of course, the foundation on which the organization must be built. However, business owners open their doors every day with neither goals to reach for nor benchmarks to tell if they are getting there. And it is not simply a matter of poor financial planning, albeit no small evil, but the failure to adequately plan every phase of the business whether it be marketing or staffing.

The major conclusion reached in one study is that strategic planning in small business is incremental, sporadic, reactive, and primarily in the mind of the entrepreneur. While large firms have the advantage of specialists with the expertise to put together coherent (if not always successful) plans, the small business manager works in an environment where he or she is too preoccupied with the daily tasks to worry about the future—if only one or two years hence. It then should not come as a surprise that many of these companies discover they have no future.

MANAGEMENT AND OTHER MYTHS

While any of the 10 managerial blunders can be disastrous to the health of the company, most companies do not die a natural death but are instead murdered through managerial incompetence.

Running a business is admittedly no easy matter, but far too many entrepreneurs bravely venture forth without appreciating just how difficult it can be. So countless businesses fail because of owners unwilling to put in the long hours, unable to cope with the pressures, or too undisciplined to keep their hands out of the cash register. This is certainly true where the business is the owner and the owner is the business. Then, too, small businesses are frequently destroyed through death, sickness, or disruption in the owner's personal affairs.

We may also see a mismatch between the owner and the business.

Far too often people choose the wrong business for all the wrong reasons. Instead of asking whether they would enjoy the business and can effectively manage the business, they instead look to the profit potential—or the prestige—the business represents. The net result is that we have become a nation of entrepreneurial misfits who give far less thought to the business we should be in than the car we should be driving. Not surprisingly, a good many small business owners are forced to reassess their career objectives. There are an enormous number of small businesses that perform poorly only because the owners lack the motivation to run them properly.

Even when owners have the aptitude for their business they may lack essential skills. It is not uncommon, for example, to find a plumber who thinks he has the experience to operate a plumbing supply firm. What the plumber does not realize is that managing the supply firm requires far different and broader skills than he acquired as a plumber. For that reason we frequently see a company out of balance. The owner may bring to it a strong sales orientation but have no financial know-how. Or the owner may have creative talents but is weak in implementation. While major weaknesses can often be corrected or supplemented through staff additions, the owner must recognize his or her limitations and somehow bring those missing skills to the organization.

As companies grow larger the management problems also change. The organization is no longer the sum and substance of the owner's strengths and weaknesses but instead depends more on the organization structure the owner creates, which may be the underpinning of other weaknesses. The management team may be out-of-balance, uncoordinated, or improperly staffed or structured for its intended mission. Basic problems within the company may be traced to basic problems in the management structure.

Conflict within the management team is a chronic problem when the company is headed by partners. Partners constantly in the midst of squabbles or power battles cannot solve the company's problems and generally cause the problems. Partnerships are a leading cause of business failure. Not only does the business remain exposed to the hazards facing other companies but its survival equally depends on the ability of its partners to blend different personalities, objectives, and styles into a cohesive management team.

Ultimately, failure rests with the individual at the top. Whether he or she is the owner of a mom-and-pop enterprise or leads a major corporation, they must remember the words of Harry Truman, "The buck stops here." And as one cynical observer of the business scene would add, "and often they run the business so badly the buck doesn't even get there."

Much has been written in an attempt to personify the ideal manager or executive against which other mortals are to be measured, and while we may catch a glimpse of successful managerial personalities and styles, there is no ideal management style. For example, we are warned against "one-man" rule and yet companies such as McDonald's flourished under the autocratic thumb of Ray Kroc. Conversely, Harold Geneen performed superbly in delegating authority to his divisional managers, content to make them fully accountable. As we observe managers with very different management styles we can draw no correlation between style and results, and when you are in business, results are all that count. Style, in this case, is not substance.

Still, even the most sophisticated companies can suffer—if not flounder—because of managerial deficiencies. Many of America's corporations are subperforming because management is inbred—secure and complacent after too many years on the job. These firms are characterized by a corporate rigidity—a reluctance to try new ideas, a resistance to change, and a low tolerance for independent thinking within the ranks. While these firms may wallow along under their own momentum they will eventually come to understand the difference between success and mere survival, and later between mere survival and failure.

The sins of management can be endless. Just as we encounter the stagnant bureaucracy, we conversely see management that can run blindly in an impulsive syndrome. Characterized by a power-hoarding chief executive, the company embarks on strategies that are overambitious and oblivious to the excessive risks. These are firms hell-bent to break past records and take inordinate risks in order to grow.

Nor can we overlook the headless firm—the company that suffers a leadership vacuum and the consequent absence of a clearly defined strategy. The firm is expected to run itself on "automatic pilot" with no direction from the top.

Managerial failure then can be summarized as being the result of extremes: too much ambition or too little, too much emphasis on centralized control or too little, an overly powerful CEO or one who is a benign figurehead.

No business operates without its blemishes. Some weaknesses are too trifling to be of serious consequence and are more than offset by important strengths. Sometimes, however, weaknesses have a cumulative effect. An aggressively innovative product/market strategy coupled with an entrepreneurial chief executive whose power remains unchecked is a dangerous combination. A rule-bound bureaucratic management in a rapidly changing industry may also be deadly. But it is hardly surprising that a company is out of control when there is no control in the executive suite because it is there that the seeds of destruction are typically sown.

3

Early Warning Signals

THE one lesson we soon learn is that most businesses fail not because they cannot solve their problems but because they cannot *see* their problems.

When trouble strikes, even the pragmatic manager can develop functional blinders, failing to take decisive action until it is too late.

Convincing management to take action even when the signals are clear that a serious problem exists can be difficult. It is unusual for management to pick up on its own initiative and willingly recognize the facts. A declining company seems to first need a crisis, and until it reaches the crisis stage poor performance is readily tolerated.

FIGHTING REALITY

All turnaround consultants and workout professionals share the frustration of clients who resist the reality that their business is in a threatening decline. Most businesspeople prefer instead to cling to the illusion that the company is simply encountering one of those nasty bumps in the road all companies experience from time to time.

Al Cook, a management consultant with the Worcester, Massachusetts, Lazarus Corporation, recounts an all-too-typical scenario:

Our first contact with the owner of a troubled business is when the situation becomes uncomfortable. Cash is running low, morale is slipping and credit is tightening. But there are still sufficient assets and resources to revitalize the company. Somehow it's always too soon to begin the turnaround effort in the eyes of the client so they disappear for several months until they can no longer ignore the problem. Eventually, they return in a panic, but only after the bank levies their account, the IRS padlocks the doors, or some other catastrophe hits. However, by then inventory is depleted, cash and credit is gone, employees and customers have abandoned ship and creditors are outright hostile. In short, there's nothing left of the business to save.

As with any progressive illness, the simple fact is that companies alert to their problems and anxious to respond early in the decline greatly improve the chances of a successful recovery over companies that delay action until the terminal stages. It is during this critical time when the company is in the earliest stages of its downward slide that managers can make either the right decisions to position the company for a turn-around or play ostrich and further dissipate assets. The aware manager works feverishly to conserve cash and assets so the company can approach the turnaround in the strongest financial position possible. The company playing ostrich simply squanders away its future.

Why then do managers so strenuously fight reality? The primary reason is ego. Few of us accept defeat graciously. As long as the turn-around effort is delayed there is no self-admission of failure. And there is no shortage of executives who actively hide the dismal facts from their corporate boards, lenders, creditors, and stockholders by draining the company until the balance sheet can no longer absorb the losses. Usually it is nothing more than a prolonged effort to save face.

Optimism is the fuel behind most start-ups and it is this same optimism that propels the company through the growth stage. Yet this same optimism may dangerously dissuade management from reacting to the early warning signals. Often we see managers ward off the rescue attempt while they futilely scan the horizon for that one new major customer, product breakthrough, or other business-saving miracle—a miracle that never seems to appear. Ironically, it is the same optimism that fuels a start-up that leads it to its eventual failure.

Then, too, management may be so close to the problem and the deterioration so gradual that they just cannot easily see the changing picture. Problems simply become accepted as a way of life. And, of course, there are the inexperienced or ever-oblivious owners and managers who never spot the gathering storm because they keep looking for the wrong signs in the wrong place at the wrong time, if they bother to look at all.

Harold Geneen, whose no-nonsense managerial style shaped ITT, the nation's most successful conglomerate, was guided by the philosophy that the ability to spot and act on problems at the earliest possible stage is the essence of management. Geneen measured his own executives by this standard, constantly warning them that the cardinal sin of management is not the error that is made but the error that is not quickly spotted and cured. Geneen well understood what so many other managers must learn—small problems are far easier to solve than big ones. While good managers stand up to trouble when they run into it, great managers are constantly on the prowl for trouble.

THE GATHERING STORM

Very few companies fail without adequate warning. For the most part the company in decline throws out a wide range of operational and financial signals—warnings that are weak at the beginning and become both more frequent and more powerful as the company approaches collapse.

No two companies generate precisely the same pattern of early warnings, because corporations—like ships—do not sink in exactly the same way. While some go down at the bow others go down at the stern, and for every company that suddenly vanishes there are many others that seem to endlessly linger before rolling over.

Rolls Royce and Penn Central are two companies that appeared to fail with little warning—less than one year from the first signals that all was not well to the day they filed for bankruptcy. But for most companies—even the small privately owned corporation—there is typically a two- or three-year "window of opportunity" where management should clearly see trouble is brewing, allowing more than ample opportunity to avert disaster.

The majority of managers mistakenly believe that the first signs of failure will appear in the financial statements. But the earliest and clearest signs are not financial, they are managerial and they can be seen long before—perhaps years before—the company's financial position begins to deteriorate.

Just as the causes of failure will depend largely on the size, age, and nature of the business, so too will its symptoms of failure and the early warning signals it will cast off.

High-technology firms, for example, who often fall victim to a competitor offering more advanced technology, can look first to a downturn in new orders from the sales department, although the financials will not reflect the drop in sales for perhaps three to six months. Even here there can be disagreement on how far ahead management should reasonably look to foresee distant problems. Philip Order, a vice-president at Loral Electronics, a leading New York based defense contractor, argues that with a technology-based firm it is too late to spot problems by measuring current sales activity. He suggests:

> Instead, you have to see what's going on in the labs; how much is being spent on R & D and whether you are staying ahead or falling behind of your competition in new product development. Today's sales only reflect the effectiveness of yesterday's research just as tomorrow's income depends on today's inventiveness.

The causes of failure and its symptoms can be so intertwined that it is difficult to tell one from the other. Iacocca, for example, never accepted the myth that Chrysler's near downfall could only be predicted in the late 1970s when sales slumped by 50 percent or more. The earliest warnings, Iacocca reasons, came in the early 1970s with the oil embargo, long lines at the gas pumps, and the automakers' stubborn allegience to continued production of oversized, gas-guzzling cars and vans.

If the gathering storm can be traced to the very causes of failure, then the earliest warnings can take several forms:

- ☐ New and more formidable competitors.
- ☐ A shrinking market or decreased market share.
- ☐ Legislation that could jeopardize the entity's ability to profitably operate.
- ☐ Dependence on one product or too narrow a product line with weakening demand.
- ☐ Dependence on, or loss of a key franchise, principal customer, or principal supplier.

□ A lag behind the industry in technological developments or in commitment to research and development.

□ Adverse consumer or market trends.

□ Dependence on "one-man" rule or key personnel that cannot be easily replaced, and a weakening of their management effectiveness.

Companies, then, move through several stages on their way to failure. The first stage encompasses faulty management decisions or failure to respond to change that weakens its strategic position. The company may begin to lose market share, suffer reduced growth, lag behind in technological advances, or generally begin to slip from its competitive position, as its overall performance drops.

As the company enters the second stage of decline, operational and financial symptoms become clearer. Sales slip further as more customers are lost; advertising, promotion, and new product development may be cut back; morale within the organization dips, and the financially weak company begins to experience more chronic economic difficulties. This second stage is best characterized by a shift from positive, long-term thinking to a preoccupation with short-term operational problems.

As the company advances to the third stage, it shifts to a defensive position. Losses mount, inventories dwindle, credit is curtailed, and cash flow becomes increasingly scarce. At this point the company begins the "bankruptcy spin"—a viscious cycle where a shrinking asset base means fewer sales, greater losses, and a further dwindling of assets.

Finally, the company enters the fourth and terminal stage—a point from which few recover. Continuing its defensive existence, lawsuits from creditors regularly appear, lenders threaten or attempt foreclosure, taxing authorities press for overdue tax payments, current assets are all but gone, and key employees and customers have long abandoned ship.

It is typically no sooner than the third stage, or even the fourth and final stage, that distressed managers begin to recognize that the company will not turn itself around and that a drastic reorganization effort is needed if the company is to have a hope for long-term survival.

The most difficult decision managers must make as the company continues its gradual plunge is to determine the precise moment the company passes a point of no return beyond which it has no realistic expectation of internal rehabilitation—reliance on a change in the profit picture alone—and a full-scale turnaround program is needed. The dilemma is not unlike the plight of the pilot of the disabled aircraft with one foot out the door while wondering whether the plane might not straggle its way back to base after all. Most turnaround leaders agree that once a company is well into the second stage of a downturn it is unlikely the company will correct course on its own. Something *has* to happen to make the company correct course and managers must begin to think of some fundamental changes in the company.

AN EAR TO THE GROUND

No matter how closely management may keep its ear to the ground, its efforts to detect operational problems must come through a constant and candid flow of information from line employees, customers, and suppliers.

Good communication does not just happen. It has to be cultivated, organized, and become part of the corporate culture. In short, employees have to know that bad news is as welcome as good news—and, in fact, is considered even more important.

If a front-line employee senses something is wrong and it can only be corrected at the top, he or she must feel confident the message will quickly reach the top, and be acted upon. In short, the company must have an open-door policy.

In practice, of course, it rarely works that way because top managers create needless barriers between themselves and the front-line troops— barriers made up of layer upon layer of middle managers who may be incapable of resolving larger problems and may be reluctant to relay bad news to the top, particularly when the boss welcomes and rewards only good news.

One of our first steps in a turnaround situation is to interview employees from various departments in an effort to cross-sample the corporate condition. Frustrated people finally have someone to talk to— a sounding board to get pent-up frustrations off their chest.

Top managers may not realize that these front-line troops can be a wealth of information about the true corporate condition. They know what the problems are because they constantly live with them. They share with us endless tales of shoddy products, inventory shortages, lost accounts, low morale, and the countless other ills that may befall the stricken company. Typically, they know more than headquarters about what is really going on with the company.

Smaller companies with shorter chains of command do not necessarily have an easier time with communication. An owner of a small firm with 10 employees may be as distant as the CEO isolated from thousands of employees. As Harold Geneen advises: "Check your corporate communications. When operating people quit coming to you with problems that doesn't mean you don't have problems. The truth is that may be the biggest problem of all."

KEEPING SCORE

An eagle eye for trouble can be meaningless without the solid financial controls necessary to accurately measure a downturn. All other signals are intuitive. When the financials continue to bleed red there are serious problems.

Financial warnings usually appear after operational signals. But even when management is willing to come to grips with developing problems, it may lack the financial controls necessary to be forewarned of approaching danger.

Failed companies can often be shown to have either nonexistent or woefully inaccurate financial statements. It is important to note that we are talking about accounting information, not necessarily physical data such as units sold, items in stock, production per hour, or other operational data that many managers rely on. Instead, the failed company will most likely suffer from lack of accurate information in three critical areas: profits, costs, and cash position.

The first weakness may be a deficient budgetary control system without which management never knows how well or poorly it is doing or whether it is operating above or below its break-even point. Also, the company many have a poor costing system, so management fails to understand the relationship of key activities to bottom-line profits. Finally, the company invariably operates without a cash flow plan so management never anticipates the next peak demand for cash or how it is to be met.

Although the company's financials will certainly get progressively worse as insolvency approaches, it will not normally be possible to see the deterioration take place simply by inspecting the accounts. The sad fact is that too many failing companies resort to creative accounting to disguise a pathetic performance. Rolls Royce, for example, deferred millions of dollars in losses over a span of years simply by capitalizing its enormous research costs. Simple though the play may have been, it was nevertheless totally successful in leading the most sophisticated analysts to believe that Rolls Royce was performing well when in fact it had awesome operational losses.

Smaller corporations frequently operating without audited statements are even more vulnerable to intentional or unintentional inaccuracies in financial reporting. Their statements typically contain a wealth of erroneous information. Small losses may actually be whoppers. Conversely, losses that may spur panic may, in reality, be profits. A small business with noncertified statements must allow for a considerable margin of error. The error may be in overestimating inventories, overvaluing receivables, capitalizing items that should be expensed, and a host of other accounting distortions which may navigate management toward the wrong decision.

Even when small companies have strong financial systems they may lack the ability to effectively use their financials as warning devices, because of built-in inaccuracies. For example, decreasing inventory levels may disguise losses, yet many businesses fail to conduct annual inventories to detect this early warning signal. At year's end the owner estimates the inventory and conveniently places it at the same level as the prior year's. Decreases in inventory can go unnoticed because they happen so gradually. Even experienced managers may not notice a decrease in inventory from $70,000 to $60,000, but that decrease represents a $10,000 loss.

Conversely, an owner may be reasonably accurate in estimating assets but inaccurate in reporting liabilities. Good managers watch liability levels closely. They have regular payment schedules and can easily detect when bills remain unpaid longer than usual, which itself is an important warning signal. It does not take long for a record of prompt payments to turn into a stack of dunning notices. Yet owners or managers may have no idea what they owe. An owner may guess $50,000, but when insisting on an updated list of accounts, the actual amount owed may exceed $100,000.

Then, too, untrained or inexperienced owners and managers may pay too little attention to their financial statements because they do not know how to use them as management tools. Only a small percentage of small business owners can intelligently interpret their financial statements. This is a recurring theme. Businesspeople everywhere cannot tell you whether they are making money or losing money. Books and records do not exist, lay in shambles, or are buried away unused. As one accountant serving a number of small companies admits with a quizzical laugh, "Financial statements may be the closest thing to a precise guess."

If managers are unable to make sense of their financials, the firm's accountant cannot always be relied upon to toll the warning bell either. Too many accountants are little more than year-end tax preparers who never provide their clients the needed financial guidance. We can recount story after story of companies deeply in debt who came to us after several years of substantial losses without as much as a mutter from their accountants. But this is not a blanket indictment of the accounting profession. Many accountants are on the ball and yell loud and clear at the first signs of trouble. These accountants work hard to help their clients achieve a turnaround and often drag their confused, reluctant clients to outside help. Still others defend their lack of navigational involvement by reporting, "The client didn't want my help, he paid me only enough to do the taxes, nothing more."

According to Charles Morneau, an accountant specializing in turnarounds:

> When we are called in to a case we begin by asking whether the company's financial reporting systems are adequate and trustworthy. If we have any doubts about the reliability of the information we reconstruct the financials. Then to determine the gravity of the downturn we will focus on the following:
>
> ☐ Are losses mounting or profits decreasing at a steady rate, and over an extended time period?
>
> ☐ Are losses significant when measured against sales? Can the company absorb the losses and for how long?
>
> ☐ Are current assets—cash, receivables and inventory—at an acceptable level? How do current assets compare to the current liabilities?
>
> ☐ Where have the changes in the financial position occurred?
>
> ☐ What is the present cash position of the firm? Will projected cash flow be positive or negative?
>
> ☐ Are the underlying problems—and solutions—observable through the financial statements?
>
> Once we obtain answers to these questions, we establish a schedule of critical dates for follow-up evaluation. Oftentimes the

company will have a turnaround program already underway so we want to periodically measure whether the downdraft is continuing.

THROUGH THE LOOKING GLASS

A distressed company can never keep its secret, no matter how hard it tries. In fact, creditors, suppliers, and customers are often the first to be aware of the company's problems.

Creditors have as much stake in the early detection of financial difficulty as does the troubled company. In fact, creditors may have the greater stake when we consider that they ultimately foot the bill for excessive losses through the needless buildup of excessive debt.

Faced with growing problems, the normal reaction of debtor companies is to conceal their difficulties from creditors as long as possible. This hopefully keeps the flow of credit open from unsuspecting suppliers and avoids the scramble to collect overdue bills by more aware creditors.

While the strategy temporarily helps cash flow, it only buys time and certainly does not solve the overall problem. In many cases buying time from unaware creditors is counterproductive as owners may make other costly mistakes—such as throwing in more of their own money—before both they and the creditors realize a workout is the only possible solution.

On the other hand, early detection by creditors can be a valuable ally in a successful workout. One reason is that creditors, by their own coercive influence, can push the troubled company into a badly needed turnaround effort before it becomes too late. Also, creditors are more likely to be cooperative in a workout when they do not feel debt was needlessly incurred by the reluctance of management to face its problems. Finally, creditors (particularly secured lenders) can often provide needed support and assistance—both managerial and financial—to the cooperative debtor firm that stands ready to accept its problems and take constructive steps toward recovery.

Creditors rely on a variety of techniques to detect problems, although not always efficiently, as attested to by the countless billions of dollars lost each year in the bankruptcy courts. Visits to the debtor's premises, phone calls, rumors within the trade, and a close review of financial statements are all standard detection procedures. In addition, each type of creditor has a distinct opportunity for spotting early signs of financial difficulty.

For the trade creditor any change in either payment or purchase patterns should indicate possible financial trouble. A company that has customarily discounted its payables but ceases prompt payment may be in as much financial difficulty as the debtor who gradually but consistently extends the terms of payment. Likewise, customers who suddenly buy abnormally large quantities on credit may simply be anticipating a near-term shut-off on credit. Trade creditors are also in an exceptionally good position to hear about customer problems through rumors that permeate every industry. Alert credit managers tend to have their information network of customers and other suppliers all too anxious to spread the bad news.

Conversely, banks and other secured lenders seldom have access to trade sources and are therefore more dependent on financial rather than operational signals. Since troubled companies usually stay current on secured loans long after they become delinquent on trade debt, reliance on payments is a relatively poor indicator of advancing problems. If a secured lender extends funds on the strength of the borrower's accounts receivable and inventory, it is in a good position to observe the early signs of trouble. Reviewing these items together with shipments, purchase orders, accounts receivable collections, and inventory changes on a frequent basis may confirm that the borrower is or soon will be in financial difficulty.

There are other operational and financial signals that creditors can rely upon as reliable indicators of stress:

- ☐ The company is encountering personnel changes with many of the best people leaving the company.
- ☐ The company has made changes in its accounting or other reporting methods.
- ☐ The relationship between the amount of accounts payable and purchases is adversely changing.
- ☐ Buying patterns have become erratic and seemingly tied to cash flow rather than inventory need.
- ☐ There is a marked decrease in inventory based on observation or financial reporting.
- ☐ Checking account overdrafts and returned checks appear.
- ☐ The company requests the return of goods for credit or demands other unusual trade concessions.

☐ Inventory purchases have shifted to other suppliers who may have offered more lenient credit terms.

☐ Credit reports disclose an increase in collection claims and lawsuits.

☐ New security interests to secondary lenders, tax liens, or other creditor attachments recently occurred.

☐ There is a known loss of a key customer or other cause for a decrease in sales.

☐ The physical plant is in deteriorating condition.

☐ Advertising and promotion is curtailed.

When a creditor spots one or more of these danger signals its natural instinct is defensive; the creditor will attempt to secure past-due payments and protect itself on future shipments. These creditor actions can in turn be useful signals to the troubled company that creditors perceive it to be in difficulty whether in fact it is true or not.

Customers have their own ways to sense all is not well. While a customer can easily abandon a poorly performing supplier, the defensive position of the beleagured supplier may actually work in favor of the customer, encouraging it to remain with the supplier to its own advantage. It is not uncommon for customers to take advantage of the troubled firm by withholding payment or by demanding lower prices or greater concessions—mindful that the crippled supplier may have greater dependence on the continued business relationship that would stronger, more independent suppliers who can afford to hold their ground. Major customers can easily cannibalize a small, struggling supplier and do not hesitate to move in for the kill at the least signs of vulnerability, which typically include:

☐ Frequent and deep discount promotions to raise needed cash.

☐ A willingness to discount receivables.

☐ Chronic out-of-stock situations.

☐ Erratic delivery or reduced service.

☐ Rapid turnover of personnel.

☐ Failure to grant credits, extend trade concessions, or pay rebate allowances.

☐ Tightened credit policy—or factoring of receivables.

☐ Decline in product quality.

On the firing line, employees are perhaps in the best position to watch the drama of decline unfold. They, more than any other group, most quickly feel the impact as they encounter:

☐ Employee cutbacks and terminations.

☐ Reduction or elimination of fringe benefits.

☐ Resistance to conventional raises and pay increases.

☐ Cuts in overtime.

☐ Delays in capital expenditures.

☐ Deferred maintenance.

☐ Inability to obtain goods on credit.

☐ Creditor pressures.

☐ Increased desperation and decreasing morale within the organization.

Eventually each of these groups falls victim to what I call ethical collapse. In the final throes of desperation management begins to weave the same web of deception around others as it has around itself. During this stage the company begins to engage in a growing pattern of shabby dealing:

☐ Defective or poor quality products are shipped.

☐ Product warranties and service commitments are no longer honored.

☐ Vendors are conned into shipping more product on credit.

☐ Existing and new investors are foolishly encouraged to throw more capital into the venture.

☐ The company draws down all available lines of bank credit.

☐ Wages and fringe benefits due employees go unpaid.

Miraculously, these strategies work—for a little while—because they each in their own way add to the cash flow and therefore help the company stay afloat. Yet, to allow the company to reach this stage only forces the company to lose the confidence and support of the people it most needs to rebuild.

4

The Leadership Challenge

ONE common characteristic of all successful turnarounds is a leader—someone who can energize the organization, overcome the obstacles, and head the company toward a new beginning.

Could the once-ailing Chrysler have survived without Iacocca? Would the giant Wickes company be in business today but for the turnaround talents of Sandy Sigiloff? We can only wonder, but I believe the leadership these men brought to their organizations was the decisive factor in their successful corporate turnarounds. While the heroic attempts of turnaround leaders such as Iacocca and Sigiloff are legendary, there are scores of less notable companies blessed with equally determined and capable managers at the helm.

Perhaps it is impossible to describe the typical turnaround leader. They do not share a physical stereotype. They do not necessarily have the same background or experience. And they typically have very different managerial styles. To meet the soft-spoken Robert Wilson, who in his own subdued way rescued Memorex Corporation, is a very different experience from shaking hands with the cigar-toting, super-energized Lee Iacocca.

The search for the ideal turnaround leader is clearly as illusive as is the search for the ideal entrepreneur or ideal manager for the stable firm. While there can be a shopping list of traits that would appear desirable, the specific managerial strengths that are most in need will depend on the organization and its own unique problems and opportunities.

Turnarounds do, however, require a very different breed of individual than do stable, well-performing enterprises. Good custodial managers are content to keep the company on path, steering the organization in a straight line measured by occasional and predictable gains. They run the business by the book and usually with an abundance of resources. Essentially, custodial managers are safe as long as they avoid serious foul-ups. In short, good custodial managers are good caretakers of the corporate fortunes.

The turnaround leaders, in contrast, are "blood and guts" types. They take the big risks because big risks are needed. They kick butts and snub their noses at the board of directors. They are tough-minded enough to fight everyone within and outside the company who stands in the way of change, because they know more than anyone that change is what the organization needs. A good turnaround leader is comfortable as an SOB because he knows popular decisions are seldom the right decisions. Turnaround leaders are the General George Pattons of the business world—unlovable but effective.

Very few custodial managers can be converted into turnaround leaders, and the reverse is equally true. Custodial managers have been programmed for success rather than adversity. America's 600 business schools churn out 80,000 budding executives each year. One institution even offers the MBA program on New York commuter trains causing one pundit to comment, "They might more usefully offer the course on the subway leading to the bankruptcy court." Yet business schools continue to turn out managers who quickly become disoriented when things go wrong, because business schools have long neglected the subject of turnarounds, and few provide a focus on the downside of entrepreneurial life. Recalling my own days in business school, our case studies invariably dealt with the problems of the plush *Fortune* 500 corporations, causing one of my classmates to later confide, "I didn't know companies could lose so much money until after I got out of business school and took my first job."

Even experience in troubled companies may not be enough to qualify for a leadership role. While there are numerous managers who have been deeply involved in corporate workouts, many of these managers have a narrow perspective of the turnaround process only because they had narrow responsibility. And even if the manager has broad experience in turnaround situations it may not be sufficient. Although the tasks of general management are often described as planning, organizing, implementing, and controlling the turnaround process, perhaps the definition devalues the difference between the concepts of managing and leading by reducing something exciting and dynamic to a series of managerial banalities. We may use the terms "manager" and "leader" as if they were synonymous. But this is a misconception. While a leader must be able to manage, a manager does not necessarily have to lead, and in a turnaround situation leading is the only task a turnaround leader has time to accomplish.

STARTING AT THE TOP

The large corporation can—and usually does—replace a floundering top management team with a new turnaround leader and workout team. Once stabilized, the turnaround leader—always on the prowl for new challenges—moves on and a custodial manager is again brought in to take over the controls. More often than not the top managers are kicked out not on the objective assessment of whether they can turn the company around but because they happened to be in charge when the mess occurred. Whether they created the mess can be irrelevant. Often the decision to replace top management comes from lenders or creditor groups who may engage in their own power struggle to determine who will lead the turnaround. In search for replacement management, the corporate board may mistakenly look for another custodial type and not recognize either that the company needs bonafide turnaround leadership or the type individual best suited to the situation.

Not surprisingly, while corporate boards are quick to use top managers as the scapegoats for corporate misfortunes, few corporate boards candidly assess their own complicity in the downturn. When we thoroughly evaluate the many companies that do fail we can invariably find a corporate board that poorly served its organization either in its ability to shape an effective corporate strategy or to control the actions of its managers.

Unlike the larger corporation that can play musical chairs with its CEO, the owner of the privately held corporation is the boss and the boss is irreplaceable. As Scott Dantuma, a Chicago turnaround consultant, says:

When called to bail out a floundering small business, the success of the turnaround inevitably has to rest on the ability of the owner. We may have to give him an inordinate amount of support, delegate to more capable employees or rely heavily on outside professionals to bolster the management effort, but sometimes management is simply too weak at the top and the turnaround fails. Typically, it was this same managerial weakness that got the company into trouble in the first place. In a small company we are forced to accept the capabilities of the top people as we find them. There is no changing of the guard.

Therefore, the ability of the business owner to mastermind his or her own turnaround is critical in designing the overall strategy. Many of the companies we consult to can be successfully reorganized, but not by their present owners. Whenever we come across an owner clearly incapable of managing his or her company through a turnaround we push him or her toward alternatives: a partner, outright sale, or even liquidation. If the turnaround promises to be a quick process and the owner has strong custodial skills, the answer may be a turnaround consultant to head the company on a full-time basis until the company is revived. Many companies can benefit from a "rent-a-boss" approach. As worthy as the idea may seem, however, very few small business owners believe an outsider can run their business as well as they can, and these same owners become even more protective when their company is on the skids. They think their presence is all the more important even though it may be destroying whatever chances the company has for survival.

Considering that the small business turnaround must revolve around the capabilities of its owner, turnaround strategies must often be based on what the owner can tolerate and achieve rather than selecting the strategy that may be best for the company. Many small business owners, for example, lack the stamina to put up with a two- or three-year Chapter 11, requiring less demanding alternatives to the problems. And often owners must tackle more fundamental questions before they can enthusiastically commit to leading the turnaround:

1. What are the specific reasons for keeping the company alive?

2. Can these objectives be satisfied through means other than continuity of the business?

3. Is there an honest desire to see the business through its troubled times and put it back on the road to success?

4. Do I really have the interest in staying with this company, and the capability to manage it properly?

Playing part-time psychologist to the misguided owner can be a challenge. Everyone knows the owner is unhappy in the business and so does the owner. Lead the owner back to the salvaged business and he or she continues on with a life of misery, managerial neglect, and eventual stagnation or failure.

Motivation is the thrust behind leadership and when it no longer exists the only solution for the unmotivated owner is to divest himself or herself of the business and select a new career path. And this is equally applicable to the CEO of the large corporation whose enthusiasm may be waning.

That advice may appear to be contrary to the thrust of this book. Actually, it is what this book is about. Saving a business requires management and leadership. Leadership requires motivation and enthusiasm.

Probably 30 percent of all small business owners eventually decide they are in the wrong business. A case that started out as a "turnaround" is transformed into a sale or liquidation. It goes beyond the question of whether the owner can effectively manage the business. More commonly these frustrated people simply have "no stomach" for the business. Many of these owners inherited the business or fell into it not deliberately, or by reasoned choice, but by chance. In other instances, the owner had a misconception of what the business would really be like. Reality can be somewhat different than expectation. Those who for years have successfully operated the business may question their own motivation to lead the organization out of the woods. While the business once matched their needs they may suffer from burnout, the desire for a career change, or, as is typically true with those who have worked the business for 20 to 30 years, they may simply be tired and no longer need the business. Leadership for the smaller organization must start with the owner understanding his or her own personal objectives, which must be an overwhelming desire to turn defeat into victory.

THE LEADERSHIP ROLE

What is it that the turnaround leader must bring to the stricken business? What is expected of him or her? How can he or she perform most effectively?

First and foremost the turnaround leader is the architect of change. He or she must shape the organization from what it is to what it can or must become. As architect, the leader must clearly and objectively assess the present condition of the company, create a realistic vision of its future, and develop the game plan for getting it there. Unquestionably, the role of architect carries with it the need for more than a modicum of entrepreneurial talent, broad business experience, and creativity.

Creativity may be even more important than business "know-how." Often managers become so steeped in their own experiences that they stop thinking creatively—which by definition means trying new things. Fortunately, there are unending lines of adventurists willing, even eager, to breathe fresh ideas into tired companies. Sometimes it only takes someone with a different perception to see opportunity where none was seen before. There is the long-enduring tale of two market researchers who were independently dispatched some years ago to one of the world's less-developed countries by one of the larger shoe manufacturers. When their telegrams arrived at corporate headquarters, one message dismally read, "No market here. Nobody wears shoes," whereas the other promised, "Great market here, nobody has any." Turnaround leaders are very much opportunity-oriented, not problem-oriented.

Being a visionary is not enough, however. The second and perhaps even more important role of the turnaround leader is to implement the strategy. For every 10 managers with a clear vision of what their company can become, only three can fulfill it (in the immortal words of Robert Burns, "The best laid schemes o' mice and men ..."). It is indeed their ability to make the right things happen that distinguishes the true turnaround leader from more mortal characters.

Recently I was asked to speak before the American Electronics Association on "The Role of the Turnaround Leader," a talk that prepared me well for this chapter because it forced me to think back over hundreds of successful cases to distill the essence of turnaround leadership. Having given the question adequate reflection, I concluded that the effective turnaround leader must perform six vital functions:

☐ Motivate
☐ Activate
☐ Communicate
☐ Aggravate

□ Negotiate
□ Innovate

Motivate: Creating a Climate for Success

Turnaround leaders do create a climate for success. Most important is the ability of the turnaround leader to reinstate a sense of purpose and motivation within the organization. Not surprisingly, employees, customers, suppliers, stockholders, creditors, and even the corporate board are disenchanted with the company and there may be few believers left. Everyone associated with the company believes the company will fail, often a self-fulfilling prophecy.

To counteract slumbering spirits, the turnaround leader has to be a bit of evangelist. "You have to put a smile on your face so others can restore the smile to theirs," reminds turnaround consultant Al Cook. "People have to believe and *want* to believe."

President Franklin Delano Roosevelt, navigating the country through its own massive turnaround during the Great Depression, will be forever remembered for his inspiring and confidence-building fireside chats long after his social and economic programs are buried in history. Self-confidence is needed because people are scared and they must see strength coming from the top, so Roosevelt was never without his confident smile. But a leader who is imparting strength of that type cannot impart it unless he or she feels it and radiates it. Only when someone steps in who can decisively give the company that climate for success can a positive outlook be regained.

We typically find employees "blue" and demoralized. Why shouldn't they be? They do not know when they will be fired. Their pay may have been cut by 20 percent. Some of their co-workers have already been axed. They are working under the worst conditions and with too many pressures. Often these very real concerns have been ignored by management, which can be found moping around with their own long faces.

In this environment a strong turnaround leader can make all the difference. The leader can convince people the company will succeed, can convince employees the company is heading in the right direction, and can motivate employees with the incentives and rewards for staying with the company through the hard times. These are all part of rebuilding the climate for success.

Frank Grisanti of Grisanti and Galef, a leading turnaround consulting firm, sums it up this way: "You don't turn people around; they turn themselves around. If new leadership is strong, thsoe people who are really sensitive to good leadership will recognize it quickly and change their ways."

Managers who are themselves weary and depressed with business problems may be the least able to inspire the troops. Sometimes this inspiration can be achieved by an outside consultant or someone else within the organization who can serve as its spark plug.

Dr. Barry Bleidt, Professor of Administration at the University of Texas, observes: "More than anything else, the turnaround leader must have a positive outlook, an attitude that accepts success as a foregone conclusion." Perhaps the individual is most like the founder of Osborne Computer who reported in INC Magazine: "This (Osborne) ... was no two bit start-up. I didn't have a degree in electronics and never had run a manufacturing plant, nonetheless I knew we would succeed," he said confidently in 1983, shortly before his company went bankrupt. Optimism, even when it is ill-deserved, can be a rare and precious commodity when it is otherwise so scarce.

Activate: The Organizational KITA

Turnaround leaders are people who know how to give the organization a strong "kick-in-the-ass" (KITA) because they know that the best way to shake the organization from its doldrums is to activate it with a series of actions. The effective turnaround leader beginning work in an atmosphere where complacency and lethargy have taken hold shocks the system to quickly get attention. Suddenly people realize something decisive is happening to turn the company around. One turnaround consultant starts his assignment with a number of small actions. He routinely changes offices, reassigns parking spaces, and once even ordered a cafeteria painted, all apparently meaningless gestures but designed to show employees at least something was happening when nothing had happened for so long.

Every turnaround leader seems to have a different way to shock the system—get peoples' attention and begin the process of getting their adrenalin pumping. The leader may fire a scapegoat at a highly visible level within the organization, usually a.visible scapegoat associated with the company's problems, or scrap some favorite projects.

Whatever it is the turnaround leader does it is always accompanied by the necessary fanfare to spread the word that things are happening. The turnaround leader uses both symbolic and substantive shock to shake the company out of its lethargy. It may be with negative motivators or positive motivators, and various techniques to activate the organization can be used, but a requisite of effective turnaround management is the need to show that the turnaround leader's words mean business. The turnaround leader is characterized by this willingness to make the fast, tough, and always visible decisions. Giving the organization a swift KITA means letting the troops know a leader has finally arrived.

Communicate: Spreading the Word

The great turnaround leader is also a great communicator. He or she knows how to keep up a continuous stream of information both within the organization and to the various constituencies outside the organization.

In a sense, the ability to communicate is essential if the leader is to motivate and activate. Communications—two-way communications —are as essential in a turnaround as is having a product to sell. Yet many turnarounds have failed only because the leader failed to build adequate communication within the company and with creditors, lenders, customers and suppliers outside.

To the extent the turnaround depends on cooperation and the continued confidence of the various constituent groups, the leader must keep them both thoroughly informed and actively involved with a constant flow of meaningful, accurate data. Equally important, the leader demands the same constant flow of information into his or her office to quickly determine organizational response to the turnaround effort.

The effective leader does more than communicate for purposes of obtaining or providing information. Communication is seen as the way of solidifying relationships which can be easily strained in a workout.

Bill Van Buskirk, who has orchestrated several notable turnarounds in the retail trades, recounts that on a typical assignment he spends two days a week in the stores and three days out talking to suppliers and lenders. "The most important thing I can do is take a major supplier to lunch because that's the only way you maintain confidence in this business. And without confidence you don't get your next shipment of goods," he adds. Being a good communicator means being a goodwill ambassador.

Most turnaround leaders agree that communication is an important part of holding the troubled business together.

Good communication in a turnaround does not just happen. Most managers are poor communicators and are reluctant to communicate because so much news can be bad. Managers of the troubled company have a natural reluctance to come in contact with those viewed as hostile to the company, which may easily include just about everyone involved with the company. The turnaround leader is not afraid to take heat in face-to-face meetings with angry employees and creditors, because he or she understands that when you need these people to rebuild the company you begin by communicating.

Aggravate: On Becoming the Resident SOB

Turnaround leaders do not win popularity contests, and the struggle to keep the company alive certainly cannot be accomplished by a "sheep-in-sheep's clothing." In short, the effective leader is usually the resident "bastard" because he or she is the one who has to make the unpopular decisions if the organization is to survive—the leader who must make and enforce the nasty decisions to lay off workers, cut salaries, scrap pet projects, withhold payments to creditors, and say "no" to a hundred people who press him or her to say "yes."

The turnaround leader must be a tough-minded manager with an equally "thick skin" because the decisions he or she makes are usually painful. For example, many people will shrink from the task of firing an older employee who has been with the company for 25 years simply because that employee can no longer pull his or her weight. And it takes a tough soul to withhold payment to a small and long-loyal supplier whose own existence depends on the check. But those are the difficult decisions turnaround leaders face every day, and they must be willing to spread some blood and guts around the organization if it is to survive. The true turnaround leader understands that sacrifice is part of survival and that what he or she does today may be essential if the company is to be around tomorrow.

But not everybody has it in them to orchestrate a massacre, or step on more than a few toes. In fact, the major problem with most people is that they tend to be kind, sensitive souls who want to keep their company alive while "doing the right thing by everyone else." Of course, they eventually have to make a choice—be charitable and give away the shop or put on the bullet-proof vest and stay in business. Turnaround leaders understand there is no middle ground.

Sometimes the organization needs more than tough decisions, it needs a bona fide massacre, and it takes a rare individual indeed to pull it off. One such individual was George Trimble who turned the mammoth Bunker-Ramo Corporation topsy-turvy by throwing 1100 people out of work in the first week. As George Trimble might say, "The meek may inherit the earth but its the SOBs who keep it in business."

This does not mean turnaround leaders cannot be sensitive souls themselves. They are perhaps as sensitive as anyone else but they make decisions while painfully aware of the fact that they have no alternatives. Bob Kuzara of Kuzara and Associates admits that he often feels like a cross between Genghis Kahn and Attila the Hun when he performs mayhem to rescue a corporate client, but he says, "When it comes to turnarounds, nice guys don't finish last. They don't finish at all."

Negotiate: Corporate Yin and Yang

A turnaround has been described as the process of negotiating. What else can we call a process where the few remaining corporate assets will be pushed and pulled between the countless players who each want a piece? So a key talent of the turnaround leader is the ability to be a winning negotiator. During each stage of the turnaround, negotiating skills are tested. The leader begins by negotiating authority from the board of directors. The leader then negotiates with lenders and key suppliers. Eventually, the leader negotiates with general creditor groups. And during the long turnaround process the leader endlessly negotiates with labor unions, key managers, and, finally, if circumstances require it, prospective merger partners and acquirors.

Chrysler's Lee Iacocca boasts his major strength to be his negotiating ability, a self-assessment few people quarrel with. The flashbacks to Chrysler's stormy turnaround has Iacocca negotiating loan guarantees with the government, major concessions from the United Auto Workers, and not insignificant assistance from its dealer network. It was not Iacocca's "equality of sacrifice" pitch that saved Chrysler but his masterful skill in selling the pitch.

The role of the turnaround leader as negotiator is critically important because of the divergent interests and perspectives of so many groups. Moreover, the company's survival is dependent on the continued support of each. To pull these divided—often hostile—factions together to share and endorse an overall workout plan is rarely easy. To keep good relationships intact while it is being attempted is borderline magic. "The tact of Henry Kissinger, and the wit of Will Rogers, is needed to get a creditor to accept 10 cents on the dollar and still shake your hand," suggests Mark Tilden, a Boston lawyer who has negotiated countless workout plans.

The ability to persuade is equally important within the organization when dealing with employees. For turnaround leaders, this crucial talent entails the ability to get satisfaction from results when one's part in the process must necessarily be indirect. Achieving results through others requires persuading them of a particular course of action and then staying out of the trenches. But as tough as they may be, turnaround leaders try to avoid coercion—flamethrowing and bulldozing—when conciliation and negotiation are available. It is through this power to effectively negotiate that the turnaround leader controls the coordination of people, ideas, money, and other resources needed to reshape the troubled company.

Innovate: Much Ado from Nothing

A motivated, capable work force, merchandise on the shelves, plenty of cash in the till, and more than enough cash coming in are the sine qua non of successful companies. Unsuccessful companies innovate.

The most intriguing characteristic of the turnaround leader is the ability to make something from nothing—because nothing is all there is to work with. Innovation may apply to new policies, new procedures, new ways of doing business, or new people in new jobs. It means more than change because even healthy companies undergo change. Instead it means improvising to counteract the chronic shortages of everything that plague every troubled company. The turnaround leader is an innovator because innovation is borne of desperation.

The innovative leader is not shackled by traditional procedures because traditional procedures no longer work. Innovation is making the organization respond to the resources available today instead of the resources that were available yesterday.

Many companies fail because management cannot adapt to changing circumstances. This is particularly true of managers who have become too accustomed to a set way of doing business, or have narrow experience, or simply cannot use creativity in place of cash.

Yet, while leaders innovate to survive, it is this same innovation that can lead them to enormous success. Such was the case when Mattel, Incorporated was forced to subcontract manufacture of toys—formerly produced themselves—only to discover the decision freed up considerable cash for even more profitable retail growth.

It is through this process of constant innovation that the leader navigates the company through the turnaround. However, no matter how carefully planned the turnaround may be, the turnaround never goes quite according to plan but ends up a series of zig and zags as the company repeatedly bumps up against unexpected obstacles. Sometimes the smallest obstacle stops the largest corporation cold in its tracks, unless it is an organization with an innovative leader.

Perhaps the greatest turnaround leaders are those who know when to *abdicate*, because they have the good sense to recognize their own limitations and willingly move over so more capable management can take charge. Yet leadership characteristics defined in this chapter are not chiseled in stone. Turnaround leaders, like other mortals, bring to the organization their own weaknesses, which fortunately give them a more human quality which adds to their overall effectiveness.

The turnaround leader must, however, bring two other important attributes to the sick company. The first is the capacity for a great deal of hard work. Very little of what we call turnaround management is glamorous. Almost all of it calls for tedious attention to detail and the ability to work under intense pressure from every direction. Leaders routinely work 16–18 hour days, seven days a week. Sandy Sigiloff's team reportedly worked 90-hour weeks during the first year of the Wickes turnaround. It is that commitment to the turnaround that can mean the difference between failure and success, since a turnaround can easily require twice the management effort as required by the more stable enterprise.

Many otherwise capable managers shrink from the leadership role simply because they do not share the enthusiasm for endless hours, the pressure-cooker environment, or the raw toughness we spoke about earlier. Perhaps it would be more accurate to say that a turnaround depends more on a leader with certain personality traits than with certain managerial skills.

Perseverance is the second essential attribute. More than anything else the company needs someone at the helm who will not quit and hastily throw in the organizational towel when the situation becomes bleak. Turnaround leaders are seasoned optimists and perpetual believers because all they have to trade on are their hopes and expectations. When optimism gives out there is nothing left to that word we call "leadership."

We have all seen many very ordinary management types eventually pull their companies out of trouble against overwhelming odds. On the other hand, we have all observed many companies fail when they had far greater resources, more chance for survival, and more talented leadership. Perseverance was the difference.

Turnaround leaders are opportunistic and exploitive. They see the opportunity first and then find the resources to exploit it. The opportunity comes from their own ingenuity and knowledge of the territory. And what they do not know about the territory they quickly discover. Turnaround leaders are flexible and adaptable, ready to change course, dropping one activity for another with greater promise. They are not only visionaries but realists as well. They must see what can be done but also understand the limitations of the organization as well as their own limitations. They willingly take the first step without knowing where the next step will take them. And whether they head a large corporation or a small one they will always be enthusiastic and involved, role models to be emulated throughout the organization.

Yet for all that turnaround leaders must be, they are best described as very ordinary men and women who have in them all that is necessary to do an extraordinarily difficult job.

5

White Knights and the Turnaround Team

A TURNAROUND is seldom a one-person show. A well-orchestrated corporate comeback requires a team of trained people, a blend of talent both from within and outside the organization.

A successful turnaround can often be traced to an owner or manager not too proud to recognize his or her own limitations and reach out for help. Ready with a helping hand is a growing army of consultants, lawyers, accountants, and other workout specialists who each in their own way make an important contribution to the revitalization process.

Timing is critical. Just as managers may wait too long to recognize the severity of their problems, they may also wait too long before seeking professional assistance. By then the business may have reached a point of no return.

Operators of troubled businesses hesitate to call in consultants and attorneys for several reasons. Many shy away from professionals as a symbolic admission of both failure and their own inadequacies in solving their problems. Turnaround consultants, like psychiatrists, routinely have to convince their clients that there is no shame in leaning on someone's shoulder. Businesspeople still cling to the ridiculous notion that they are supposed to be omnipotent and that business problems are loathsome diseases.

Cost may be another factor in an owner's hesitancy to seek help. The cash-shy business owner who cannot meet payroll hardly welcomes the idea of expensive consultants and lawyers who can charge upward of $150–200 an hour. These people seldom see professional assistance as a necessary investment but rather as an unaffordable cost. In the words of one reluctant client, "I don't need a high-priced consultant to tell me I'm running out of money."

Small business owners, being less sophisticated in the use of outside professionals than the larger corporation's executive, are less likely to understand how these professionals can help, even when they can help. The word "consultant" still scares people. They envision someone showing up in a three-piece suit, scanning the business for a few hours, then returning in a few weeks with a pristine report complete with charts and graphs that might just as well be written in Greek. Sometimes that happens but quite often the difference between success and failure is the ability of management to find the right outside professional talent and use it effectively. Most managers must bear in mind the painful reality that they got their business in trouble in the first place and they cannot get the business out of trouble on their own.

Consultants, attorneys, and accountants are, of course, needed for their technical skills. Management of the stable enterprise can be complex but the turnaround is far more complex and depends on unique skills and seemingly strange techniques that defy the rules of conventional management. The company going through a major turnaround needs people who understand how to put broken companies together again by playing by the rules and processes shared only by others who work in the insolvency field.

While the managerial and professional skills are obviously critical, the more valuable contribution of the professional advisor is the objectivity he or she may bring to the situation. Owners and managers usually get too close to the problems and cannot see them, much less find solutions. They are just too deeply involved emotionally and financially to "go it alone." Turnaround task forces are usually led by, if not composed of, people from outside the organization, so they will not be tainted by existing biases.

Frequently clients have the right answers but need outside professionals as a sounding board, to provide assurances that the right decisions are being made. Eighty percent of the time the client's intuition about what must be done is correct. But because the client has not been through a turnaround before, he or she do not have the confidence to follow through and press the decision into action.

Robert Cline, a Cleveland management consultant, says:

> The real function of outside professionals is to do for management what management cannot do for itself. The owner may know he has to fire people or stand up to creditors but may not have the guts to do it. Many times outside people are brought in to do the dirty work because the organization doesn't have a bastard on board.

The resources available through professional advisors can also be decisive. Consultants, attorneys, and accountants within the insolvency field form a small, closely knit professional network and are usually the best source for locating other players for the team. Most turnaround consulting firms maintain a roster of hundreds of other consulting and law firms who are outstanding within their specialities, and through this list they routinely match up difficult-to-find professionals with anxious clients. Professional advisors, in turn, maintain affiliations with banks, lenders, liquidators, business brokers, and others who administer to the troubled firm.

No two troubled companies will need exactly the same professional assistance. A firm that is losing money but is still solvent with no creditor problems may need a consultant to regain profitability but will have little need for an insolvency attorney to reorganize the company or defend it against creditor actions. Conversely, a company with weak financial controls or a poor marketing strategy will require different and more specialized operational skills than can be provided by a general turnaround consultant. Possibly the most important decision management can make is to determine precisely the type of assistance it most needs from:

☐ Turnaround consultants
☐ Business or operations consultants
☐ Insolvency attorneys
☐ Auditors and accountants
☐ Key personnel

TURNAROUND CONSULTANTS: THE WHITE KNIGHTS

Names such as Iacocca, Sigiloff, Grisanti, Galef, and Argenti are well known as white knights ready to ride to the rescue of the company in distress.

They have brought to the forefront the image of the turnaround consultant who, as the rugged individual, magically transforms corporate losers into winners.

Although turnaround consulting is a fast-growing specialty within the broader field of management consulting, there are still relatively few turnaround consultants and far too few to handle the many companies who need their services. Less than 1 percent of all management consultants consider themselves specialists within the field of turnarounds. Despite the fact that business bankruptcies are at a record high, these corporate fixers are so rare that there is not even a word for the trade they ply. One of the best-known practitioners, Stanley Hiller, Jr., even has difficulty explaining what he does. He describes it as "R & R–the repair and rebuild business."

The problem of finding the right turnaround consultant is further aggravated by the fact that the specialty is highly segmented. No two consultants seem to excel in the same situation or work the same territory, since they tend to operate in a narrow niche.

Many consultants, for example, confine themselves to a certain type of business: manufacturing, wholesaling, retailing, or service. Others confine themselves to particular industries such as textiles, real estate, or nursing homes. Virtually every consultant can characterize his or her practice by the size of the client, with the fewest consultants available to the smallest business—the one least able to afford the staggering fees charged by the better-known consultants. Victor Palmieri, another well-known corporate doctor, admits that he only looks for interesting and financially rewarding problems. "And that means they have to be big problems," says Palmieri. And for his efforts, Lee Iacocca pocketed nearly $20 million last year.

Consultants also bring to their clients very different skills. While most turnaround consultants consider themselves generalists adept at every phase of the workout, it is seldom true. Consultants, for all their aura and mystique, are no more omnipotent than the clients they serve. This same observation caused one cynic to declare, "All consultants offer impeccable credentials which can easily lead to misinterpretation by the unwary." Consultants, like everyone else, have certain strengths and weaknesses based on their own training, experience, and interests. Many consultants with a brilliant capability for stemming losses are woefully inadequate in straightening out the company's balance sheet. My own firm—Galahow & Company—built its nationwide clientele on its expertise in restructuring corporate debt but does not involve itself in operational matters. Sometimes the consultant will perform only one function, in one stage of the turnaround, as is the case with Robert Kuzara & Associates which steps in to stabilize the cash flow of companies in the severest financial crisis before turning the ailing client over to other consultants who can take the stabilized business to long-term rehabilitation.

The condition of the client company can be an important consideration in shopping for the right consultant. Some consultants do not function well under crisis conditions and prefer still healthy clients at the early stages of the downturn. Others—like the Kuzara firm—enjoy the challenge of a company on the edge. There are firms that thrive in the pressure-cooker climate characteristic of a firm a step away from bankruptcy. And along with the exhilaration that comes from stress, they enjoy high visibility, which, for most people who like this work, is its own reward.

Turnaround consultants also work in varied ways. Some follow the path of Sandy Sigiloff and nimbly rescue floundering giants such as Daylin and Wickes by taking over management of the ailing firm until it is fully revitalized. Fixer-uppers such as Sigiloff rely heavily on teamwork, bringing in their own crew of experts to chart the course. And while their financial rewards are not staggering, they bet on themselves, and when they win—as they always seem to do—their take can run into the millions. In contrast are consultants who remain part-time advisors simultaneously servicing many clients on a per-diem or hourly basis.

And not all turnaround consultants work for the troubled company. Nearly one in two represent banks and other lender or creditor groups whose interest is recouping as much as possible from the stricken debtor. Almost every major commercial lender has on its roster one or two workout consultants who attempt to breathe new life into a dying borrower with the hope that prolonged life will mean prolonged payments. Unwary debtor companies often mistake a workout consultant provided by the bank as someone who will look out for the company's interests—which is akin to the chicken looking to the fox for comfort. In a workout situation the interests of the troubled company and its creditors are necessarily adversarial, requiring the troubled business to retain independent consultants free of allegiance to creditors.

Turnaround consultants, for all their differences, tend to have one thing in common: a career that accidentally happened when their own company fell onto hard times. Virtually all consultants I know can recount earlier days when they wrestled for themselves the same problems they now wrestle for clients. From the experience they discovered the enjoyable challenge of saving a sick company.

As rare as they may be, there are several ways to find capable turnaround specialists. The Society for the Advancement of Management and the American Society of Consulting Engineers are two national organizations that have turnaround consultants within their ranks. Court-appointed bankruptcy trustees are frequently people with a track record in rehabilitating financially troubled companies. Credit associations are another particularly good source, as are banks and lenders, provided they can offer consultants free of conflict. The Small Business Administration, through its SCORE (Service Corps of Retired Executives) program, provides at no cost consultants with skill in this area, and it is not necessary to be an SBA borrower to qualify for this valuable assistance.

Talk to several consultants before engaging one. Probe their ideas, check their references, and investigate their track record with similar situations and comparable companies. A good consultant will gladly provide references of former clients. While the professional skills are important, the client must also develop a comfortable and compatible relationship with the consultant and therefore personalities are equally as important.

Selecting the right consultant is only half the battle. Unless the consultant is effectively used, nothing worthwhile can be accomplished. In fact, a poor working relationship between consultant and client can be more harmful to the organization than no relationship at all.

Admittedly, it is often difficult for someone who has operated his or her own business for 10 or 20 years to suddenly accept direction from a newcomer to the scene, even if the consultant has impeccable credentials. There is a natural tendency to resent an "outsider" interfering. Frequently the resistance to a consultant is because the consultant is forcefully imposed on management by creditor groups who have lost confidence in the ability of management to rescue the operation.

And there are times when the owner or senior management welcomes a consultant but other key employees resent or resist his or her involvement. Every consultant is looked upon by employees with a certain disdain, seeing the consultant as a threat to his or her job or authority.

On the other extreme are owners and managers who happily abdicate all managerial responsibility and decision making to their consultants. The owners may simply be to weary to continue the battle or foolishly believe the consultant has magical managerial powers. While consultants may better understand the turnaround process, the consultant needs the owner to assess the impact of turnaround decisions on operations. Consultants, for their part, may unduly dominate the decision-making process when the company needs the owner's active input if serious mistakes are to be avoided. It is these same owners who so readily turn control over to consultants who are most likely to have unrealistic expectations about what the consultant can accomplish. When the results are not achieved, friction between client and consultant frequently sets in.

The effectiveness of the working relationship, then, depends on the consultant and client each understanding their respective roles in the workout. The authority and functions of the consultant must be clearly communicated to key people within the organization so the chain of command does not become blurred. Essentially, it must be decided whether the consultant will have direct decision-making authority over operational decisions or whether he or she will serve only in an advisory role to top management.

To be effective, the consultant must not only understand his or her role within the management team, but must also understand his or her role within the turnaround team. The turnaround consultant must be able to develop a good working relationship with both the corporate and insolvency attorneys, accountants, and other advisors. Consultants may be as inclined to overstep their managerial roles as lawyers who mistakenly believe they are qualified to give business advice, and accountants who pretend they are lawyers. Good professional teamwork starts with a definition and mutual respect of the respective professional roles.

For consultants to be accepted, they must be presented to the corporate constituencies in the correct way. Employees who might otherwise view the consultant as a sign of managerial inadequacy must instead see the consultant as bolstering management's capabilities. Creditors concerned that the consultant's fees may erode cash otherwise available to pay their bills must instead feel the consultant is their best hope not only for a corporate recovery but for a greater recovery on their outstanding debts. Finally, everyone with a concern about the company's future must look upon the consultant as a source of credibility—a voice to say exactly what is—when management can no longer be taken at its word. An effective consultant knows not only how to repair a faltering business but is also a credible communicator to employees, suppliers, creditors, stockholders, and lenders as he or she both foresees and satisfies their respective concerns.

The turnaround consultant's life is rarely easy. Management may have unrealistic expectations of how rapidly or smoothly the turnaround should proceed, and the various interests may simply expect too much from the turnaround consultant. Robert Korb of Korb & Korb, a New York based turnaround consulting firm, speaks for all of us when he says, "Those involved with the troubled company oftentimes think a consultant can be a substitute for bad management. He can't be. The consultant can only help good managers better handle the turnaround."

BUSINESS CONSULTANTS:
BACK-TO-BASICS MANAGEMENT

Business consultants are an entirely different breed than turn-around consultants, but hold an equally important place in the turn-around process. While the turnaround consultant can cure the corporate ills, business consultants are frequently needed to attack the root causes. For example, our firm is now handling the turnaround of a Texas kitchen cabinet manufacturer. Within two months, we stabilized cash flow and are now completing the debt restructuring, eliminating over $600,000 in trade debt. But the basic reason for the company's difficulties are its woefully inefficient production methods and a nonexistent marketing program. To transform the company into a profitable enterprise we called in a production engineer who improved productivity 200 percent, and an advertising agency, now ready to roll-out with a hard-hitting marketing program designed to dramatically boost sales. Many troubled companies share these very basic operational problems in production, merchandising, marketing, or distribution that can only be solved by consultants with very specialized skills, not usually offered by turnaround consultants.

As turnaround consultants we can often see obvious problem areas within client companies but rarely do we know enough about the operational aspects or the 101 tricks of that particular trade that can make the difference between a failed or successful turnaround.

As another example of the importance of a seasoned industry veteran, we recently turned to a highly successful Boston restaurateur to consult with a struggling Cape Cod restaurant operator who suffered three consecutive years of poor profit margins. The right answers came with a new menu, strict portion controls, improved buying, and a greatly improved waste-prevention program that only someone with hands-on restaurant experience could provide. From a profitability standpoint, a turnaround may require nothing more than correcting some very basic problems within the business—problems that only someone experienced in the particular industry could possibly recognize.

For that reason, the best people to help with specific operational problems are the strongest operators within the industry. These are typically successful business owners who will lend their expertise to troubled, noncompeting companies within the same industry. And they can make a critical difference in corporate performance.

Because consulting needs vary greatly among companies, begin with a candid assessment of the specific needs. Does the company have a wide range of problems or specific difficulties? Does it need help with creditors, finances, cash flow, and curing the overall condition of the company, or are the problems operational? Is full-time or part-time support needed? Is a long-term or short-term consulting arrangement likely? These are the questions that must be answered before the search for a consultant begins.

LAWYERS: RIDING SHOTGUN

While consultants and workout specialists are invaluable, competent legal advice is vital. A turnaround is always law-related, even if bankruptcy or complex legal issues are avoided. At the very least an attorney will be necessary to forestall and defend creditor suits and, through his or her presence, remind creditors that bankruptcy is always the backdrop when a more pleasant and cooperative workout is unsuccessful.

Speaking as a bankruptcy attorney, I can say without misgivings that too many troubled small businesses are lost due to inexperienced legal representation. Small firms are more likely to struggle through their problems without a consultant and instead rely on their attorneys for guidance. And that is where costly mistakes are often made. As John Naisbitt, writing in *Megatrends*, asserts, "Lawyers are like beavers. They get in the mainstream and damn it up." Very few attorneys have experience rehabilitating troubled companies. Frequently real estate lawyers, criminal lawyers, and probate lawyers who would not recognize a balance sheet from a cash flow statement are advising clients on complex business and insolvency matters. Just as medicine is specialized, so too is the law. In reality there may be no such thing as a competent or incompetent attorney, as all attorneys are both competent *and* incompetent, depending on the area of law involved. The company needs an attorney well experienced in "saving" troubled companies, a legal gunslinger defending the beleagured corporation from its numerous foes. A rare breed? There may be even fewer practicing attorneys who can legitimately claim specialization in this area of practice then there are turnaround consultants. There are, of course, a number of lawyers who have handled business and personal bankruptcy cases, but Chapter 7 liquidating bankruptcies are relatively routine matters, requiring far different skills than demanded by a complex corporate turnaround or reorganization.

We see otherwise salvageable businesses liquidated every day because the attorney representing the business did not know the alternatives. If the attorney cannot offer workable rescue strategies, then other attorneys may offer solutions. Clearly, no business should be liquidated or thrown into bankruptcy without a thorough review by both turnaround consultants and experienced counsel.

A seasoned practitioner will not only know the legal strategies, but will know his or her way around the insolvency system as well. He or she has battled with creditors' counsel before and knows what to expect. Creditors' and debtors' counsel interact on hundreds of cases, developing a curious working relationship among themselves while still protecting the interests of their respective clients. As Dan Mandel, a bankruptcy lawyer with the Fort Lauderdale firm of Mandel and Weisman, says, "It's a lot easier negotiating a plan of reorganization with counsel for the creditors' committee when you are on a first name basis." The familiarity even works its way into the courtroom. A bankruptcy judge may be more inclined to trust the word of a lawyer who appears before him or her regularly, and this judicial leeway can make a difference in the outcome of a case.

Expect an established insolvency attorney to have a network of resources that can help the business survive. Such an attorney knows the banks that lend to troubled companies. He or she has dealt with accountants who can perform magic with a jumble of numbers. Consultants? The attorney is probably the best source. Many of the same lawyers are present at each workout; a few always represent the same parties, while others have different roles in each new situation.

Typically the general counsel to the business will refer the bankruptcy lawyer. While many clients are reluctant to ask one attorney to refer another, few lawyers will resent a referral to a colleague outside their area of practice. The clerk of the bankruptcy court can also provide the names of local practitioners as can state and local bar associations, which usually maintain rosters of qualified bankruptcy attorneys.

There are, of course, those who argue with some justification that lawyers are counterproductive to the turnaround effort since they tend to think in terms of legal solutions and not business solutions, on which the turnaround must be based. But I agree with the more balanced view proposed by Phil Weitzer, a Miami bankruptcy specialist, who says, "The lawyer has his place. He shouldn't be driving the stagecoach but is great riding shotgun."

ACCOUNTANTS: THE NUMBER-CRUNCHERS

Accountants are frequently changed when a company begins its workout. The existing accountants may be as tainted as management, and credibility and creditor confidence can only be restored when new auditors take over the financial controls. Change is absolutely essential when the accountants concealed the corporate decline through manipulative accounting or were slow to alert management of the financial warnings. Accountants who are more equipped to prepare neat balance sheets with exhaustive footnotes than they are to let management know how untidy those numbers really are, should not be part of the turnaround team.

All companies require basic financial controls to stay on course, but the need for accurate, detailed, and timely financial data is far more critical with the company in crisis. To be effective, the auditors must understand the business and plug in the right controls. For example, Charles Morneau, the certified public accountant who specializes in non-profit institutions, has achieved a national reputation in the workout of financially troubled nonprofit schools. To bolster his capabilities he designed a remarkably efficient financial information system that has proven invaluable in navigating schools back to health. Although this level of specialized expertise is rare, it demonstrates how the accounting field is nurturing its own brand of specialists.

Even the once-stodgy Big Eight accounting firms are setting up "boutique" consulting divisions to specialize in turnarounds—albeit their performance remains focused on the financial end and not the managerial end.

To dig out the important numbers you need accountants who thrive in a world of cash flows, cost analysis, break-even projections, forecasting, and budgeting. They anticipate the critical questions: Where are we making or losing money? What is our new break-even point if we drop a product or shut a plant? What is our forecasted cash position over the next 60 days?

The perfect financial navigator can skillfully analyze operations. He or she is a rare breed, a blend of comptroller, visionary, and magician who can coordinate the numbers to navigate operational change.

Considering the importance of the financial function to a workout, we frequently hire full-time or part-time comptrollers for small client firms who ordinarily would operate without comptrollership in more normal times. Larger firms may have people in place, although not necessarily the right people, and they too must obtain new financial support.

The larger firm may also have its own accounting efforts verified by the creditors' own accountants. Lenders and trade creditor groups can be expected to retain their own auditors to check for fraud, embezzlement, and creditor preferences, and to undertake other investigative work. The company's financial controls, monitoring systems, and cash flow projections on which creditors may determine further credit are other review areas. Prior to debt restructuring the creditors' auditors will perform liquidation analysis and determine the feasibility of performance under any proposed payment plan.

While accounting firms seem eager to compete for work in the turnaround field, not all firms are prepared to make a commitment to provide the time and personnel to adequately complete the project. It is not unusual for a workout to require an extensive amount of accounting work, particularly at the early stages of the turnaround or when a bankruptcy proceeding is involved, and then pass through a long period of inactivity before picking up for a hectic finale. The accounting firm must be able to commit the resources to match these inevitable spurts.

Because a strong finance function is so important during a turnaround, many turnaround consultants bring in their own accounting staff to insure the correct and timely flow of financial data. Even when the company has adequate accounting systems in place, the consulting firms may have its staff monitor the reports to verify accuracy. Our own experiences tell us that many companies are unduly optimistic in their projections, forcing us to challenge the assumptions on which their rosy cash flow is based. Perhaps the most important qualification of an accountant is the ability to see things as they really are rather than as how management would like them to be.

KEY MANAGERS: TALENT FROM WITHIN

The turnaround team also needs key managers from within the organization to work closely with the outside advisors. The number of insiders selected will, of course, depend on the size and nature of the company and its organization; however we recommend no more than six insiders as part of the formal workout committee since a larger group becomes unmanageable.

Select people who cut across operational lines so that there is a balanced input and a more accurate assessment of how decisions will affect all business areas. Line managers are preferable to staff since they best understand the impact of a decision and must implement the decisions.

Key managers for the workout committee must be encouraged to express their own views and to freely disagree with top management. The existing management team may have too many followers to be useful. So, too, an evaluation of key managers may uncover weak managers unable to initiate or carry out the changes that must take place, and when they are found on the turnaround team they must be replaced.

Another vital qualification of key managers is their willingness to accept change. Incumbent mangers typically resist change because change appears to discredit their prior actions, or even threaten their own authority within the firm. Frequently managers with excellent capabilities for their jobs impede progress because they constantly resist change. Sometimes you have to look deep within the organization for mavericks who can objectively and forcefully send the company on an entirely new path.

Getting a feel for the right key managers for the turnaround team means knowing the people within the organization. The advice of the Business Planning Institute is:

> To evaluate your management staff you must plan with them, work with them and encourage them to freely communicate with you. Are they results oriented? Can they work well under crisis conditions? Can they carry out difficult orders? Can they implement and improvise when resources are lacking? Can they motivate the people beneath them? Do they have any unusual skills or strengths for specific areas of the turnaround?

Over time, if the company's problems become intractable, primary players may tire and even more effective replacements may be found within the organization. Steven Miller, an assistant treasurer who became the financial point man for Chrysler, won particular praise for his skill in handling the complex financial and creditor relations problems and is only one of a number of rising stars whose opportunity came in a moment of corporate need. Many of today's corporate leaders won their stripes in the combat of a turnaround. Few return to the boring luxury of working in normal companies that simply make money.

6

Code Blue: Taking the Corporate Pulse

THE legend is that the great turnaround leaders can accurately assess the corporate pulse before they walk in the door. In short order they measure overall corporate viability, grasp the problems, and magically produce solutions to seemingly hopeless problems. Much of the legend remains legend except perhaps for the ability to quickly assess the corporate condition. To turnaround veterans the evaluation process is largely instinctive. Experienced corporate doctors can tell in their gut what the company is all about, just as a physician can rapidly assess the severity of a flesh wound. When the company is badly hemorrhaging, time becomes the one precious commodity. They are the turnaround leaders who realize they must first know "where we're at," before they can know "where we're going." The small but seriously troubled company may require immediate turnaround action and therefore the evaluation process cannot extend more than several days. Complex but reasonably stable companies may, in turn, require months of detailed analysis before the scope of their problems are known, but even then seriously crippled corporations can hardly afford the luxury of crossing the "Ts" on endless reports. Too many companies die on the operating table while their surgeons linger over the x-rays.

The evaluation process cannot, however, be considered an event that occurs only at the beginning of the turnaround. In reality, evaluation

71

is a continuous process. Within moments the turnaround leader must measure the severity of the crisis. Is the company in cardiac arrest or merely suffering an unglamorous case of acne? Within hours an assessment must be made whether the company has the staying power for a turnaround. The trained eye can also quickly form an opinion as to how the company can best restructure its debt. Formulating the profit strategy is what takes time as the tedious probing of the corporate strengths and weaknesses continues throughout the turnaround.

The scope of the evaluation will also depend on the party undertaking the evaluation and its specific objectives. While management is interested in the long-term viability of the company, creditors are more narrowly interested in the ability of the company to liquidate its debts. Secured lenders may be even more narrowly focused on the value of the collateral. Suppliers will be primarily interested in the ability of the company to pay future bills, and employees will wonder whether the company will be forced to retrench, thereby cutting jobs and salaries. Meanwhile, stockholders are predictably worried whether they will ever see a return on their investment in the company.

The very diverse objectives and perspectives of these groups can encourage greatly different conclusions about the corporate condition and what can and should be done with the company. Perhaps the only objective they share is to see that the company survives, although each for a very different reason.

GATHERING INFORMATION

Depending on the size and type of business, the apparent nature and gravity of the problem, and the extent of the crisis, the turnaround leader must define clearly all the information needed for an appraisal and must understand the role and importance of each key indicator. Very often the company must produce data never before compiled and implement controls thought to be beyond its capabilities.

Having the right information is more important than having a lot of information. A "quick fix" on any company can be obtained with remarkably little information. The need for more detailed and sophisticated information only becomes more necessary during the strategic turnaround when the company positions itself to make money.

For the "quick fix" certain basic financial information is needed. At the least it will include the current balance sheet and profit and loss statement and comparative statements for the prior two or three years. The past and projected change in financial position is also extremely useful. Finally, and of greatest importance, are detailed cash flow statements for the forthcoming year.

Critical information concerning business operations and legal relationships may also be required at the initial stages of the evaluation, although the specific target areas will again depend on the company and its many variables.

However concise the financial and operating data may be, it is imperative that it be accurate, current, and realistic. "Realism" particularly applies to forecasts and projections which typically reflect the always-present optimism of management.

Key managers, employees, suppliers, creditors, and customers may also be approached, as each has its own perspective of the company's strengths and weaknesses and can often provide essential insights not apparent from the financial statements and operating data.

An inspection of the physical plant is equally important during the preliminary stage. The overall condition of the physical plant—inventory, fixtures, equipment—and the observable efficiency and housekeeping are all vital to get an adequate feel for the overall situation. No company can be precisely measured by sitting in an office. If the turnaround leader is from outside the organization he or she has to kick some tires.

CODE BLUE: THE COMPANY IN CRISIS

The initial step in the evaluation process is to determine the extent of the crisis, the urgency of the situation, and how drastic the corrective action must be.

The two most serious threats to continued operations are: (1) cash flow problems, and (2) threatened action against the company by creditors.

Which is the greater problem rarely requires much investigative work. More often than most people ever realize, companies do not come to grips with their problems until creditors force them into bankruptcy, a lender forecloses, or a tax agency seizes the business. The objective then, of course, is for the company to regain possession of its assets either through Chapter 11 or a workout with the involved creditors.

While the troubled company may be able to block creditor action, a serious cash flow problem is less easily solved and therefore must be quickly and precisely measured with three vital questions:

1. What is the company's present cash position?
2. At what point will the company run out of operating capital?
3. What internal or external sources of financing exist to cover the negative cash flow?

Chapter 7 deals with specific strategies to solve the cash flow problems, but at this stage the focus is on whether the company has the ability to stabilize itself and survive long enough for a long-term debt restructuring or strategic turnaround plan to take hold.

DEFINING THE VIABLE CORE

Once it can be seen that cash flow can be stabilized, attention must turn to finding the "viable core" of the business—that nucleus of activity that is both a cash generator and profit generator, and can serve as the foundation for rebuilding the company. Essentially, the company must separate its winners from its losers.

The definition of the "viable core" necessarily and conversely identifies the superfluous business activities that drain the company and must therefore be quickly excised as the company downsizes to its more essential and productive activities.

The identification of the core business, or "motherlode" as it is often called, is critical at the earliest stages of the turnaround because both short-term and long-term planning will revolve around the preservation of the viable core and the shedding of all extraneous activity. Often the viable core is the least visible part of the organization and may well be its smallest. For example, Dart Industries incurred sizable losses in its retail drug divisions (Rexall) and in its real estate and cosmetic divisions, but its far smaller Tupperware division threw off enormous amounts of cash and therefore it was around its Tupperware division that Dart was rebuilt. Similarly, the Penn Central—long thought of only as a railroad—turned to the net worth and stability of its valuable Manhattan properties to rescue it from its long-ailing railroad business. And Braniff Airlines' rescue was clearly a result of its rapidly identifying its most profitable air routes. In each of these cases, survival was possible only because the company was able to quickly identify and protect its own vein of gold.

However, finding the "viable core" of a business is not always easy. Management must often sift through a maze of detailed financial and operating data before it fully understands where the profits and losses are coming from.

Nor does it imply that a "viable core" necessarily exists. In a great many companies no one definable business unit or activity stands apart as a future moneymaker. Small businesses—retail stores and service companies, for example—are hardly complex organizations that can be easily divided into component parts.

Even when a profitable nucleus of activity once existed, the company may have depleted its assets to the point the "viable core business" is destroyed and cannot be recreated. Finally, the company may be completely without potentially profitable activity or *raison d'etre*, making it apparent there is very little worth saving. For instance, it was finally concluded that W.T. Grant could not be reshaped into a profitable company and without a "core business" to trim the giant retailer to, the decision was made to liquidate.

The evaluation must not only identify core operations that can produce profits but those that can finance the company through the turnaround. Sometimes one unit serves as a temporary "cash cow" and another offers long-term profit potential. The role and value of each unit must be clearly understood before the turnaround goes into full thrust.

RCA, for example, was a bloated casualty of the pell-mell rush for diversification that infected American business in the 1960s and 1970s. From its base as a leading maker of home-entertainment products and owner of NBC radio and television networks, RCA had over the years added such diverse and unrelated businesses as Hertz rental cars, Banquet frozen foods, a huge financial services business, and even a carpet maker. Under its new chairman, Thornton Bradshaw, RCA was forced to rid itself of those various offshoots, bringing it back to the company it was a decade before: a company built around a strong technological base.

The viability of a company as a whole then can be assessed by understanding both its strengths and weaknesses. The strengths are those that are going to have to be preserved come hell or high water. If there is an operation that is making money everything possible must be done to insulate it from the losers.

THE FINANCIAL REVIEW

The next step in the evaluation process is to grasp the overall financial condition of the company. The preliminary mission is to determine whether the company has only a profitability problem requiring a strategic re-structuring, an insolvency problem requiring a debt restructuring, or, as is more typically the case, whether it is a company that is both insolvent and unprofitable.

While there are countless books dealing with the financial analysis of a company, for purposes of turnaround evaluation certain key points must be highlighted:

Balance Sheet

The troubled company may reflect a poor balance sheet that can be considerably worse once all the dirty financial linen that accumulated over the prior years is uncovered. Assets may be overvalued, inventories may be partly obsolete and in need of major write-downs, and a number of expense items may be capitalized, particularly when management attempts to cover up losses. Conversely, on the liability side, payables may be grossly understated, with significant contingent or disputed liabilities unlisted. In short, the balance sheet must be reviewed with the cold, jaundiced eye of a pawnbroker, forcing accurate answers to a host of questions:

■ Assets

- [ ] Is there a complete inventory of fixed assets?
- [ ] Have the accounts receivable been verified?
- [ ] To what extent is the collectability of the accounts receivable related to the completion of contracts by the company?
- [ ] When was the last physical inventory taken?
- [ ] Are there patents, trademarks, or other special assets?
- [ ] What assets are leased?
- [ ] What is the inventory mix of raw material, work in process, and finished goods?
- [ ] Are the finished goods salable or is a substantial portion obsolete or slow moving?
- [ ] To what extent is the equipment salable?

☐ To what extent is the equipment utilized?

☐ Are there substantial assets that are not essential to the continued viability of the company that can be disposed of to produce working capital?

■ Liabilities

☐ What is the nature and aging of trade obligations?

☐ What is the effect of slow pay or nonpayment of accounts on continued supply?

☐ Are the trade obligations unmanageable to the point of requiring significant adjustment?

☐ How is the company presently handling the payment of payables?

☐ What past-due tax obligations are owed to tax authorities?

☐ What actions are threatened by tax authorities?

☐ Is there personal liability for officers and parties for tax obligations?

☐ What debt is secured or items leased?

☐ Are secured debts and leases current or in default?

☐ Is there a threatened foreclosure or repossession of secured or leased equipment?

☐ Does the company have a pension plan? Is the company up-to-date in its contributions?

While the nature of the company and its apparent problems will largely dictate the approach to the balance sheet evaluation, the overall review should focus primarily on two issues:

1. Does the company have adequate financial stability and resources to sustain itself during the workout?

2. Will creditors give the company time for a long-term workout or is immediate protection from creditors needed?

The answers to both issues may require more than a cursory look at the balance sheet; they may require a closer examination of the basic relationships between the company and its creditors, suppliers, and finance sources.

Profit and Loss

The income statement may undergo only a sketchy review during the emergency stage. Turnaround consultant Bob Kuzara says:

> I only want to roughly identify where we are losing and how much we are losing when I step into a turnaround case. Once I'm satisfied we had shut down the major cash drains I may not return to the income statement until the company is totally stabilized and can afford the luxury of thinking in terms of profitability instead of mere survival. But to quickly tell the winners from the losers management has to provide precise and accurate income statements broken down by company or division and product line and plant, or whatever breakdown makes sense. The reason so many companies are in trouble is because they do not know where they are making or losing money and the reason they don't know is because they have poorly designed financial information systems that must be corrected for an intelligently planned workout.

A threshold question is to determine whether there is one easily identifiable cause for the company's operating losses. Often the cause *is* a one-time problem. Certainly, companies such as A.H. Robins and Manville Corporation can pinpoint their problems to their product liability problems, and once these nonrecurring problems are segregated, the income statement can again be projected with a rosy hue. For these one-problem companies no complex strategic planning is needed.

At the early stages, however, the multiproblem company may not be able to do much more with the income statement than determine whether there are significant opportunities for expense reduction. But management must carefully consider whether expense reduction can be undertaken without serious side effects or destroying the "viable core" of the business. A more important question may be whether management will be receptive to and can implement the operational changes necessary under a major expense reduction program. Faced with a continuous pattern of substantial losses, there can be no alternative but to thoroughly review each item on the income statement to identify trends and relationships among elements of cost, volume, and profit. The company may necessarily go through a financial modeling, projecting the new bottom line under various scenarios. Essentially the income statement evaluation is one more example of back to basics as we try to find out how to make money in the business.

EVALUATING THE HUMAN RESOURCES

Crunching numbers is not enough if the business is to survive.

People, both in groups and as individuals, have to be good if the organization is to perform. Many turnarounds are nothing more than a turnaround of the human resources.

The logical starting point is with top management itself. Chapter 4 outlines many of the skills a turnaround leader must possess. And often the success of the turnaround depends on the willingness of top management to step aside and put the organization in more capable hands. Turnaround consultant Scott Dantuma suggests, "The most important question in the whole evaluation is the one top management must ask itself—can *I* really turn this company around?"

If top executives have difficulty in evaluating their own performance, they may not do measurably better in evaluating the performance of their subordinates or employees. This difficulty may stem from the failure to evaluate people against the demanding standards of what the company will require under a turnaround. According to industrial psychologist Elliot Fine, "Managers think in terms of asking whether their employees can adequately do the job they are doing, instead of asking whether they can do significantly better to improve results."

A turnaround leader recruited from outside the organization can be far more objective in assessing the people within the organization. Yet even he or she may judge people too soon or judge them too harshly simply because they are a tainted part of the old regime that got the company into trouble. When replacement is decided on, the turnaround leader can do it in remarkably arbitrary style. Consider James Hawkins, who straightened out Hewitt-Robins: "Junk the 'yes men,' " he recommends. "You say something to them that's almost right. But its wrong. If they agree with it then you can them," Hawkins advocates. The evaluation of key managers and employees can, of course, only be accomplished through open and candid face-to-face meetings; however, general employment problems within the organization may be determined by inquiring about:

□ Employee turnover rate
□ Difficulty in recruiting new employees
□ Number of unfilled positions
□ Employee protests or grievances

☐ Employee productivity changes
☐ Overall morale changes

However, in an age when employers must think twice before axing people, the evaluation may turn from the assessment of the people to the assessment of whether the company can easily make required employee changes. Then the important questions are:

☐ Does the company have union contracts?
☐ Will the union be cooperative or hostile?
☐ Are there employment contracts? What are their terms?
☐ Are there restrictions in labor or employment contracts relating to merger, change of location, duties, or changes in the operation of the business that would be relevant when considering options in the workout?
☐ Are there employees who are of critical importance to the company because of special knowledge, special relationships, or unique skills?
☐ Do any managers have "golden handshake" contracts?

Axing people is not the only solution to poor performance, because replacing people will have its own disruptive effect on the organization. Moreover, poor performance may also be the result of the corporate condition, indicating the need to motivate rather than terminate.

Special attention must be paid to the politics within the organization, and in times of extreme strife the politics can become bizarre and totally disruptive. For instance, I once consulted to a $20-million-a-year shipping firm. I met in one office with the young president who inherited a half-interest in the business from his father. In the very next office sat his disgruntled sister who, serving as treasurer, inherited the other half-interest. Neither brother nor sister spoke to each other for over three years and each functioned through their separate management staffs, who blindly but loyally followed them in their internal feud. The roadblocks to a successful turnaround effort can be quite obvious.

Power plays within the troubled organization can take many forms but they are always disruptive. Top managers must closely work together, and when basic harmony does not exist changes are needed to develop a cohesive team. Also, the board of directors may be too passive or domineering and either fail to adequately control the efforts of top management or prevent management from operating with sufficient flexibility. And, of course, other political realities may exist that in one way or another impede the ability of management to make the changes necessary for survival.

Conflict may also exist because of poor organizational structure. The company may be too top-heavy or conversely not offer enough support to its front-line troops. Of greater importance, the structure of the organization must be shaped so that the necessary changes can be swiftly implemented and the results of change more accurately measured.

Changing the organizational structure alone is never sufficient without the right people at the key points. The evaluation must consider whether the key people can take direction from the top and force needed change to the bottom of the organization. Managers who think the answer to the people problem is simply to play with neat little boxes on a piece of paper are fooling themselves, prompting one observer to remark when handed the fourth draft of a newly proposed reorganization: "Different tree, same monkeys."

EVALUATING THE MARKET POSITION

Before the turnaround is too far along, the company must be evaluated in terms of its basic market position. An objective analysis tells the turnaround leader not only where the company presently is but where the company is likely to go.

Very quickly management has to face the naked truth about the company's current competitive condition. For younger companies that have never been off the ground, it may be a moment of truth that there is no sound economic *raison d'être* for their continued existence. In short, they may reach the bitter point in the evaluation when they accept the reality that there is just no sense in going on. This frequently is the conclusion of smaller entrepreneurial firms built around a new or unique product or service. Once tested, hopes for its future success can quickly vanish.

But just because a young company has never made money certainly does not mean that it cannot. Many small companies are recent start-ups based on a sound business concept but which suffer the financing or strategic problems most young companies face. To avoid throwing the "baby out with the bath water," it then becomes necessary to closely evaluate the products and services in addition to the company.

The mature company that falls on hard times because of marketing problems has no less a challenge. There can be no end to the number of possible marketing errors or the extent to which the company may have to go to evaluate and correct its marketing strategies as it considers:

☐ Does the company occupy a unique position within the particular industry?

☐ Does the future viability of the company depend on moving with the identifiable trends within the industry and is the company positioned for the necessary change?

☐ Are the company's problems shared by others within the industry?

☐ Are there identifiable causes for declining sales or decreased market share?

☐ Is there a particular product or product line responsible for dragging the company down? Are there products that are performing well?

☐ Are there new competitors responsible for sales decline?

☐ What are the realistic possibilities of regaining the competitive advantage?

Essentially the company has to uncover the reasons for slumping sales or decreased market share, whether segmented by product, channel of distribution, end-user customer group, or geographic area. The evaluation may also take the company through an often dismal historical review of innovation in new products, markets, promotional approaches, and price strategies.

Given an assessment of the market position of the company, the evaluation may next center on the effectiveness of the marketing strategy:

☐ Does the company have a defined management strategy?

☐ Is the marketing group staffed and integrated so that it can effectively carry out marketing analysis, planning, implementation, and control?

☐ Are marketing results measured and strategies corrected? Companies, of course, do not operate in a vacuum.

Frequently the turnaround support can be found in the public and political dimensions of the company:

- [ ] Is there widespread support or opposition to the company?
- [ ] Is the company a large employer in its geographic area?
- [ ] Is the company a significant supplier of goods or services to governmental entities?
- [ ] What would be the effect on the public, business, industry, or government if the company were to cease operations?
- [ ] Will business groups or government agencies take an interest in or assist in the workout?

EVALUATING THE LEGAL FACTORS

A turnaround involves itself in a maze of legal considerations, many of which must be considered early:

- [ ] Is the business operated as a single entity or are there multiple entities? If there are multiple entities are some entities healthy and can they be legally safeguarded from the problems of the remaining organization?
- [ ] Is there an immediate prospect of litigation that would disrupt the business? Is there an immediate prospect of attachment or repossession of an important asset?
- [ ] Is the company a defendant in burdensome litigation? Is there potential litigation from shareholders, franchisees, customers, or governmental entities arising out of the company's failure to comply with applicable laws and which may not be resolved through a workout?
- [ ] Does the company itself have major claims against third parties? Are these claims likely to yield sufficient proceeds, or be resolved in time to help rehabilitate the company?
- [ ] What existing contracts or affiliations may control the nature of a workout?
- [ ] What legal obligations does the company have with respect to its warranty obligations and service policies?
- [ ] Can the business successfully defend itself against any major claims, and if successful would the need for a turnaround continue to exist?
- [ ] Are there any regulatory issues that would limit the turnaround options?

☐ Are there any legal issues that seriously cloud the ability of the company to reorganize or achieve a successful turnaround?

PUTTING IT TOGETHER

The various evaluations must be synthesized into an overall assessment of the company's position before a turnaround plan can be formulated.

Through the evaluation process management must integrate sufficient facts to resolve five issues:

1. How serious is the overall problem? Is the company in critical condition or is it still relatively stable and in fair health?

2. What is the gravity of the downturn? If the company has a deteriorating financial condition, how rapid is the deterioration and with what speed must the turnaround be accomplished?

3. What are the causes of the downturn? Are the problems reoccurring or are the causes of decline continuing? Can the causes be clearly defined? Is there more than one cause, and, if so, what are the more significant causes?

4. Does the company primarily need a strategic turnaround (profit improvement) or financial restructuring (debt reduction)? If both are required, which should occur first?

5. What are the relative strengths and weaknesses of the firm? Is the company sufficiently strong to withstand a turnaround? Are any weaknesses likely to be fatal to the turnaround effort?

What this all boils down to is that someone is finally in the corporate cockpit gauging the tailspin with one eye while scanning the cockpit dashboard with the other. But if the turnaround leader has been in the cockpit before, the dashboard will not reveal anything he or she did not know before.

7

Staying Afloat

CASH is lifeblood for the ailing company and the one commodity it has most trouble getting its hands on. Therefore, the first task in stabilizing a financially troubled company is to stop the cash drain and replenish the corporate coffers with a reasonable cash cushion. This is usually the most critical stage of the turnaround process as adequate working capital and a positive cash flow are essential if the company is to buy the time necessary to revitalize its profits and restructure its balance sheet. Many firms unable or unwilling to stem the cash drain literally bleed to death before they can apply long-term turnaround remedies. Unfortunately many of these failed firms are those that waited too long before coming to grips with their problems.

PLUGGING THE CASH DRAIN

Negative cash flow is both a result and a cause of the financially troubled company's difficulties. The problems leading to and arising from negative cash flow are identifiable and, to a large extent, predictable. The most common factors that contribute to a negative cash flow include:

☐ Lower sales volume
☐ Poor accounts receivable collection

☐ Shorter credit terms or COD payments to suppliers

☐ Customer reluctance to provide advance funds or deposits

☐ Reduced lending against accounts receivables and inventory by secured lenders

☐ Holdbacks on trade discounts and other supplier concessions

☐ Borrowing at higher interest rates

☐ Demands for accelerated payback on outstanding loans and off-sets against compensating balances

☐ Buying defensively—at higher prices or less satisfactory terms

☐ Increased costs and expenses associated with managing the troubled firm

Many more causes and results of cash flow problems may be identified. Each business will have its own list of factors, but most of the causes on this list are almost always present.

The cash flow problem only becomes more aggravated with time because it is both a cause and result. The objective then is to reverse the process before it reaches the point where the cash drain becomes a torrent and there is too little left of the company to save. Businesses that fail to reverse their cash flow problems end up in a "bankruptcy spin." Lack of cash or credit starts the cycle. Inventory shrinks as it is depleted to cover the cash commitments, and the cashless business cannot replenish the inventory. Reduced inventory in turn causes lost sales which in turn creates even less cash to the increasingly anemic business.

The cash flow problems are generally far-reaching and take their toll on every phase of operations. Employees soon tire of dealing with irate customers complaining of inventory shortages or cutbacks, equally angry creditors clamoring for payment, or suppliers who refuse to ship. The company with a cash crisis becomes totally defensive. It is no longer a performing company but a reactive organization preoccupied with protecting itself from being picked clean.

TURNING THE TOURNIQUET

The troubled company does not need a bandage but a tourniquet to stop it from bleeding to death. The first and most important step is to put a hold on all but the most essential disbursements and make a drastic cut in every conceivable overhead item.

This is likely to be the most painful phase of the entire turnaround program because it is here that management is forced to dismantle pet projects, terminate long-standing and loyal employees, and say "no" to a host of people lined up with their hands out. Stopping the cash drain is more than an operational exercise, but one likely to change the strategic direction of the company as well. The company often is forced to trade a planned future for the present, but the exercise is necessary if the company is to have a future.

While the organization may understand and support the overall objective, there is typically resistance to the degree and extent to which it must be carried out. For example, when we are first called in to a case, we immediately stop payment on all outstanding checks until we can determine which payments are absolutely essential. In some companies we may recoup $20,000–$30,000 in payments that should never have been made, and this can help spell the difference between a successful turn-around and a failure. Still, most clients watch us go about our work in silent horror, unaccustomed to the "hard-ball" techniques that must be employed if the turnaround is to have a chance.

Before management can do anything about a severe cash problem it has to understand the steps necessary for solving that problem. Taking control of cash flow means understanding the organization's cash flow pipeline so management can control both what goes into the pipeline and what comes out. That means that everything must be stopped that can affect cash, including purchasing, new hirings, and capital projects. Basically, all movement of cash stops except payroll, essential overhead items, and critical purchases. For most organizations, turning off the cash spigot means turning off all payments to creditors, coupled with a cost-reduction program.

Freezing Creditor Payments

Creditors head the list of targets when it is necessary to stop the cash drain. Yet this is seldom easy because when creditors know the company is in trouble they push as hard as possible for as must as possible before the business collapses.

Many businesses fail only because they allow themselves to be "bled" to death by anxious creditors. Creditor A who is owed $4000 agrees to accept $200 per week. Creditor B, owed $7000, gets $350 per month.

Creditor C, not to be outdone by the others, squeezes $500 monthly payments on its $12,000 bill. Creditor D decides to recoup its $6000 by withholding trade discounts on future payments. Without realizing it the company is paying out two dollars for every dollar in sales. Meanwhile, the company has to replenish inventory on a COD basis, cover operating expenses, and pay down loans. The end result is predictable failure.

To compound the problem, the business will pay out many thousands of dollars over several months before it realizes that it can never hope to fully pay down its debts from operating income and a total debt restructuring is necessary. Instead of restructuring the original $150,000 owed, perhaps it ends up negotiating a settlement on $120,000. But what was accomplished by paying creditors $30,000 when it should have been apparent at the outset that surgery was needed to pare down the trade debt? Clearly, it is as easy to restructure $150,000 as $120,000, and as any veteran of corporate turnarounds will tell you, "Creditors will still call you an SOB and still won't extend credit. Whatever you pay creditors before you restructure your debt doesn't help a bit. It's money down the drain, and money critical to strengthening your business."

Until such time as the company can approach creditors with a workout plan creditor payments should stop. During this period the company must withhold payments of all past bills owed trade creditors while future shipments are on COD or order-to-order credit. Conversely, creditors should not be allowed to withhold trade or cash discounts or other concessions as these incentives have a cash equivalency. Similarly, returned goods should be credited against future payments, not past debts.

Creditors will not always display great patience and will have their own strategies to press for payment. Under creditor pressure the troubled company may be asked to secure the indebtedness with a mortgage on business assets or the personal guarantee of its principals. This invariably is a costly mistake as the creditor is now in a far stronger position than if it remained an unsecured general creditor, and moreover the owners may have incurred needless personal exposure.

Creditors can also be intimidating. They will threaten bankruptcy (less than 1 percent follow through), they will file lawsuits (generally a futile exercise), and they will threaten a report to the credit association (by now the company has no credit anyway). In reality, creditors can do little damage and are eventually forced to accept the reality that they will not be fully paid, just as management must accept the reality that it cannot fully pay them.

This does not suggest that the relationship between the debtor company and its creditors should be adversarial, and it is certainly counterproductive if it turns hostile. Creditors must be approached in a way that will encourage their cooperation toward a mutually satisfactory workout plan.

Creditors rightfully complain that cash-shy customers are less than candid about their problems. "We do get tired hearing 'check is in the mail' stories. If a customer is in trouble he should come clean and say so. He will at least preserve his credibility," says Robert Sammarco, credit manager of New England Wholesale Drug Company.

Creditors also turn against customers who load up and order as much as possible on credit just before announcing the bad news that they cannot pay. One rightfully upset supplier reports that an account ran up a $20,000 bill only two weeks before filing for an obviously planned Chapter 11 bankruptcy. These are the tactics that cause creditors to turn their backs on even the most generous workout plans.

Creditors must also be assured that no other unsecured creditor is gaining preferential treatment—a policy that must be rigidly enforced. Creditors will stand by provided other creditors are not gaining ground at their expense.

The troubled company will also encourage creditor patience by remaining loyal to the supplier during the workout period. No supplier enjoys being stuck on a bill while a new supplier is shipping and getting paid.

Finally the creditors must be convinced through a series of progress reports that the company is working in good faith.

Realizing a debtor's credibility with its creditors may be shaky following months of excuses and storytelling, our firm often sends "moratorium" letters to the creditors shortly after entering the case. The moratorium letter advises creditors of the company's financial difficulties and request that the creditor defer collection efforts while we review the company's affairs and can propose a payment plan. Through this letter creditors have the assurances of professional involvement and the comfort of knowing the debtor company is finally doing something constructive about its problems. Equally important, by dealing directly with creditors the management of the client firm can concentrate on running the company free of creditor pressure.

Cost-Cutting

Truly significant results can almost always be achieved in cutting operational costs when the pressure is on. Since opportunities exist in every operational area, it is difficult to provide more than general approaches, leaving specifics to several excellent books on cost control.

Operational costs are often summarily slashed by shuttering entire divisions or plants, such as when Penn Central quickly abandoned cash-draining railroad operations to protect its more lucrative real estate holdings. Similarly, Food Fair Supermarkets credits its turnaround victory to its rapid action in immediately closing scores of cash-draining outlets.

Downsizing the company at too early a stage is not always possible because management may not yet know where the cash drain is occurring. Frequently they must do extensive cash flow analysis on every measurable activity—whether it be by division, product, or project. Once they understand how it affects cash flow, they can begin to prioritize and make reasoned decisions as to what stays and what goes.

Payroll costs must be singled out as the one overhead item deserving special attention because 70–85 percent of overhead is payroll related, and it therefore represents the greatest cost-cutting opportunity.

The vast majority of companies are overstaffed. Frequently the company can cut payroll by 25–30 percent within the first 60 days and perhaps reduce payroll another 10–15 percent over the workout period. Most of these cuts will come from within executive and staff ranks and will initially be through staff reductions rather than payroll or fringe benefit cuts, which may occur later. The company may also switch to a compensation program where wages are directly tied to productivity or sales. Other companies have achieved considerable savings by subcontracting work and deciding to "buy" rather than "make." And in virtually every troubled company overtime and other perks are eliminated.

When tough discipline is applied, enormous cost reductions are possible, as when Phil Ziegler turned around the ailing Hyatt Bearing Division in Sandusky, Ohio. In the span between 1970 and 1975 employment at the division's three plants decreased from over 12,000 to 8000 employees. The division not only became more profitable but also more productive. As with all successful turnarounds, Ziegler managed to get 120 percent out of 100 percent of his employees.

The basic cost-cutting strategy is to reduce or eliminate fixed overhead items. While the downsizing of large corporations can show how rapid and dramatic the downsizing process must be, managers may not sense the need to sacrifice. Fancy offices, first-class travel, company cars, country club memberships, and the other trappings are all symbols of success no longer appropriate when the signs of success no longer exist.

THE GREENING OF THE CORPORATION

Plugging the cash drain is only half the battle. The company must then rebuild its cash reserve so it can start the turnaround process with maximum financial strength.

Large corporations may not have to go far for their cash transfusion. A paternal parent company, an affiliated division, another stock issue, or timely governmental intervention can usually be counted on to keep the floundering corporation afloat. Smaller companies have fewer external resources to lean on. If they are to survive their cash crunch they must look inward for needed operating capital.

Troubled companies are full of cash-raising opportunities. We successfully turn chronic cash flow problems into a sustained positive cash flow in the vast majority of client firms. Typically the cash position is greatly improved within two weeks, using nothing more than the most basic asset management techniques.

The management of working capital deals mostly with receivables, inventory, and fixed assets, and the need to convert some or all of these assets to cash through reductions or improved efficiency. Often each phase of cash management has been mismanaged or undermanaged, leading to an overall condition that can have significant impact on a bank balance.

Accounts Receivable

Start with accounts receivable because it is the quickest and best source of cash. Calculate the average collection period. If the company sells on 30-day terms its receivables should not exceed 45-day sales. If it does, there is work to be done. The analysis of receivables may, however, be distorted as old and uncollectable receivables may remain on the books of companies that have not earned a profit and therefore have no tax incentive to write off uncollectable accounts.

Develop a "no-nonsense" collection policy toward delinquent accounts. Only an aggressive attitude can turn old receivables into cash. The few antagonized customers must be sacrificed as their future purchases are less important than their present cash. Current and marginally delinquent accounts are best approached with an extra cash discount for immediate payment. The customer who ignores a 2 percent discount may be motivated to pay if offered 5 percent.

The collection policy must walk a fine line. On one hand it must be sufficiently forceful to bring results. On the other hand the company cannot appear to be desperate. Sensing financial problems, accounts often withhold payments hoping to negotiate pennies-on-the-dollar settlements with liquidating receivers.

The credit policy must also be tightened. Granting extended terms as a sales incentive must be eliminated and cash sales encouraged. Cyclical billing and strategic lockbox locations can also create a faster flow of cash. Slow payers must be eliminated or granted reduced credit limits and shorter payment periods. As with any credit policy, a balance must be reached between sales (and profitability) and cash flow, but unlike the well-heeled company that can comfortably finance its receivables, the cash-starved company must choose cash flow.

Consumer credit to retail customers is another matter. Few small retailers can afford to maintain charge accounts. "Plastic" is the alternative. If a customer is without a MasterCard, Visa, or other major credit card, this same customer is probably a poor credit risk to begin with.

Similarly, the company should consider factoring unpledged accounts receivables. Many cash-poor companies are sitting on a wealth of receivables that can be easily converted to cash through factoring. Understandably, few companies relish paying 6 or 7 percent as a factoring expense, but again it may not be a matter of what is desirable but what is essential.

If the receivables are pledged, there may also be opportunities to negotiate more liberal financing which may free up additional dollars. It is not unusual to borrow 70 percent against receivables when 80 percent is available from other lenders. For the company with $200,000 in receivables, the added borrowing leverage of 10 percent will put $20,000 in the bank.

Inventory

A surprising number of merchandising and product-oriented firms are in financial difficulty only because they never learned the basics of inventory control.

Many of these firms operate with grossly excessive or inefficiently managed inventory, gradually built up over the years. Their profit may be "on the shelf" but so is their cash flow. Less experienced operators often buy too heavily, concentrating on extra discounts and gross profit when the safer strategy is to focus on turnover and cash flow. These firms may discover that a drastic inventory reduction program can be both a short-term and long-term solution to chronic cash problems.

It is difficult to believe just how poorly managed inventory can be until you come face to face with the situation. Not long ago we consulted with a hardware retailer plagued with the chronic problems of too many bills and too little cash. Based on sales of $1.2 million, an efficient inventory level would be approximately $150,000. Yet this same hardware store had $160,000 on the selling floor, $90,000 in the basement, and $80,000 warehoused, for a grand total of $330,000. Cartons of merchandise, much of it stale and shopworn, were stacked to the rafters as one more puzzled businessman wondered where his money went.

A greater challenge is the firm with an out-of-balance inventory. A normal inventory level may mask the problem of being overinventoried with a large number of slow movers while short on fast-moving items. Out-of-balance firms require a remerchandising program if they are to maintain an acceptable instock position, sustaining sales and retaining customers.

Adjusting inventories to free up cash is seldom enough. Left to their poor buying practices these firms typically repeat their errors, ending up in the same situation a year or two later. Therefore, the cause of the problem becomes as important as the cure, requiring a complete overhaul in purchasing procedures, accompanied by a new merchandise plan, rigid inventory controls, incoming and outgoing inspections, and constant monitoring of inventory. When 70–80 percent of a firm's assets are tied up in inventory it cannot receive too much attention.

Fixed Assets

Managers are less likely to consider fixed assets in a cash-raising program. Somehow equipment, machinery, and real estate seem sacred. When depreciated, these assets may have little book value but can often generate considerable cash.

A cardinal sin of management is overspending on fixed assets. Fancy offices, fancy equipment, and fancy cars can spell big trouble. I recall finding a woefully insolvent client behind an $8000 marble desk. Surgery on his business included stripping his business not only of the desk but the designer lamps and rugs and over $100,000 in nonfunctional trimmings. Today this same individual is sitting behind a used $50 desk, but at least he has a desk to sit behind.

Survival under a turnaround means stripping the company of every item of unproductive equipment. From ceiling to floor, if it is not nailed down, it is a candidate for sale or a less costly replacement.

Functional assets—particularly equipment and real estate—lend themselves well to a sale-leaseback arrangement. Many investors are looking to buy and lease back property for its tax benefits. And as with receivables, fixed assets may present the possibility of additional borrowing with a more liberal lender or a more creative financial package. However, borrowing to raise cash during the cash crisis is not always desirable. Even if the collateral can support more financing, banks and other asset-based lenders will usually decline loans to the financially weak company. Once the company is forced to turn to high-interest secondary lenders, the cost of borrowing may outweigh the benefits.

The more fundamental problem with borrowing is that borrowing only buys time while dissuading management from taking decisive action. Borrowing only defers corporate death but the funeral is seldom avoided. Existing lenders frequently fall into the same trap, throwing more good money after bad in the hopes of rehabilitating the company and its own loan. When it is clear the firm's problems are temporary and will be internally corrected without debt restructuring, the loan becomes sensible. But mere hope is no substitute for reasoned judgment.

Once the opportunities to borrow from external sources dry up, owners through sheer desperation often begin to dig into their own pockets. This is almost always the one biggest mistake that can be made because it not only fails to rescue the company but typically wipes out the owners as well. And unfortunately it happens all the time. The business starts its long slide downward, and its owner keeps plugging holes with money. First the savings go, then there is another mortgage on the house. Finally, the owner cashes in his or her pension and life insurance until there is nothing left to throw into the business. Check writing is easy, problem solving is far more difficult. Cash transfusions should be considered only after the business is stabilized and on a profitable course.

CREATIVITY AND THE CASH CRISIS

Desperate people do desperate things, but desperate people can also do creative things:

- ☐ A financially distressed sundry goods rack jobber decided to retrench and stop sales to accounts in a neighboring state where delivery costs made them unprofitable. But the accounts were not abandoned. They were "sold" to another supplier for $80,000 and a percentage of the first year's profits.

- ☐ A health club advertised a special one-year membership fee of $300 payable in advance. It was a bargain compared with the regular $480 membership fee, prompting 200 new members to join and adding $60,000 to the coffers.

- ☐ A distressed pharmacy tapped its tobacco supplier for a $25,000, three-year loan. The selling point? The pharmacy owed the supplier $40,000 and agreed to give the supplier a mortgage on the business to secure the entire $65,000 indebtedness.

- ☐ A supermarket, hard-pressed for cash, sublet space to a branch bank, raising $12,000 in prepaid rent. Three weeks later it rented its basement area to a local newspaper publisher for another $20,000.

- ☐ An Indiana-based burglar alarm firm's financial plight required fast thinking to raise fast cash. It licensed its potential alarm system to a dealer in Arizona for $70,000 and today has 32 licensees paying over $850,000 a year in royalties.

These examples, of course, only scratch the surface of an endless list of cash-raising possibilities. The point is that each of these businesses were hard-driven to find money when money seemed impossible to find. Virtually every business has its own unique opportunities that are bound to remain untapped until its management becomes both determined and disciplined enough to see and act on the opportunities.

MEASURING THE CASH CRISIS

Each of the foregoing exercises must be guided by a singular objective: to put the company in a positive cash position and keep it there. And, of course, the more positive it is the better it is.

Therefore, we must at the earliest stages quickly assess the severity and speed of the downturn, forecast our existing cash flow, and program the required cash flow if the company is to become stabilized and stay afloat. Once we can assess the required correction in cash flow we can begin to develop a battle plan centered on four questions:

1. What actions will bring the most immediate and significant results?

2. What actions will have the least adverse effect on long-term profitability?

3. What actions will be least disruptive to the organization?

4. What actions can be most readily achieved?

Stabilizing the cash flow of a company that has run aground is seldom an easy task. Management must work against nearly insurmountable odds and resistance from every corner. Results at first will seem slow and you will return to these same questions time and time again to chart a corrected course and look for fresh alternatives when earlier ones prove unsuccessful.

Yet, during this emergency stage in the turnaround, cash is king and the cash flow statement becomes the road map to the kingdom. The intense preoccupation with cash flow will continue until the enterprise safely passes through the period when survival is no longer in question and revitalization is underway.

8

Planning the Turnaround

HOW do turnaround leaders reshape floundering corporations into healthy enterprises? When we closely examine the great comebacks of the past we see there is no one formula. That is the true challenge of the turnaround: each enterprise must find success in its own way.

One reason there can be no precise turnaround formula is that there are so many different types of turnarounds, and companies—like people—exist with vastly different resources and under widely varied circumstances.

Yet when we closely examine successful turnarounds we find they each:

1. Define clear objectives and a vision for the company.
2. Develop the strategies needed to achieve the objectives.
3. Implement the turnaround program with a vigorous action plan.
4. Measure performance and constantly monitor progress.

SETTING TURNAROUND OBJECTIVES

The organization without clear objectives is as hapless as a ship without a rudder. Yet a sizable number of companies operate without clear objectives—or even a rudimentary business plan articulating even fundamental goals—and somehow they expect to succeed. Developing and communicating a unified sense of direction, to which all corporate constituents can relate, is probably the most important concept in management and yet it is often ignored in turnaround management, where it is most needed. Unless the company has an objective, a corporate purpose, identity, and vision of what the organization should become, it will either remain adrift or be channeled in the wrong direction.

The strategic plan must begin with a statement of mission, a clear objective of what the business is expected to become within a measurable point in time. Turnaround leaders who have masterminded brilliant comebacks have made over their companies into dynamic entities hardly recognizable when compared with earlier incarnations, only because they knew where they wanted to go. They were architects of change. For instance:

☐ When Jack Welch took over the reigns of General Electric, GE was a stodgy old pipestack company with old-fashioned product lines and an old-fashioned philosophy of doing business. But Jack Welch had a different vision for GE—to have GE become the pacemaker and trendsetter for a wide variety of consumer products, building GE into a $29 billion business on the leading edge of the changing markets in which it competes.

☐ RCA, unlike GE (which later acquired RCA), created a different vision for its future success by downsizing to the basic consumer electronics field it knew so well—divesting itself of a bevy of nonrelated companies that dragged RCA down.

☐ Transformed by a dash of the old Disney magic, Walt Disney Company has become alive in the past couple of years as one of the most vital, exciting, and successful companies in America. Disney's objective was crystal clear: Move out of the time-warp productions of the 1950s and into the mainstream of American entertainment. The result? Blockbusters such as "Down and Out in Beverly Hills," "The Golden Girls," and the "Disney Sunday Movies," and a rejuvenated Disney Studio with record earnings.

General Electric, RCA, and Disney are very different companies with very different problems. And each company turned itself around in a very different way. However, each of these companies had a clear picture of what it must become if it was to succeed. Seldom do companies "stumble" into a new beginning. More often it is the result of an architect who knew how to take the corporate components and build a new house, if not a new castle.

Corporate transformation need not be radical to be effective. The future may be only a minor modification of the past. Often the turnaround objective can be summed up less dramatically. For example, one of our clients, a manufacturer of wood-burning stoves, has grouped together a series of objectives which together provide a clear mission for his young but struggling firm:

1. To increase sales in the Midwestern states from $2 million to $3 million per year, over the next three years.

2. To finance growth from internally generated cash.

3. To increase utilization of plant facilities from 70 to 90 percent.

4. To reduce salaried payroll from 12 percent of sales to 9 percent over the plan period.

Constantly eye-balling this game plan, the young entrepreneur knows exactly where he wants to take his company. Integrated marketing, financial, physical resources, and cost-reduction objectives were rolled into one coordinated goal, and the company has a blueprint for success.

The corporate mission provides the base upon which the organization's efforts are structured. This in turn gives the managers and employees their sense of corporate destiny, without which the company is doomed to muddle along, devoid of pride, spirit, and purpose.

Every turnaround company needs goals and objectives. They define the specific performance, results, and standards that the revitalization efforts of the organization are designed to produce. Objectives are the milestones guiding the organization along the path toward the fulfillment of its corporate mission. They are the means for measuring group and individual performance and the means for measuring corporate recovery and growth.

Good turnaround objectives are singular and specific and they avoid platitudes and generalities; they define a result to be achieved, not the act of getting there; they are measurable; they contain a deadline for achievement.

Yet turnaround objectives must also be simple, not complex or ponderous. Often MBA types produce 300-page strategic plans that nobody could easily understand and fewer still could execute. The trap here is that massive planning efforts often consume valuable time, time needed more for action than reflection. A turnaround plan is too complicated if it cannot be completely understood by key employees within a 15-minute meeting.

A greater danger in setting turnaround objectives is that they may be unrealistic. Optimism is a valuable commodity in a turnaround situation but not when it encourages fantasy and delusions about what the company can soon become. The objectives must be achievable from both a financial and operational viewpoint, after realistic reflection of both the prior track record of the company and the resources now available to it. In short, the objectives represent a degree of "realistic corporate stretch." Many companies fail to achieve a satisfactory turnaround because of unattainable objectives. While organizations with considerable resources have great flexibility in how they can be reshaped, the smaller or resource-poor company has obvious limitations. Often the managers of these firms believe they will have more outside support in rebuilding the company than turns out to be true.

To design meaningful objectives, the company must also begin with a clear understanding of priorities. For example, a company may be both losing money and deeply insolvent and therefore include in its objectives a plan to improve profitability and solvency. But which objective is more important to the immediate survival of the company? Which objective should have priority? The company may well set as its short-term objective the return to a positive cash flow during the emergency stage and defer its profit-improvement programs to the stabilization stage, when the company may also undertake a debt-reduction program.

Defining objectives is a constant process involving the interaction of key management members, a process in which self-interests compete and philosophies may clash. Few tasks so effectively put the collective nervous system through the wringer as setting turnaround objectives. To reduce the conflicts that often characterize objective-setting sessions, long-term goals may be reached first, since a consensus on long-term goals is generally easier to reach than one on short-term goals. Once long-term objectives are reached management may begin to work its way back to short-term objectives, which can then be easier reached. Under proactive management guidance, the objectives are shaped through healthy interchange, feedback, and fine-tuning.

The objective-setting component of the turnaround process requires the thought, analysis, imagination, and judgment of top management. But in planning objectives the input of line managers is also required. Frequently the front-line troops are more accurate and realistic in their assessment of the corporate future. Top managers tend to be visionaries and line managers pragmatists. Achievable objectives need both.

Just as objectives and an overall turnaround plan must be the consensus of those within the organization, it must also be supported by lenders and other groups outside the organization whose support is essential. Often management must "sell" the plan to lenders and creditor groups who may see the plan as a threat to their own positions. In a turnaround situation, management cannot plan in a vacuum but must usually develop the plan together with lenders, creditors, suppliers, distributors, and dealers, each of whom provides an integral piece to the overall jigsaw puzzle.

STRATEGIC ACTIONS

The strategies define how the company will achieve its objectives and are therefore the thrust behind the turnaround plan. Since most turnaround plans encompass profit-building and debt-reduction objectives as their cornerstones, the combinations of strategic moves are endless. However, management will typically consider broad-brush strategies that include:

☐ Liquidation or divesture of unprofitable activities
☐ Cost-cutting programs
☐ New marketing strategies
☐ New product development
☐ Sale or merger
☐ Acquisition of new companies
☐ Shrinkdown of operations

The strategies employed may change as the company goes through the various stages of the turnaround. For example, during the emergency stage the company will necessarily focus on strategies most closely related to cash flow. At this juncture the company may center its strategies around cost-cutting and divestment of cash-draining activities. As the company enters the stabilization stage the strategies will focus away from the earlier crisis issues and center more on renewed profits. At this stage the company may focus on improving operations, reshaping its product mix, and modifying its marketing strategies as it begins to reposture the business for long-term survival and growth. The process of divestment may continue since the company is far from "out of the woods," but at least newer strategies emerge that indicate the company has a future. Once the company reaches the return-to-growth stage, the strategies may focus on acquisitions, new product development, or increased market penetration to name a few of the possibilities. The strategies become strategies of opportunity for the company, just as prior strategies helped shed the problems of the past.

To develop sound strategies two obstacles must be overcome that may produce poor decisions. The first is that planning specific strategies requires reasonably accurate short- and long-term forecasts, and such forecasts are almost always impossible to produce in a turnaround situation. Most strategic plans are, in practice, nothing more than extrapolations of past management practices and neither capitalize on the strengths of the company nor create a realistic bridge between where the company is and where it is supposed to go because the strategies are too rigid to be responsive to the rapidly changing corporate condition. For turnaround strategies to work they have to be extremely flexible and adaptive. Strategies in a turnaround are often reactive.

The second obstacle is that the strategies may not be realistic. If the objectives tell us where we want to go, and the strategies are to tell us how to get there, the various combinations of strategies that comprise every turnaround plan must be both coordinated and achievable. For example, a marketing strategy that calls for doubling plant and equipment might be in conflict with lack of funds.

Troubled companies must be particularly cautious to select strategies consistent with the limited resources available, and should err on the side of caution. Few distressed companies generate cash as quickly or as copiously as its management would hope, and when the strategic plan is based on the expectation of available capital, there is at least a presumption of faulty thinking. Consider the old Underwood Corporation which, after years of losing money as a typewriter manufacturer, decided to journey into computers. It appeared to be a sensible strategic move except that Underwood seriously underestimated the money it would need to enter this capital-intensive field and promptly ran out of money before it could accomplish much of anything. Underwood discovered what so many other companies also discover—the pursuit of opportunity can be a prelude to disaster when the selected strategies are unworkable.

The selection of specific strategies will also depend a great deal on the corporate culture and the philosophies and personalities of its management. Many troubled companies are run by daredevils willing to risk the corporate jewels on a bold turnaround strategy. This was certainly the style of Bill Ylvisakar, who took Gould, Inc., a $1-billion-a-year maker of auto parts and electrical equipment, and tore it apart to start all over again. Revived from its latest incarnation—after the sale of $1 billion in assets—Gould is a high-tech company with interests in semiconducters, microcomputers, and factory automation. While the strategies selected by such adventurists is to "atomize and synthesize," others such as GE's Jack Welch is a "fix 'em, close 'em, or sell 'em" strategist. The characteristics of the turnaround are often the no-nonsense characteristics of its leader. But each company must decide for itself how much risk it wants to live with, and therefore how bold the strategic move will be.

However, a strategic plan can be bold and assertive and at the same time allow for a "fall-back" position. In fact, it must provide for a "fall-back" position: Murphy's law has not yet been repealed. If something can go wrong, it will. For that reason the overall turnaround plan must include alternative strategies when the central strategy fails. Prior to launch, the plan should define and quantify the circumstances for aborting the present plan and implementing a substitute plan. This underscores again the need for flexibility in designing both objectives and strategy. No turnaround company ever achieves precisely the desired results or accomplishes them precisely as planned. Although the turnaround may seemingly move ahead along a particular path, the path is never straight but a series of "zigs" and "zags." Nor does the strategic plan move ahead at a predictable or even speed but inevitably proceeds through a series of pauses and spurts. Since no strategic plan can contemplate every contingency, the turnaround leader must work in an environment of constant reaction to "what is," which may be far different than "what was supposed to be."

In a recently completed study by Northeastern University, it was found that two out of three of the 86 turnaround companies studied failed to implement agreed-upon strategies because:

☐ Major problems arose which had not been predicted.
☐ Competing crises and activities within the organization absorbed and deflected management attention.
☐ Coordination was sloppy.

Strategic planning for well-performing companies can be difficult enough, without superimposing the additional problems of the troubled company. Perhaps the reason strategic planning has become what *Fortune* called "bedraggled" is that many managers invest their misplaced faith in the infallibility of planning for planning's sake, often becoming the victims of what Pearson Hunt wrote about in the *Harvard Business Review* as "the fallacy of the one big brain":

> The study of business management . . . is seen whenever people act as if business problems were solved by a single entity having one big brain. All too often, we design schemes of analysis that assume that problems can be recognized, defined, analyzed, and solved by one brain of enormous capacity, which operates in a completely objective manner, searching for and comparing all possible alternatives in one thinking process . . . to arrive at the best possible answers.

To manage a turnaround effectively, therefore, we must arrange our strategies in some order, with simplicity and with the understanding that people will make decisions at different levels, at different times, and from different perspectives based on differing judgments. Possibly the ideal strategic approach for a turnaround is that voiced by Napoleon: "Unhappy the general who comes on the field of battle with a system." He knew the value of keeping strategic options open.

IMPLEMENTING THE PLAN

A third element in any turnaround plan is the action plan through which turnaround strategies are implemented. A well-designed turnaround action plan includes:

1. *Who* is to do it?
2. *What* is to be done?
3. *How* it is to be accomplished?
4. *When* it is to be completed?

The first step is to properly organize the company so that the plan can be implemented. A turnaround is typically time-consuming and requires skills unlike those needed for day-to-day operations. For that reason larger corporations may organize specific turnaround task forces that primarily orchestrate the turnaround while the remaining organization continues with normal operational responsibility. Of course, even when a "platoon" system is inaugurated, there must necessarily be a great deal of coordination between the turnaround team and the line managers to insure that the turnaround program is carried out and meshed closely with ongoing operations.

A major reason for turnaround failure is that people within the organization simply do not know what is to be done or what their respective roles in the workout are.

Execution is largely a matter of management control. Management cannot take it for granted that line managers will necessarily know how to transform management's broad goals into practice. And this is particularly so when the required actions go contrary to existing operational practices and employees are required to go beyond routine procedures.

Good communication is part of the answer. The job of top management is to make the strategic implementation credible and appealing to all of the organization's employees so that the widest possible commitment to fulfilling the corporate objectives is secured. This is accomplished by providing a clear explanation of the process to all staff members.

Responsibility must also be pinpointed if the turnaround plan is to work. The turnaround plan must define who is responsible for each phase of the turnaround. Key managers must understand in advance the expected results, and this must be followed by a strict review and accountability mechanism to see whether results were achieved.

For the plan to work, strict accountability cannot be overemphasized. Line managers must have quantifiable standards by which to measure their own performance and the performance of other key managers responsible for implementing the turnaround. Pinpointing responsibility is, of course, a component of any good management system but it is an absolute must in a turnaround where areas of responsibility may shift or authority lines can easily become blurred. Without strict accountability, planning is just a gesture in the right direction.

The second phase of the action plan is a clear definition of what is to be done. How management chooses to spell out the specific actions will, of course, depend on many factors. However, the action must be defined in such a way to avoid confusion or misdirection.

A major problem is that top management may prescribe sweeping changes and the organization may not be programmed to achieve those changes, creating what I call "operational gap."

Lack of resources is another reason for "operational gap." This "operational gap" may be the most troublesome spot in a turnaround because of the obvious difference between management creating broad-brush changes in the organization from the comforts of its penthouse suites and the ability of the front-line troops to respond to those changes.

To implement the turnaround then, it may be necessary to walk in small steps. The organization is likely to adapt to change far slower than management would hope. The greater the measurable detail of each step, the easier are the managerial tasks to control organizational behavior and to exercise the organizational power needed to successfully execute the plan.

Further, the more thorough and detailed the turnaround plan, the more line managers will understand what is expected of them. The more precise the communication between the turnaround team and line managers, the more each will understand the expectations, potential problems, and alternatives. Building a company, as with building a house, requires the architect, builder, and carpenter to not only work from the same detailed blueprint, but also talk to each other.

Implementation of the plan will necessarily depend on line managers having the resources to get the job done. This too can be a stumbling block to effective implementation. Management, for example, may demand operational changes for which additional labor or equipment is needed, and yet refuse or fail to provide these resources. On the other hand, line managers and employees, passive in their attitude toward change or hostile to management, may sabotage the turnaround effort, create false obstacles, and demand unneeded resources. In large measure, this can be resolved through candid communication, a mutual understanding of the problems, and a clearer understanding of what the organization can realistically deliver.

The resources an organization will need to achieve results can vary dramatically depending on the attitude of employees. Enthusiastic, motivated employees learn to innovate, particularly when the turnaround leader sets his or her own standards for innovation. Apathetic employees who could care less about the eventual success of the organization look for excuses and reasons to justify nonperformance. And for this management is usually at fault. Richard Sloma, in his best-selling book *No-Nonsense Management* (MacMillan, 1977) reminds us, "Don't expect change in results if you haven't changed conditions." And it is for that reason that employees may resist the turnaround effort or create false obstacles.

Although we discuss motivation in Chapter 9, the entire process of implementing the plan may be no more complicated than building enthusiasm for the plan within the organization. Yet, notwithstanding the issue of motivation, an effective implementation plan recognizes there may be new tools and resources needed to quantify, identify, isolate, and carry out the turnaround program. The processes by which an organization goes about transforming itself need not be overly complicated.

In short, an effective plan enables a manager to control change and to make it orderly. A plan is a series of steps that provides the means for the firm to go "from here to there." "Here" comprises one set of operating circumstances and "there" constitutes a totally different set of circumstances. This is seldom an insurmountable challenge for turnaround leaders who can make good things happen.

MONITORING THE PLAN

Because the turnaround organization is a change-sensitive system based on feedback, it is alert to threats and opportunities as the plan evolves and is implemented. Management must carefully monitor the entire process, and move swiftly and decisively to refine and modify the turnaround program when changes are detected that will affect the achievement of the corporate mission.

Turnaround objectives should, whenever possible, be quantified. Once the plan is put into action, effective management control depends on being able to compare actual performance against planned results. A turnaround plan is worse than useless if actual performance progress cannot be tracked and its impact upon corporate recovery evaluated.

Corporate information systems already in place may not be adequate for monitoring the turnaround. First and foremost is the need for timely data. Turnaround situations rely on weekly reporting systems for key indicators. Cash flow, expense budgets, and purchasing are continuously monitored. We frequently require clients to provide sales figures on a daily basis, and have even tracked cash positions on an hourly basis. How timely the reporting information must be will, of course, depend on the nature and condition of the company and the characteristics of the turnaround plan itself. However, when the company is financially troubled, any change can have a pronounced effect on performance, and management must understand how each change affects performance before it becomes too late to correct course.

No less critical is the need for the correct type of information. A major error, however, is to become bogged down with too much information, when management should define—and focus on—the few essential performance barometers. It is considerably better to constantly monitor the key indicators than to become immersed in extraneous detail that can only cloud matters. One turnaround leader claims he can measure the progress of a manufacturing firm by watching just three items: the break-even point, the amount of the orders shipped, and the amount of the orders in process. And more than a few successful turnaround leaders record corporate progress on the back of an envelope. While most turnarounds require somewhat more sophisticated information, simplicity can be a virtue, particularly when it is likely to mean increased speed and accuracy.

The actual-to-plan measurement need not—in fact, should not—be limited to information available only through the accounting system. Wherever and whenever possible physical measurements should be used. Instead of only measuring dollars, consider units of sale, orders received, or units produced. These may provide a clearer expression of the corporate condition and are often the best feedback for monitoring and controlling the turnaround.

The ability to measure performance is in itself meaningless unless management couples it with realistic and set benchmarks. Corporate progress must be tracked against a predetermined plan. And a "damage control" program is needed to repair the organization when plans prove faulty. The commitment to key milestones is essential. While the organization may constantly modify its expectations it must also know what to expect from the organization next week, next month, and next year.

The organization may quantify progress in terms of sales, profits, reduction loss, or debt, but as the corporation goes through its transformation it must have a clear vision of what it should look like at reasonably spaced intervals along the way. When this vision is shared by everyone within the organization it is an exhilarating feeling, but never as exhilarating as getting there.

9

Creating the Climate for Success

COMMITTING corporate plans, budgets, policies, strategies, and objectives to paper does not make them a reality.

The skilled corporate leader creates an environment which those involved with the organization recognize as a climate for success. This is the corporate ambience in which employees are inspired to achieve ambitious goals and outstanding performances. It is a climate within which customers do not abandon the organization but instead throw their support behind the organization because the organization has become user-friendly. Creditors and lenders revel in this climate for success with greater confidence that the problems of the past will remain in the past.

Just as the turnaround leader must create financial stability, he or she must also create organizational stability, which in the minds of most turnaround veterans is a considerably more difficult feat than rebuilding financial stability. Ultimately, management must develop a people-oriented philosophy if the turnaround is to succeed. The failing of too many managers is that they deal with people as if they were things.

For these ailing companies the predictable crisis will be their eroding relationship with employees and customers—the two groups the company most relies on for its existence. Yet these two important groups have their own stakes in the success of the organization and the ability

of management to "right the ship." When these groups see their interests
as adverse to the company or their needs no longer satisfied, a struggle
results. When they see their interests in alignment with those of the
organization, cooperation and support result. The difference is inevitably
the corporate climate created by the turnaround leader.

This turnaround leader has the priceless ability to pull together
employees, solidify relationships, and throw a cloak of support around
the organization.

A classic case of organizational dry rot was encountered by John
Mahoney when he came aboard as president to rescue a failing $20-
million-a-year Washington-based retail chain. Mahoney recounts:

> Employees were either jumping ship or just didn't give a damn.
> Suppliers shut off credit and with dwindling inventory we were
> losing sales and good will. Once a customer comes into a store and
> sees empty racks, she won't come back. Competitors? They were
> hovering around us like vultures. One was waiting for our auction
> so he could pick up our inventory at a knock-down price, and two
> others were busy soliciting our best employees. Our landlords were
> beseiged with phone calls to throw us out so our competitors could
> move in to our best locations.

Every troubled company is embroiled in much the same crisis. How
management goes about the task of relieving organizational stress by
creating a climate for success makes all the difference whether those
affiliated with the company begin to pull together or continue to pull
the company apart. And after a successful rescue of his own corporation,
Mahoney will tell you, "Creating a climate for success under such circumstances is seldom easy; the turnaround leader must be a dealer in
hope."

MOTIVATING THE ORGANIZATION

In a company where a climate has been set for success, employees perceive and experience this positive environment. They know theirs is a
company that both wants and intends to succeed. Such an environment
alerts employees to the reality that a climate exists in which top management both *wants* and *needs* their help to shape and share in this
success.

The attitudes of the people within the organization are more critical in a turnaround situation than at any other time in a company's life. Every company has problems motivating its employees and galvanizing them for greater productivity, but a turnaround company is in a particularly difficult situation because morale is usually rock-bottom. While the company can be ruthless in eliminating extra people and achieving salary cutbacks, it is nearly impossible for a company to sustain a long-term turnaround unless it can also turn its people around. However, there are countless "people" problems to overcome.

It is in the shakeout stage when the company first begins to come to grips with its problems that employees will be most demoralized. They are no longer primarily concerned with their work, but with their own security. Everybody is blue because they are working in a bad work environment and they never know when their own job is on the line. The comments of a middle manager for Allis-Chalmers, which just went into Chapter 11, are typical: "How am I supposed to be excited about the company when I may be handed my pink slip next week and rumors of 20 percent pay cuts are in the air?"

It is correctly feared that when large cutbacks have to be made, motivation will be most affected. Most turnaround leaders agree that the best prescription is to get the staff reductions over with as soon as possible, and to make them all at once. Employees cannot function well when their own future security is threatened. But once the layoffs are made, management must let the remaining employees know no further cutbacks are planned. Rumors abound in a troubled organization and employees must hear the facts straight from the top. The answers to uncertainty, anxiety, and fear are the leader's personal integrity and his or her ability and willingness to communicate the straight facts.

Many organizations do not have to go through the pain of laying off employees. Unfortunately, the best employees may leave of their own accord, leaving behind those who are less valuable and less employable elsewhere. Sometimes the turnaround has to be achieved not only with fewer people but with the least capable people. A strong turnaround leader will anticipate the defection of the best people, retaining them by giving them added responsibilities in the turnaround effort and particularly attractive incentive programs.

Another question that plagues management is whether it is better to go with across-the-board pay cuts and preserve jobs or to sacrifice jobs and maintain salary levels. Many companies, of course, cannot afford the luxury of options and must undertake both. But when the company has alternatives, pay cuts are preferable to layoffs when the pay cuts are temporary, and layoffs are advisable when long-term cost reduction is needed. Elliot Fine, an executive recruiter, observes:

> You can't take an employee earning $30,000 and expect him to hang around forever for $25,000. He may put up with it for a month or two to avoid the upheaval to a new job but after that he'll probably move on. An employee may be more tolerant of cutbacks in fringe benefits than a salary reduction because it has less impact on his paycheck and is less visible.

Labor unions may to a large extent dictate how personnel cost reductions will be handled—typically preferring salary cutbacks to layoffs. But bargaining with a labor union for concessions can be difficult since it expects significant sacrifice on everyone else's part before salaries or jobs are to be sacrificed. The threat of Chapter 11—and its powers to negate collective bargaining agreements if obstructive to the company's survival—can be a formidable weapon in negotiation. In recent years labor unions have become proactive in the workout of employer organizations, and assert an enormous influence on how employees respond under adverse corporate conditions. In larger organizations employees will be more inclined to take their cue from union officials than from top management. Within these organizations management may first find it necessary to instill the climate for success in the union representatives before it can be transmitted to the rank and file. Chrysler, the first major corporation to appoint a union official to the corporate board of directors, well understood the power of union influence.

The tolerance of employees to layoffs and salary cutbacks may be governed more by the psychology than the economics of the situation. It is one thing to go before a crowd of employees to announce a 10 percent salary cutback; it is another when management first tells how top management is taking a 40 percent pay cut and creditors may end up with 20 or 30 cents on the dollar. Employees, more than anyone else, must be convinced of the "equality of sacrifice." But there really must be a perceived "equality of sacrifice," reminds Leonard Buckle, an industrial psychologist: "An employee earning $25,000 and cut to $20,000 may not be overly sympathetic to a president whose $250,000 salary is lowered to $200,000." The sacrifice must be functionally equal and not just mathematically equal.

Moreover, cost-cutting should begin at the top through reduction in support and staff positions where there is likely to be the most overhead flab. "You can't sell the idea of layoffs on the shop floor unless enough heads rolled in the executive suite," reminds Leonard Buckle. Demonstrating that the top managers can take it hard on the chin with cutbacks in the executive suite will be quickly noticed. It will revitalize morale and at least neutralize antagonism, if not foster cooperation. But even the show of blood from the executive suite may not be sufficient to pacify employees now asked to shed some of their own blood. Employees —with some justification—believe that of all constituent groups, they are in the least favorable position to make sacrifices on behalf of the organization. Again, it is a matter of relativity. An employee who measures his or her salary by counting $10 bills cannot relate to sharing the sacrifice with lenders and creditors who routinely deal in millions.

Eventually management must go beyond stabilizing morale and begin to shock the troops toward more positive thinking. For the turnaround leader to orient the company away from failure and toward success the leader must believe in the future of the company and clearly and continuously convey that belief. The attitudes of management play a decisive role in the attitudes of the front-line troops.

Employees who have long been conditioned to think only in terms of problems must gradually be conditioned to again think of opportunity, profits, and growth. "It won't happen overnight," Elliot Fine cautions us, "but it must happen as the corporate culture is transformed from a defensive posture to one of forward movement." But getting employees to think of profit and opportunity can be as difficult for the troubled enterprise as it is for the stable firm. Most employees do not associate their work with bottom-line profits. Although most employees sincerely want their organization to become more prosperous, in reality they seldom work harder to make it happen. Employees only perform better when they derive a direct benefit to themselves.

Incentive compensation and performance feedback can most directly get results. Just as employee wages and benefits may necessarily be cut when cost savings are imperative, a system of recognition and rewards must be plugged in as benchmarks of recovery are passed. A company may, for example, provide incremental bonuses for predetermined sales increases. And management should certainly commit to restoration of salary and benefits as the company progresses.

The incentives must be meaningful if they are to be effective. Wherever possible incentives should be tied to individual performance instead of overall corporate performance. A bonus on sales commissions and productivity incentives tied to each employee, for example, is preferable to across-the-board incentives.

The incentive program must be designed in advance—preferably when the initial cutbacks are made—so employees can see the upside as well as the downside of the situation. Employees will not only be more inclined to stay with the company but will show far greater enthusiasm if they know they will be amply rewarded for that loyalty.

But if incentives are a "carrot" the company must also carry a bigger "stick," cautioning employees that the company will be less tolerant of poor performance and then following through with terminations when performance standards are not met.

Leading employees with the carrot and stick has to make employees believe that either they yank their oar harder or they are out. And it must be a very powerful force in a turnaround. Kicking the organization may mean moving or replacing people or bringing new people in, all of which may be long overdue. While turnaround companies are people-sensitive they must also be performance-sensitive and survival-sensitive. This means management must often terminate loyal and long-standing employees who cannot adequately perform. It also means management may scrap affirmative action and other social programs when they restrict its ability to hire or retain the very best employees.

Maintaining a climate of success cannot be achieved with an incentive system alone. A system of monetary rewards, while vital, is in itself inadequate to create a crucible of enthusiasm. Barry Sullivan is a superb example of a corporate leader who knows how to create a climate for success. Sullivan took over controls of First Chicago Corporation in 1980, when First Chicago, then the nation's eleventh-largest bank holding company, was under heavy attack by such financial services giants as Merrill Lynch, American Express, and Sears Roebuck. In addition to numerous marketing changes, Sullivan reshaped the corporate climate by encouraging an open atmosphere and a teamwork approach through a collegial management style, a new compensation strategy, and personal example. It is Sullivan who can be found delving into every corporate nook and cranny—from budgets to selecting the art that will decorate the bank's walls. Sullivan created a new corporate climate by changing just about everything from the physical environment to internal communication to employee participation in managerial decision making. In exchange, Sullivan is blessed with people who show up to work each morning with a refreshingly positive attitude.

Leaders like Sullivan understand how well employees can respond to even the small "wins" in the turnaround process. Management must constantly spotlight the gains, even if the gains are modest. One of my own clients makes it a point to take the 12-employee crew of his cabinet shop to lunch whenever something positive such as a sizable new order or sales increase occurs. Another company on the rebound from slumping sales raffles away to a lucky employee a free vacation trip whenever sales reach a certain mark. These may be seen as nothing more than symbolic gestures but symbolism can lift spirits. Shortly after the devastation of Pearl Harbor and months of defeat in the Pacific at the hands of the Japanese, General James Doolittle launched a stunning bombing raid on Tokyo. As expected, the raid inflicted negligible damage but for a first time since the war began, Americans had cause to smile. Victory can come with small punches.

Honest, open, and frequent communication may be the cornerstone for creating this new corporate climate. The communication I speak of is not through fancy corporate bulletins or through five tiers of management, but in face-to-face meetings between top managers and clusters of employees. Managers who want results roll up their sleeves and talk *with* their people instead of talking *to* their people.

Management all too often forgets that employes may have the greatest stake in the survival of the company, and with remarkable insensitivity often leaves employees in the dark as corporate events unfold. Nothing can alienate employees more than a distant management unresponsive to their own concerns. The constant theme we hear from employees in every size and type of organization is, "We have given this place years of our life and depend on it to feed our kids and keep a roof over our heads. We damn well have a right to know what's going on." And, of course, they are right. Telling them is, of course, what good communication and courageous managers are all about.

Managers often believe they are effectively communicating, but they may be giving nothing more than lip service. Employees have a natural cynicism to whatever management tells them, and this may be particularly so when the company is in deep trouble and the truth may encourage employee defection. After all, managers understand that even rats have the good sense to jump ship when it is about to sink. Still, good managers accept the right of employees to share the bad news with the good, albeit with a dose of optimism.

Look upon a chance to meet with employees of a turnaround company not only to keep them abreast of developments, but to learn from them. The tendency of top management to insulate itself from the front-line troops may be tolerable when times are good, but fatal in the bad times when management is critically dependent on constant feedback from every level of operation. Management must listen to and get employees' input if it is to have a clear sense of what is really going on. Often it takes a crisis to bring management and employees together, and it is management that finds itself surprised with the many valuable ideas employees can indeed contribute.

To truly energize the organization it is not enough to simply communicate with employees. Employees must actively participate in the turnaround program. There are various ways to increase employee involvement. One company divides employees into task force groups, with each group assigned a specific project. Another appoints key employees to serve on a special workout committee on a rotating basis. George Trimble of Bunko-Ramo successfully instituted a philosophy of teamwork based on a 10-member employee counsel that meets with him monthly for shirt-sleeve sessions. Giving employees greater responsibilities and say in corporate governance is not a novel idea; however, there is no better time to implement it than during a turnaround when employees rightfully believe they should be more in control of their own destiny.

When we put it all together a four-point strategy emerges:

1. Establish stong leadership.

2. Establish clear goals with strong incentives and severe penalties tied to those goals.

3. Constantly communicate.

4. Encourage employees to participate in the turnaround process.

The mandate for management is to create the atmosphere within which these strategies can flourish.

THE USER-FRIENDLY CORPORATION

Managers who recognize and believe that the customer is number one also energize their organization toward the needs of their customers. Of course, firms with customer-driven philosophies seldom fail in the first place because they believe that the customer is the life-source of all profit-making enterprises. These firms continue to put the customer before all others even in troubled times and therefore are in the strongest position to maintain customers and preserve the sales base upon which to rebuild.

Penn Central, Baldwin-United Corp., Rolls Royce, W.T. Grant, and numerous other famous corporate relics, however, are classic testimony to the ostrich approach to customer satisfaction practiced by so many firms. These are the firms that can to a large extent trace their failures to their bureaucracy-driven philosophy to serve organizational needs before customer needs. For these firms to survive they need more than cosmetic marketing and customer service strategies; they need a new sense of corporate philosophy where the customer does come first. In short, they must learn to march to the beat of a different drummer.

Companies in financial difficulty are particularly vulnerable, and are far more likely to lose customers to more aggressive competitors better equipped to satisfy the customer.

Yet many troubled companies allow their sales to erode because they succumb to the pressure to demarket rather than market. Cash-shy, these companies are inclined to cut back on advertising, promotion, and other marketing efforts seen as less vital to the continuity of the business. These same firms are also likely to raise prices, slash customer services, reduce product quality, and engage in a wide number of business practices to increase short-term cash flow at the expense of long-term survival.

Maintaining strong sales is critical in a turnaround and yet may be the most difficult challenge to a management preoccupied with so many internal problems. Customers leave the stricken company in droves once they experience problems in receiving products or service. Customers naturally gravitate to winners and away from losers. And stronger competitors will show little reluctance to move in for the kill once aware of the troubled company's inability to fend off attack.

It is because the company is so vulnerable that a more powerful marketing program and increased emphasis on the customer becomes imperative. "Marketing is a powerful expression that the company is alive and well," says Ben Fishman of Philadelphia's Professional Marketing Associates. "Customers often leave faltering companies because they no longer believe the business can properly service them. A well-designed marketing and customer service program can dispel that image," he adds.

This experience is shared by a large Boston wholesale drug firm that recently emerged successfully from a Chapter 11 reorganization. But while the company was in Chapter 11 five competitors hit the road to tempt away their retail accounts, dangling everything from lenient credit and extra discounts to paid vacations to those shifting their allegiances. The firm's sales manager recounts:

> In the first several months we lost about 28 of our 465 active accounts and then began to hit back with our own marketing effort, adding three new salesmen to solidify relationships with existing customers. Then we spent $60,000 on a series of promotional campaigns to gain new customers. Our competitors who thought we were down for the count couldn't believe we could really bounce back and actually steal away their customers. At first we had too many financial and operational problems to worry much about sales, marketing, or customer retention programs. We simply became sloppy in dealing with our customers and when you are in business you can't afford to become sloppy . . . no matter how many other problems you have.

If a renewed advertising and promotional program is needed to energize the company it must be done more effectively. Promotion costs in most troubled companies must often be realigned to match the basic strategies set for the turnaround. The old concept of "smother 'em" marketing must be replaced with a well-conceived, targeted marketing campaign. Pareto's law—that 20 percent of all activity produces 80 percent of the results—has no greater applicability than in the design of the new marketing strategy where the most productive 20 percent must be defined and concentrated on. When cash is tight it must be focused on the most important customers even if it means neglecting the smaller, less profitable accounts. The troubled company can no longer be all things to all people. It must decide which customers are vital to its continued existence and use the shrinking resources to build even stronger relationships with these accounts, and constantly monitor their satisfaction level. Usually the company will undergo retrenchment during the turnaround so many of its marginal accounts will be shed anyway as the company shrinks back to a "viable core" business. What is critically important is that the company hold on to those few big customers as a nucleus for moving forward.

Because they do not directly generate revenues, soft expenditures such as public relations, community image-building programs, and institutional advertising should be eliminated. Advertising can only be supported to the extent it produces direct, measurable results. Promotional or sales aids such as samples and other incentives must also be reviewed with careful cost/sales assessment. The sales department—long accustomed to support from the home office—may have to realign its own compensation to match performance. A number of ailing companies switch salespeople from salary to commission, which fortunately serves to eliminate many of the less productive salespeople who could not justify their salaries in the first place. Salespeople whose workday was less than productive often find more efficient, profitable ways to sell when their paycheck depends on it. In fact, a study of retrenchment policies of troubled companies disclose that the sales staff typically undergoes the largest cutback of all personnel categories, and the cutbacks appear to have very little impact on sales. The health of a company may be gauged by its dependency on the sales function. Healthy corporations are market-oriented; their managerial energy is directed at meeting customer needs. Weaker organizations will harness large sales forces to the task of finding replacement customers.

Pricing is another area that requires examination in a troubled company and must be looked at as part of revamping the overall marketing program. Many companies, of course, get into trouble because they underprice. In fact, underpricing occurs about five times as often as overpricing, another situation easily corrected during the turnaround.

Not surprisingly, the pressure to increase sales often leads these firms to lower prices. The mistaken theory is that additional sales can be profitably added to the existing sales volume, even when the prices are too low to cover a proportional share of the overhead. These companies do not realize that gross margins on sales seldom rise enough to cover the creeping costs associated with the added sales.

A&P was a classic example of how a faulty pricing strategy could sabotage a turnaround. After years of struggling A&P decided to go "deep discount." The result was near disaster, leading to the costliest price war in food retailing and additional losses of over $40 million to A&P in just six months. A&P discovered that lowered prices only cause competitors to meet the threat with their own lowered prices. And when competitors decide to slug it out on the basis of price alone, the victor is typically the company with the greater staying power.

While the natural tendency in a turnaround is to cut prices and maintain costs, the central strategy of virtually every successful turnaround is just the opposite—increase prices and cut costs. Rational and properly introduced price increases rarely hurt sales but can add considerably to the bottom line, when coupled with a program of improved service and other customer-retention strategies.

Energizing relationships with customers, then, typically means a new commitment to product quality and customer service. Companies make a dangerous mistake when they cut back on product quality and believe they can get away with it. The introduction of shoddy products is always noticed. American automakers are noticeably reducing product quality in an attempt to stay competitive with lower-priced import cars, but this strategy may simply trigger more lost sales as domestic automakers accomplish nothing but producing more poorly made products without even gaining a price advantage. Iacocca may well have saved Chrysler by taking just the opposite approach—insisting the new K-cars are so well made that Chrysler stands behind them with an unheard-of 7-year, 70,000-mile warranty. The lesson we learn from surviving companies is that the turnaround may be an opportunity in disguise to look at the continued quality of their products or services with the same objectivity customers will, and to gain the competitive edge with products of enhanced quality.

If energizing the company means energizing the product line, the company with a proliferation of product lines will again have to remember Pareto's law and focus on the key lines essential to rebuilding the company. Unfortunately, product or product-line proliferation is synonymous with growth in many companies, but many of these companies remain unable to fully develop or profitably exploit every product line simultaneously, with the net result that they do poorly in all. For the turnaround company, shrinking the product line is usually the surest route to higher profits and higher return on investment, particularly if the company can easily eliminate low-margin lines consuming a disproportionate share of the overhead.

The energized turnaround company stresses its strong customers, strong product lines, and strong service and distribution policies. A company going through a turnaround has too few resources to waste on the weak. Simmons Company—manufacturers of mattresses and sofas— shrunk from over 8000 dealers to fewer than 5000 dealers, reasoning the company would do far better giving its attention to those dealers who are the most productive. Simmons concentrated all its corporate resources on building stronger dealer relations and stepped up both its own and its dealers' promotional programs to generate more sales. Simmons products were improved in quality with corresponding price increases. Simmons in its comeback followed a survival strategy followed by countless turnaround companies: "Thick on the best—to hell with the rest."

"Energizing the marketing program of a turnaround company is essentially a matter of coming up with the right answers to basic questions," according to Stanley Stewart, President of Market Makers, Inc., a Tennessee-based marketing consulting firm:

1. Who are the customers we should be concentrating on?

2. What are the product lines or services essential to our survival?

3. What marketing vehicles (advertising, promotion, etc.) will allow us to most effectively and efficiently reach our customers?

4. What added services or programs will strengthen our relationship with key customers?

5. What things can we do now to look like a survivor?

6. What resources can we commit to the marketing program?

ENERGIZING FROM THE TOP

If the purpose of business is, as Peter Drucker says, "to create a customer," or as Stanford's Harold Levitt puts it, "to buy a customer," then the responsibilities for energizing these philosophies throughout the organization rest on the shoulders of the turnaround leader. The turnaround leader has the primary responsibility to the company's major customers. It is the turnaround leader who must appreciate the potential contribution that *every* employee can offer in a company that is keen to acquire new customers, keep existing ones, and rebuild on a foundation that focuses on the customer as the reason for the employee's paycheck. It is these same turnaround leaders who energize both employees and customers, with a linkage between them through which improved products, services, systems, and policies flow.

Indeed, the involvement of all employees in the care and custody of customers is an important asset for any company, but it is particularly important for troubled companies where employees and customers must often be adaptive and flexible in their dealings as they each cope with the limited resources of the organization.

Corporations in trouble become user-friendly because their customers not only remain their most valuable asset but may be the only asset left relatively intact. Corporations that survive learn how to keep their customers by keeping very close to them. Corporate winners listen to their customers and service the socks off them, and make sure they always feel very important. The continued ringing of the cash register creates the sweet sound of corporate success.

If we believe, as we should, that the business of business is customer service and satisfaction, the primary function of the turnaround leader is to energize the organization in that direction. Energizing the organization describes a managerial philosophy which embraces a particular collection of skills and techniques used by executives who are the movers and shakers of turnaround companies:

1. Developing a sense of purpose—a shared view of what the company is about.

2. Instilling a sense of pride—that the company is the best at what it does.

3. Creating a climate for success by heading the organization away from problems and toward opportunities.

4. Building the motivation machine that inspires employees to routinely turn in extraordinary performances.

5. Exploiting the unique competence of staff and management to fashion a high-performing executive team and then diffusing power and responsibility through a vigorous commitment to delegation.

6. Energizing the organization with a user-friendly attitude based on a customer-first, service-driven philosophy.

7. Fashioning new products, services, and programs to regain the competitive edge and to instill both the belief and reality that the company, indeed, has a future.

10

Second-Chance Financing

"SUCCESSFUL companies live within their income, even if they have to borrow to do it." These words from the humorist Josh Billings apply equally well to unsuccessful companies.

Almost every troubled company needs more than stoppage of the cash drain to survive. Massive amounts of new money and replenished assets may be needed if it is to go forward. This dependence on "second-chance" financing from external sources will in turn rest on the company's ability to internally generate cash from operations and couple it with the capital required to stabilize and position the company for new growth.

A great many companies fail only because they are unable to finance their way through the turnaround. With chronic cash flow shortages the company is forced to shut down. Many of these failed companies collapse when stability and survival could have been achieved with a more assertive approach to financing. As the expression goes, "They were a dime short and a day late."

With the debtor company pressed for money, thoughts can turn in a hundred directions. Can it be obtained from existing vendors and lenders? Is it available from customers for whom the company is an important source of supply? If not available from existing relationships, are there new sources that can be tapped? Are there assets that have substantial equity, sufficient to support additional loans? Are government sources available for immediate financing? Should the principals of the company provide a fresh infusion of capital?

The answers to these questions will rest on many variables: The size of the company, the nature of the business, the company's relationship with lender and creditor groups and their own stake in a successful workout are all important factors. Another important consideration is whether a financier will believe the company's problems are behind it and the new money will be used to propel the company forward rather than pay for the sins of the past. Therefore, a company immersed in the crisis or emergency stage of the turnaround will have far fewer opportunities to attract outside financing than will companies emerging from the turnaround with a brighter future just ahead.

Yet, even under the most favorable circumstances, financing the turnaround business is rarely easy. John Whitney in *Taking Charge* (Dow Jones-Irwin, 1987) aptly states:

> A promoter getting off the train with a cardboard suitcase and a checkered suit has a better chance of raising money for an oil well in Georgia than the going concern with a checkered past has for raising money for continuing operations. Notwithstanding the fact that oil may yet be found in Georgia, and notwithstanding the fact that the turnaround firm may indeed be turning around, there's no "story," no concept, no magic. With luck, the turnaround leader will receive wandering attention and a stifled yawn from the investment banker; otherwise he will be asked to close the door quietly as he leaves.

In most cases the company strikes out in its financing attempts because the company's long-term prospects are unchanged from those that have existed for a considerable time. If the business is in trouble because of a catastrophe or some other specific event that does not adversely reflect on the overall viability and profitability of the company, management can make a far more convincing case for refinancing. The prospects are far less optimistic when the company suffers from chronic mismanagement, prolonged losses, or is surrounded by clouds of fraud or creditor abuse.

Even when circumstances favor financing, lenders will want to see whether the company has first utilized and exhausted its internal sources of cash. And primary reliance on the company's internal resources are important, because negotiations for external financing can take considerable time and the distressed company has to inevitably live off its assets while it becomes stabilized and has the opportunity to attract outside capital. This is also important because management is more likely to find money externally if it has demonstrated an understanding of its internal resources and has performed well in harvesting and deploying those resources toward a successful turnaround effort.

None of this implies that financing the troubled company is always a conscious or voluntary undertaking by its financiers. More commonly —and particularly at the earliest stages—the company has a "window of opportunity" to draw down its credit lines from unsuspecting vendors and banks. Even when the creditors are aware of the company's plight they may have no practical alternatives but to continue financing the company. Chrysler, as an example, ran up its trade payables by $350 million during the period in which it was trying to qualify for the government's guarantee, much of it from trade suppliers who depended on Chrysler for their own survival.

TAPPING TRADE CREDIT

No company can do business from an empty wagon. When sales depend on having adequate products or inventory, empty shelves can only mean a silent cash register.

Trade credit is a principal financing tool for the product-oriented company. Therefore, when inventories are depleted, the focus should be on how inventories can be rebuilt to a satisfactory level through the use of trade credit.

Trade creditors are usually aware of a company's problems well before lenders, and by the time the problems surface, trade credit financing is usually exhausted. On the other hand, a large accounts payable exposure may be very helpful if it has the effect of locking in trade creditors. Heavily exposed trade creditors may be forced to further support the organization and can be treated as having the same vested interest as a lender. Exposure may induce them to cooperate with more credit, but only if their further risk can be favorably measured against the improved odds of collecting the old debt.

Trade creditors can be torn between the need to keep up sales and the risk of nonpayment, as was apparent in the Chrysler case. Many cling to the old axiom that the first loss is the best and therefore will not continue any credit terms. And it should not be the objective of management to intentionally or needlessly cause its trade suppliers greater risk of loss. But between this objective and the unpleasant reality that the business needs more products on credit, the supplier and company may consider various options.

One common solution is for the principals (or affiliated firms) of the troubled company to issue guarantees to secure future credit. On rare occasions, to keep trade creditors engaged, banks have provided letters of credit or subordinations as they did in the W.T. Grant workout, when banks guaranteed over $100 million in new shipments of merchandise to restock the troubled retailer. Whenever guarantees are issued, the guarantor obviously will want to limit its own exposure to what is reasonable under the circumstances, and may require that the guaranty be limited, or secured by corporate assets, or contain other protective features.

Trade creditors may also be induced into granting further credit if the credit can be secured by adequate and unencumbered assets which may be available. The company may also offer to secure past indebtedness as well as future obligations as a concession for an extension of its credit line.

Even when the company is highly encumbered, there are a variety of devices to secure new shipments of goods. Where the goods are identifiable the parties may consider a purchase money security interest, trust receipt, or even field warehousing arrangement to secure the seller. We often arrange consignment agreements and have remerchandised quite a few retail businesses from manufacturers anxious to open new outlets on a consignment basis. Frequently retail clients discover new—and more profitable—merchandise lines once they seek new sources of supply willing to sell on a consignment basis. This occurred, for example, when a three-store ladies apparel chain decided to take on consignment a line of artificial furs to augment its anemic dress lines. Before long 70 percent of its volume was from its new fur line, encouraging the revitalized chain to expand as specialty stores selling only artificial furs—another example of how companies often find opportunity from adversity.

The urgent demand for merchandise may develop even more involved relationships between supplier and customer, creating partnerships and other forms of affiliation. The supplier may see the takeover of a troubled distributor or retailer as an opportunity to sell more goods. The business in need of inventory may look upon the supplier as a lifeline for essential merchandise. Business school professors benignly refer to it as "vertical integration" but marriages between supplier and customer can be seen in more profitable and pragmatic terms. For example, the New York-based Norton-McNaughton Company—manufacturers of trendy fashions—recently acquired a 50 percent ownership interest to help rescue the 20-store Great Factory Outlet chain from Chapter 11. Norton-McNaughton plans to expand its own lines within the recently acquired retail chain and as a major stockholder of the clothing retailer it undoubtedly will see its investment returned many times through greater sales of its own merchandise.

Lack of credit and empty shelves may destroy business but enterprising people can turn even empty shelves into opportunity. Not long ago a local supermarket failed and was acquired at auction by two young chaps who took over the lease even though they had neither the money nor credit to inventory the store. Nor did they want to. Instead they leased the store's departments to established local merchants. A nearby butcher set up a "meat boutique," a local produce distributor became the "green grocer," and a bakery chain grabbed at the chance to add its tempting baked goods, all surrounding fully stocked shelves rack-jobbed by a food wholesale. The imaginative owners, busy coordinating the advertising and operating the checkout registers, are collecting over $80,000 in rents plus 1 percent of sales for their imaginative efforts. As the young partners figure it, "We'll earn about $70,000 in net annual profit from the business, and not invest a nickel in inventory." This is the innovation and imagination that we speak of as being as valuable as cash or credit.

DEFENSIVE LOAN

Lenders can only be convinced to make additional advances to a financially troubled borrower if the lender is satisfied that the borrower's trouble has been pinpointed and that further advances will be unlikely. The primary consideration is that the additional advance will increase the overall loan recovery. This decision is seldom intuitive.

"Essentially we ask ourselves if we are throwing good money after bad or whether it is reasonable bridge financing to rescue the company so it can eventually repay the loan," says Richard Sacco, who represents a number of New England-based institutional lenders in loan workout programs.

The amount of any defensive or rescue loan must be reasonable in relationship to the loan balance at risk. But how much more should be put at risk to protect a $500,000 loan? Is $25,000 reasonable? Perhaps, but would $250,000 be? The risk/benefit ratio is often judgmental.

The key to negotiating defensive loans is to provide assurance that the new money will be coming back.

Further financing is likely if the lender is offered additional collateral, subordinations, or other conditions that will insure the priority of payment, and can additionally see how the loan will increase the chances of a successful workout.

Banks and other lenders often get in so deeply that they are unable to pull the plug without endangering their loans, and are therefore forced to provide bridge financing for the turnaround. This was seen in Lockheed's brush with bankruptcy in the early 1970s. Lockheed operating with virtually no working capital was resuscitated by a cash transfusion by both the government and the banks, both of whom had tremendous stakes both in their prior loans and the continuity of the giant aircraft manufacturer.

Even in smaller companies, the key to a successful turnaround is the bridge financing provided by lenders or other creditor groups. We often have to convince banks and creditors that they really own the business because the stockholders have no equity and the financing then is more in their interests than in the stockholders'. "That should always be the approach," says Richard Sacco. "The lender must see the bridge financing as an opportunity to help save his own position in the situation."

General trade creditors can also be parties to a defensive loan, hoping that a cash or credit infusion will stabilize the company to the point where a more favorable recovery can be obtained. More typically, larger creditors will buy out the claims of smaller or more hostile creditors so an orderly workout can occur.

In several situations trade creditors have taken the place of banks threatening to foreclose. By replacing the banks they have removed the threat to the continued survival of the company, preserving it for a favorable workout. In many of these same cases, the creditors have loaned additional amounts for working capital or bridge financing purposes.

Similarly we frequently see trade creditors subsidize a troubled account by making its loan payments in order to keep it operating. For instance, a wholesale grocery firm recently advanced over $20,000 to a client struggling to meet its loan payments, to keep the business afloat until it reached its peak selling season. It worked out well. The business survived and repaid not only the $20,000 but over $80,000 in past-due bills owed the same creditor. Without the loan, the business would probably have failed and the creditor would have been fortunate to obtain 20 cents on the dollar. Similarly, a pool of creditors loaned a boat repair shop $50,000 to cover obligations payable over the slow winter season. Again, it was a smart move. Over the following two boating seasons the business not only repaid the $50,000, but a sizable amount of past bills as well.

The issue of continued support from lenders must also be looked at negatively. A bank, for example, may become anxious to be paid off, draining the company of too much of its working capital. What happens is that lenders forget that the recovery of capital should come from future profitability rather than liquidation of the assets. Instead of leaving adequate capital in the company so it can function and grow, the bank takes the money to reduce its debt position. The amount, then, that a lender agrees to leave in the company is a form of bridge financing. Management, however, may have to fight hard to keep enough of the money in the till so the company can survive. A realistic assessment of the company's cash needs, its ability to pay down loans, and the relative safety of the loan can define the appropriate cash levels.

IN SEARCH OF NEW LENDERS

New financing is commonly needed to replace existing lenders. This is particularly true when a lender compromises its debt and the debt reduction is conditional on cash payment. The existing lender then must be replaced by a new lender.

A new lender is, of course, reluctant to step into the uncomfortable shoes of another lender whose loan was in jeopardy. New lenders usually want to see several quarters of satisfactory performance demonstrating the ability of the company to perform on the loan before the new lender agrees to enter the picture.

However, new lenders may more willingly enter the picture when the new funds are used for operations and not as replacement financing. For example, a finance company or other higher-risk lender may come in and insist on priority of collateral and payment over existing lenders.

Existing lenders may agree to go forward for a limited period of time in a subordinate or junior position, rather than trying to escape the situation.

The new lender, particularly if it is a commercial finance company or other asset-based lender, may also provide the needed discipline and day-to-day financial stewardship vital to the company's cash management. Such a lender—more experienced with troubled companies—typically can provide specialized audits, monitor assets, and control cash flow more readily than can institutional lenders accustomed to dealing with stable firms.

FAST-FORWARD FINANCING

Eventually the company reaches the point when short- and intermediate-term bridge financing must be replaced by a well-designed, long-term financing package. Then management must consider the optimum debt the company can support and arrange for additional equity financing to provide any additional capitalization.

Three common errors may accompany the search for permanent financing:

1. Permanent financing may be arranged too soon. The time to go after permanent financing is when the company has proven stability and future profits (and payback capability) can be accurately measured. Far too many companies put together what they see as a final financial restructuring only to dismantle the program when projections fall short. Conversely, a premature financing arrangement may find the company selling equity and diluting the ownership of its existing stockholders when it could handle considerably more debt, leaving ownership of the company intact.

2. The troubled company may seek new financing to bail out old debts. This is perhaps the most frequent error. An owner of an insolvent company may mistakenly believe a new investor will commit his or her money to paying down excessive debt. New investors seldom invest to save a business but to build a business, a reality too many desperate owners overlook. The point is that the balance sheet must be cleaned up *before* the search for permanent financing begins. Even when the new financing is in the form of replacement debt, the company should have its "takeout" agreements in place with existing lenders.

3. The company may waste valuable time and effort approaching the wrong capital sources. Financing the company emerging from recent financial difficulty can be far different than financing the new venture. Some financiers are attracted by the pizzazz of a fresh start-up or are simply more comfortable with its unblemished past. Conversely, there are capital sources that believe the burdens of the once-troubled enterprise are not quite as heavy as building everything from scratch. Then too the troubled company carries with it a degree of desperation intriguing to the more opportunistic financiers who believe the best deal comes from those who are most desperate. Therefore, conventional financing sources and conventional financing techniques have little application to the turnaround company. However, there are many sources available:

Asset-Based Lenders

The more conservative banks and institutional lenders will shy away from the turnaround company for perhaps two or three years following the turnaround. For the cautious lender this "window" confirms that the turnaround has, in fact, taken hold and that the company has adequately distanced itself from its checkered past. Asset-based lending, then, is likely to switch to finance companies comfortable with the collateral while hoping the company can perform on its payment obligations. Not only will these more aggressive asset-based lenders extract higher interest rates, tighten controls over the collateral, and require hair-trigger default provisions, but they will also require strong personal guarantees of top management or principal shareholders, coupled with additional collateral from outside the company. Often the personal guarantees or collateral provided by stockholders have little value and are inconsequential in the overall security of the loan. However, the lender may consider it important to commit its owners to the future of the company, discouraging them from walking away too easily.

Factoring Arrangements

Firms that operate with accounts receivable financing may be forced to switch to factoring arrangements once the company goes into decline.

In certain industries and for seasonal situations, specialized fac-toring firms can provide a bridge for financing receivables, albeit with costly tolls for the turnaround company. Under the factoring arrangement the factor takes immediate title to the receivables at a discount of between 5 and 10 percent. For the business operating with marginal profits—characteristic of the turnaround company—the factors discount can eas-ily make the difference between profit and loss.

Still, the company generating sizable receivables may have little choice but to turn to factors when banks decline further advances against receivables. Larger factors, such as the New York-based Access Capital, look primarily to the quality of the receivables rather than the credit-worthiness of the company. Dealing with accounts receivable factors—although expensive—is usually a temporary expedient until the company can demonstrate sufficient financial strength to again justify the more traditional and less expensive accounts receivable financing. Yet many companies stay with factoring as a permanent arrangement, preferring the immediate cash availability and other advantages a well-designed factoring plan can offer.

Venture Capital

Firms in the $1 million to $20 million range may attract venture-capital financing, particularly if they show significant growth potential following the turnaround.

For instance, Hambrecht and Quist, a large West Coast venture-capital firm that once specialized in high-tech start-ups, is now allocating a large part of its considerable portfolio to turnaround companies. So are a number of other venture-capital firms that only now are recognizing that turnarounds can offer even greater returns and richer rewards than can start-up ventures.

Why the sudden interest in turnarounds? One reason is that start-ups—particularly in the computer and high-tech fields—have lost their luster as fewer than one in 10 turn out to be a winner. The batting average with the revitalized company has proven considerably better in recent years.

The turnaround also provides the venture capitalists greater op-portunity to get involved in the management of the firm, involvement not usually welcomed by the start-up entrepreneur. Venture capitalists, champions of their own managerial prowess, seem inexplicably drawn to the opportunity to roll up their sleeves and straighten out a corporate mess.

Duke Wynne of Hambrecht and Quist reports that H&Q routinely sends in its own management team to orchestrate the turnaround whenever it invests in a troubled company. Usually the management team will stay with the troubled firm for two to five years, leaving only when the company is stabilized and a few management team is brought on board.

Not all venture-capital firms share H&Q's success in turning around their problem ventures, however. Often venture-capital groups believe that having money automatically means they also have the required management skills. Frequently they do, but more often they do not. As one considerably poorer but wiser owner who lost his high-tech firm after a venture-capital group stepped in cautions: "You probably wouldn't hire the venture capitalist as a management consultant but for some reason when he shows up with money you blindly let him take over the helm."

Whether the venture capitalist has the magical ability for the job or not, he or she begins with the motivation of enormous rewards. A venture-capital group, for example, may easily bargain for a 60 or 70 percent ownership interest in the company while advancing its money on a secured loan basis. Additionally, the venture-capital group may be very well paid for its management efforts, with a combination of warrants or options based on performance.

Venture-capital groups increasingly attract fresh management talent from the ranks of troubled companies. For example, Richard Rifenburgh, who is credited with saving GCA Corporation from bankruptcy, has recently joined Hambrecht and Quist as a partner where he specializes in rebuilding troubled companies. At GCA, Rifenburgh masterminded a program of selling off divisions to raise cash, leaving the company only in the semiconducter business but with a net worth of over $137 million. With Rifenburgh on board, Hambrecht and Quist exemplifies one of many venture-capital firms that can offer management as well as money. Hambrecht and Quist also operates the Phoenix Fund, which has made investments in other turnaround opportunities.

A. David Silver, the proclaimed superstar of venture-capital placement, has written several excellent books on the subject of venture capital, all published by Wiley. *Upfront Financing* may be his best book on finding venture capital and it adds much to the complex issues and opportunities of dealing with venture-capital groups.

Public Issues

Several years ago an intriguing book appeared called *The Phoenix Approach* by William Grace, Jr. (Bantam, 1984) which underscored how to become wealthy by investing in financially troubled companies. The book blessed what so many sophisticated investors already knew—the near-bankrupt and once-bankrupt company can be a terrific investment. These investors well understand that the perceived value of the ailing company can be significantly lower than what the company is actually worth, and therefore their stock is likely to sell at bargain-basement prices.

Many troubled companies have creatively packaged an attractive combination of tax loss carryforward, cleaned-up balance sheet, and a hope for a brighter future into a cash-raising public offering.

Whether the public issue for a turnaround is for common stock, convertible preferred, convertible debentures, or debt with warrants, it is likely, however, that an underwriter will accept the issue only on a "best-efforts" basis. One major advantage of a successful public issue of new shares is that the ownership dilution is likely to be less severe than with a private placement, and therefore management will have less opposition from existing shareholders.

For the many companies that do go public, the tax loss carryforward (sometimes referred to as NOL—net operating loss) is often the most valuable asset the company can feature. If a marginally profitable private company wants an inexpensive way to go public, the turnaround company because of its NOL can be generous in what it pays for the common stock for the acquired company and should therefore be willing to give the acquired company a call on substantial amounts of additional stock if future performance targets are not met.

Turnaround companies can finance themself by using this same strategy to acquire the spinoff subsidiaries of larger conglomerates. A conglomerates throw-aways can provide a cash feast when an asset-laden subsidiary comes aboard on a leveraged buy-out basis. For the larger turnaround company, the best financing may come through an attractive acquisition.

NEGOTIATING THE FINANCING DEAL

Whether the providers of new financing are commercial banks, asset-based finance companies, or venture capitalists, they must be approached with certain realities in mind.

The first and most obvious reality is that the negotiating power will be held by the provider of financing—whether lender or investor. The lender is the one with greater options as there are generally many more companies in search of funds than there are capital sources looking to throw money into ailing enterprises. Al Cook, who specializes in loan placements for small and mid-sized firms, points out, "The CEO of the troubled company shouldn't beg but a dose of humility can't hurt."

However, even companies with little staying power should not cave in and reach for whatever financing deal is offered. A desperate company may be too anxious for capital and give too much away in return. The company can always strike the best financing deal by financing itself through as much of the turnaround as possible, deferring the issue of external financing until the company is stabilized and therefore has greater bargaining power. However, during each stage of the workout the company should continuously contact potential finance sources to establish a sense of the financing available.

Once the financing deal is reached, the company must also be certain that the lender will be as supportive of future growth as it will be in protecting itself from corporate failure.

Many of our deals have involved lenders with a preoccupation for various protective mechanisms such as loan convenants, board representation, and accelerated conversion of warrants, but they never consider equally important loan commitments for financing the company toward renewed growth. How the prospective lender responds when the company approaches emerging opportunities can be as important as how it will react to a prolonged downturn or rough weather.

Frequently, the mismatch between lender and borrower occurs because neither knows enough about each other. The lender must look far beyond the collateral values and cash flow projections and talk to key managers, employees, suppliers, customers, and even competitors. Intensive questioning will produce valuable information not only about the company but, of equal importance, about the capabilities of its managers.

Conversely, the company must undertake its own investigation of the lender. What relationship does the lender enjoy with other borrowers? Is the lender flexible or rigid? How long a relationship does the lender usually have with its borrowers? Are there signs of overreaching or coercive practices by the lender against its borrowers?

The parties must share a clear understanding of the financier's role in the overall workout plan. Not only must lender and borrower be in agreement on the basic turnaround strategy and future direction for the company, but must also review the possible contingencies and alternatives with a candid discussion of how each would respond should these contingencies materialize. The parties should then set benchmarks by which success is to be measured, the timetable for reviewing performance, the rewards for success, and the penalties for unsatisfactory performance.

The lender and the company must also understand in advance the degree of managerial or financial control that will be asserted by the lender. A surprising number of companies enter into major financing arrangements anticipating the same managerial and financial autonomy they enjoyed before, only to unhappily find the lender constantly looking over their shoulders.

Managers of firms who have combined with venture-capital groups may particularly feel managerial pressure as venture-capitalist groups inevitably want fast, if not spectacular, returns which may be beyond the reach of the company or the vision of its management. Few turnaround companies burst into full bloom overnight. Financiers who accept an equity position in the company may have unrealistic expectations for the company—expectations often encouraged by management too anxious to attract funds.

The relationship between company and financier should not be one of blind trust, but neither should it be adversarial. It should be based on reliable information objectively interpreted by people with the common sense and experience to build the foundation for a revitalized company.

THE CAPITAL-INFUSION DECISION

Second-chance financing for many troubled companies must come from its owners as the only parties with sufficient interest and confidence in the continuity of the business to dig deeply into their pockets to keep it alive.

In sick divisions or subsidiaries of otherwise prosperous companies, the parent will foot the negative cash flow for only so long and eventually refuse to throw more good money after bad. Companies cannot afford to become emotionally involved in their losing ventures. The corporate graveyards are littered with the bones of broken companies that were slow to cut their losses and shed poorly performing operations.

The situation is no different for the free-standing small company whose survival depends on a continuous flow of capital from its principals or stockholders.

Small business owners, in fact, are more inclined to lose objectivity and begin to make irrational investment decisions with their troubled business because, unlike large corporations, small business owners are emotionally involved in the success of their enterprises.

There can, of course, be no hard-and-fast rule for determining when a further infusion of capital from personal funds is appropriate. But losses can be controlled by considering four questions:

1. How much *can* you invest?
2. How much *should* you invest?
3. How much *will* you invest?
4. *When* will you invest more?

The first question helps define the risk that can be safely absorbed. The amount that *should* be invested, however, is determined by what the business can justify as an investment, assuming it can be turned around. A business can absorb an enormous amount of capital and yet be capable of only modest profits totally disproportionate to the investment it consumed.

Then the amount that will be invested must necessarily be that amount that cannot be internally financed from operations or from external sources. The objective is for the owner to use his or her funds only after all other sources are exhausted. The final question challenges the owner to set performance standards and definable benchmarks to measure the corporate recovery, and to advance further funds only as each benchmark is passed.

Admittedly, the decision whether to feed or starve the business is perhaps the most difficult of all management decisions. It takes a tremendous amount of discipline to turn one's back on a company that appears poised for a rebound, and many owners must objectively answer whether their business deserves a second chance.

11

Problem Loans: Workouts and Cramdowns

ONCE the company becomes stabilized, management must search for relief on the liability side of the balance sheet with a complete debt structuring program.

Development of a plan begins as the company tries to shape, "sell," and implement a program to escape the debts it cannot fully service.

The primary objective in financial restructuring is to keep the many concerned creditors at bay, reduce debt to tolerable levels, bring in new cash, and achieve the restructuring on a "voluntary" basis by convincing the creditors that the inherent and inescapable sacrifices are less burdensome than those likely under reorganization or liquidation in bankruptcy. The process of extracting a company from debt accumulated over years of unprofitable operation is difficult. The classes of creditors are usually varied so the success of the workout rests on the ability of management to convince creditors they are being treated fairly and equitably in relation to similar creditors as well as in relation to other creditor groups. The creditors must also see themselves as being fairly treated in relation to others who are expected to make sacrifices for the ailing company, and therefore the debt restructuring must be on balance with the sacrifices of stockholders, employees, and management.

Management must take the initiative in shaping the financial restructuring with an understanding of the alternative forms of relief available and the concessions that must be sought—and how it can best convince its creditors to provide this relief.

The long, tedious, and often complex process of working out these answers with creditor groups can be exhausting for managers already heavily involved in holding the business together under difficult conditions. Massey-Ferguson was typical of a number of major corporations that responded to these complexities by organizing in-house management teams to take on the debt restructuring responsibility, some on a full-time basis, for each major effort. Smaller companies usually rely on their professional advisors who better understand the available alternatives, provide greater credibility, and a more objective view of what a successful debt workout plan would look like.

The debt workout requires political and diplomatic skills, both of which depend on effective negotiation. Frequently, very similar situations may produce very different results because of the parties involved and their abilities to work cooperatively in what is essentially an adversarial situation.

The challenge of the debt workout is for each party to establish credibility and negotiate in good faith with an understanding of the other parties' interests and positions.

While good communication is essential to all negotiation, a debt workout is different from other business and legal negotiations in many ways.

The workout involves many parties with conflicting interests and rights. Creditor groups may be as hostile to each other as they are to the debtor company, just as vultures fight for their share of the spoils. The polarization of the various interests is always counterproductive to an easily achieved reorganization, and it is this same hostility that forces many companies to work out their problems in the more stable environment of a Chapter 11.

Furthermore, the workout usually continues over a long period of time and depends on relaxing the traditional lines of communication. For example, attorney-to-attorney and client-to-client lines of communication are nonexistent in the workout. All must talk to each other with a mix of business and legal judgments. Therefore, businesspeople may talk to creditors' counsel with nearly the same open candor as their own counsel.

The less experience the debtor or creditor has in the workout process, the more likely such a person will fear open discussion of intentions and disclosure of information critical to a well-planned and successful workout. The inexperienced player will not realize there are few secrets in the workout and that almost any action will bring a predictable reaction. Surprise or unexplained moves provide little advantage. Indeed, there is great similarity between a debt workout and the game of chess, where it is not always necessary to make a move to predict what the opposing party will do in response. Poor communication frequently results in either the debtor or creditor taking an action that cannot be undone, even though the futility of the move becomes apparent. Ultimately—as with all negotiations—both the debtor company and its creditors must walk away from the bargaining table believing they won a hard-fought victory.

The debt restructuring plan itself must take into consideration at least three major classes of creditors:

☐ Secured creditors

☐ Unsecured or general creditors

☐ Tax obligations

Obviously, each creditor class must be treated differently as each has very different rights, alternatives, concerns, and options in dealing with the troubled company.

Ultimately, the overall debt must be restructured in amount so the total debt bears some reasonable relationship to the assets of the company. Then, payment on the debt must be structured so it falls within the capabilities of the company to pay and service the debt from future income. When these goals are reached the company has not necessarily achieved a total turnaround, for that can only come when the company also achieves profitability. But at least the company can operate free of creditor pressure so it can concentrate on achieving the growth and profitability needed for a new beginning.

THE OVERFINANCED COMPANY

The balance sheet cleanup begins with a critical look at the secured obligations—debts on which the creditor holds a mortgage or pledge of company assets as collateral security.

These typically include bank loans, governmental or SBA loans, and acquisition loans from sellers of a business or other asset-based lenders.

Often the company will hold equipment under lease agreements, which, although legally different from secured obligations, are as a practical matter treated in much the same way.

A successful workout with secured creditors is a critical first step in the debt workout because secured creditors have the right to foreclose on their collateral, thereby terminating or disrupting business operations to the extent the pledged assets are needed for continued operations. Obviously, a bank that holds a mortgage (security interest) on all assets of the company can quickly put the company out of business at the least sign of trouble. Unlike unsecured creditors who can only sue to recover their debts, secured lenders require particularly careful handling because of their enormous power of self-help. As secured creditors, they are in the strongest position to control the destiny of the company as they begin to wonder about the best way to recoup their shaky loan.

Of course, a good many secured loans are never fully repaid because the collateral proves inadequate.

Hundreds of thousands of companies are overfinanced, victimized by what I call "nonsense loans." These are loans that make absolutely no sense when profiled against the company's assets or ability to repay. It is not unusual to see companies with marginal profits carrying loans on their books two or three times the value of their assets, and well beyond the ability of the company to ever repay.

While the majority of problem loans originally made sense, they can no longer be handled as the corporate fortunes change; many of these problem loans were based on unsound business deals to begin with. A seller sells a business worth $100,000 to an unsuspecting buyer for $300,000 and then wonders why the buyer cannot pay on the $250,000 self-financed by the seller.

A venture-capital group lends $400,000 toward the start-up of a high-tech firm and blindly accepts the optimistic growth projections of the business plan. When the business stagnates the loan goes into default.

I personally believe the SBA put as many people out of business as in business because it specializes in "nonsense loans." SBA loans are seldom made on the premise of a sound business concept and in fact the SBA exists only to make loans more prudent lenders turn down. Our own files are loaded with sad stories of people fed false hopes by overly lenient governmental loan programs.

Just as bankers and SBA officials can be blinded by faulty business concepts and unrealistic predictions about what the business is or can become, major suppliers hungry for a new account may extend ridiculous amounts of credit without adequate protection. Lulled by hope more than economic reality, both lenders and businesspeople must approach the problem loan as the offspring of their mutual blunder.

Scott Dantuma, a Chicago loan workout specialist, sums it up: "Businessmen with their hands out for loans can be like kids with their hands in the cookie jar. Lenders can be like parents not smart enough to clamp the lid back on. The businessman ends up with the bellyache but that doesn't get the lender his cookies back."

APPROACHING THE LENDER

Once it becomes apparent that the loan is unworkable or heading for default, open and timely communication with the secured lenders is required.

Typically, the business will discontinue payments to general creditors long before it is forced into default on secured loans, so it may be necessary to project ahead and ask whether the business can continue to comply with its loan obligations well into the future.

The debtor company must take the initiative in both detecting its coming problems and in reshaping its finances to match the reality of the situation. Lenders are far more cooperative if the borrower is both objective and candid about the problems. And in the earlier stages of a workout a lender may have the flexibility to grant the many concessions not available to the seriously delinquent or uncooperative borrower, or a borrower who has allowed the assets and collateral to erode.

In approaching the lender bear in mind three important questions that will shape the lender's own approach to the situation:

1. Are the loan problems temporary or will the loan require major restructuring for the company to survive?

2. What loan concessions, if any, will the lender have to make if the company is to survive?

3. Would the lender be better off calling the loan and liquidating the collateral now, or should the lender grant the company time to work its way out of the problem, or, conversely, time to find replacement financing?

Anticipating these key issues, approach the meeting with as much information as possible that will reveal the extent of the company's difficulties and its short-term needs. It is unlikely that the restructuring proposal will be finalized during the initial meeting as the workout may not be far enough along to project a final plan. Nevertheless, the company should have its own rough ideas of the long-term prospects and the scope of an anticipated restructuring—whether the loan will have to be reduced, payments extended, or both. The lender will, of course, also be interested in management's assessment of the causes of the problem, the alternatives considered, the solution, to the extent it has been formulated, and the resources available to accomplish it.

A company in financial difficulty will typically, and for as long as possible, deal with its creditors individually, attempting to shield each from the others. The company may even try to conceal defaults on other loans. This is usually a mistake when dealing with secured lenders. A successful workout ordinarily requires close coordination among secured lenders, particularly when they hold overlapping rights to the same collateral. Moreover, a primary concern of secured creditors is that other lenders are receiving preferential treatment, thereby encouraging foreclosure action to protect their own position. Through joint action secured lenders can insure parity of treatment and a unified approach to the overall problem. For these reasons a collective approach with the secured creditors can produce smoother proceedings.

BUYING TIME

The initial objective in meeting with lenders is to buy time—a grace period with a moratorium on payments until cash flow eases, the company is stabilized, and a final workout plan evolves.

The one most important decision the lender must make is whether to grant a moratorium or proceed to liquidate the loan. Lenders—particularly those relying on inventory and receivables as collateral—are always concerned that the secured assets will be depleted during the attempted turnaround. Often they are right. For example, a Pennsylvania discount chain was recently liquidated, yielding only $1.4 million for a major bank as its primary lender. Two years earlier, when the company began its workout by filing Chapter 11, the same company had a liquidation value of over $3 million. Delay and an overly cooperative attitude cost the bank over $1.5 million.

The "cooperate or foreclose" decision is never easy, presenting the lender a Hobson's choice of "damned if you do, and damned if you don't."

Lenders well understand the adverse public relations from forcing a business to close too hastily, and who can say that given the opportunity the company will not extricate itself from its problems and repay the lender far more than could possibly be realized through immediate liquidation.

It is, however, for the company to convince the lender that cooperation poses little risk. This means that the lender must have confidence in the ability of management and that the company can be stabilized without draining pledged assets during the workout.

There are many steps that can be taken: Approach the lender with a detailed cash flow so the lender can see how the company can internally finance itself from operations, or alternatively that a negative cash flow will be financed from sources other than through asset depletion. Back up representations with an agreement to submit frequent asset appraisals to monitor collateral levels. Provide the lender benchmarks by which it can determine for itself whether the company is undergoing a satisfactory recovery, or whether the downturn continues beyond the point when foreclosure action is justified.

Of course, lenders, faced with a shaky loan, will attempt to shore up their position by having the company or its principals pledge additional collateral. They may also ask for an infusion of capital from its principals to bolster the balance sheet and provide the company working capital. While modest cash infusions may be both necessary and justified, lender pressures should not create additional or unwarranted exposures for the company's principals. Likewise, pledging additional corporate collateral invariably makes it more difficult for the company to later deal with the bank should a permanent debt restructuring be necessary. It can be difficult to turn down a lender's demand for additional collateral or stockholder investment when a refusal may prompt foreclosure; however, the refusal may be the best way to test the lender's own perception of its bargaining power.

Lenders may have other problems which may explain their lack of patience and cooperation. The lender may be under pressure from regulatory agencies to decrease or "write down" their nonperforming loans. A bank may have incurred extraordinary losses during the year and decide it would rather absorb additional losses this year so it can begin clean next year.

A new loan officer may prefer to "charge" the loan against the officer he or she replaced rather than carry it on his or her own portfolio, or there may be other political considerations within the lending institution that may control the lender's position.

The financial position of the guarantors may also be a decisive factor. Despite our protests, for example, a bank foreclosed on a client's loan only one month in arrears. The bank wanted to protect itself on the loan by proceeding immediately against the owner under his personal guarantee. Why? The owner was going through a divorce and the bank wanted to attach the owner's home before he lost it to his wife. Convincing a lender of the continued strength of a guarantor is as important as demonstrating the continued strength of the company. The lender may also have strong recourse under its guarantees—such as with SBA loans— and would therefore prefer to seek recourse under its guarantee rather than engage in a protracted loan workout.

Then there are cases where the lender will be concerned over preferences granted other creditors and push the company into bankruptcy. Similarly, the lender may suspect fraud, embezzlement, or other dishonesty warranting liquidation of the loan and a closer investigation of the corporate affairs.

How a lender is approached will, in large measure, also depend on the lender's anticipated reaction to the problem loan. Prior dealings and relationships between the lender and the company certainly provide a good indication of what can be expected, as can the lender's general reputation for leniency or rigidity. Lenders, however, can react in markedly dissimilar ways to the same situation. Even within the same lending institution great variations in attitude can be found. Since we cannot dissect the attitudes of all lenders, I can only emphasize the need to know what is inside that pinstripe suit before the first meeting.

EARLY FINANCIAL ACTIONS

Nearly every overfinanced business begins with the need for major concessions on repayment until a final debt restructuring is in place. The concessions required will depend on the forecasted cash flow and the debt service the company can accommodate during the workout; however, the most common concessions in ascending order of intensity include:

1. Extend the Loans. This is most palatable to lenders because the loan remains both fully performing and is earmarked for full payment.

Lenders frequently rewrite 3–5-year notes into 7–10-year paybacks, often cutting monthly payments in half.

2. Defer Principal Payments. This is a frequent solution to reducing stranglehold payments as a large percentage of a monthly payment—particularly on older loans—are largely allocated to interest. However, it may not provide much relief on newer loans calling primarily for interest payments.

3. Defer Interest Payments. Lenders more actively resist this concession as it creates a nonperforming loan. Alternative concessions (such as extensions) that would produce the same monthly payments are more readily accepted as the loan is not considered in default.

4. Concession of Interest Payment. This provides a positive direct impact both on cash flows and on the profit and loss statement and, indirectly, on the borrower's equity position. In the more severe cases a lender may concede perhaps one year's interest but beyond that the loan should be restructured as to its principal balance.

5. A freeze on All Loan Payments. This is the most difficult proposition to sell but lenders dealing with companies in an acute cash flow crisis frequently have no choice but to go along with a total moratorium on payments for a defined time period. In a current case a stationery supply firm was able to improve cash flow and working capital by $160,000 by deferring all payments on a $700,000 loan due a Chicago bank. Lenders are more likely to forego all payments when they feel they are adequately secured, the collateral will remain intact, and the payment freeze is short-term.

The concessions granted by a lender during a workout may change, and both lender and borrower need a continued policy of flexibility. Troubled companies often start with a complete payment freeze and gradually increase the flow of cash to the lender as the company becomes more stabilized. But cash flow during the workout period can be highly cyclical, requiring both the lender and the company to constantly adjust the repayment arrangement to match the current situation.

Companies may require their payments be restructured even when the company is solvent and debts proportionate to assets. Many firms are the victims of poorly planned financing—typically a case of reaching for short-term financing when long-term financing was needed.

Under these circumstances the concessions are nothing more than a recasting of the loan to what it should have been in the first place. For the overfinanced company the initial concession is only a recognition of more significant concessions to be faced later.

CRAMDOWNS: SHRINKING THE OVERFINANCED LOAN

A more sensitive issue, and one bound to meet with more resistance, is the need to shrink an overfinanced loan by a cramdown, voluntary reduction or cancellation of part of the debt. But when is a business overfinanced?

There is only one formula for determining what the total debt must be reduced to for any workout to be successful: a business is overfinanced when the total debt exceeds what the business can readily be sold for as a "going business" concern. That is precisely the formula to be used shaping every workout. For example:

□ Beacon Packing Company, a small meat processer, owed its banks $240,000 secured by all corporate assets. General creditors were on the books for another $150,000. Total debt: $390,000. What was the business worth to its owners? They believed the business could not be sold for more than $150,000. The solution? Cut the bank loan from $240,000 to $135,000 while the general creditors in a considerably worse bargaining position agreed to accept $15,000, or about 10 cents on the dollar.

□ Amit Builders, according to an appraisal, could be sold for about $75,000, yet it owed its secured lenders $300,000 and trade creditors nearly $100,000. The secured lender accepted $60,000 and the general creditors settled for $10,000, aware they would receive even less under bankruptcy.

The need to reduce excess debt to approximate the value of the company appears elementary, yet there are hundreds of sophisticated business owners who foolishly struggle with excessive debt for as long as the creditors let them. They avoid the reality that they are not working for themselves but are instead the indentured serf to the creditors. Owing so much money it is unlikely they will ever see an equity or net worth in their own business.

In calculating what a business is worth, owners must consider the value of the business to themselves. According to Scott Dantuma, who has represented both lenders and borrowers in loan workouts:

> Don't concern yourself at this point with book value or liquidation values. Look instead at the workout as nothing more than an opportunity to buy your business back from the creditors on 100 percent financing terms because in concept that's precisely what a well-designed workout and debt restructuring should accomplish.

This is common sense and a view I share, but many business owners cannot see it. I ask them to think about their homes. What if a home had a fair market value of $100,000 and mortgages and liens against it of $200,000? Isn't it true that they would have to pay down the encumbrances by $100,000 before they began to build the first dime in equity in their own property? If they could not reduce the encumbrances, wouldn't it make appreciably more sense to forfeit the house to the creditors and buy another $100,000 house for $100,000? Of course, it is just more difficult to see this as logically when you relate it to a business.

The fair market value of the business may determine the maximum debt the business can justify but it certainly does not define how the secured lender should be forced to assess its own bargaining position in the debt restructuring process. Here the secured lender can comfortably look only to the net liquidation value of the pledged assets and whatever other recovery is foreseeable from the corporate guarantors.

Therefore, management for the troubled company must enter the negotiation process with a clear idea of what the pledged collateral will bring at liquidation. For this purpose management should retain a well-qualified auctioneer-liquidator to render a liquidation appraisal of the collateral pledged to the respective secured creditors. Ideally, the secured creditors will accept the appraiser's valuation, although most lenders will eventually insist on their own appraisal to confirm liquidation values.

There can be considerable disagreement on what the collateral is worth or what a secured lender will realize from a business liquidation. The nature and condition of the collateral, auction location, and even seasonal demand are but a few of the important controlling factors. Partially finished goods, equipment annexed to real estate, and receivables owed by recalcitrant customers add to the question. Sometimes it is only a matter of timing—and whether there is a highly interested buyer around when the assets are being disposed of. With many types of assets there is no realistic way of knowing what it will bring until it is actually auctioned.

Leases, copyrights, patents, franchise rights, customer lists, and a host of other intangible assets may have considerably greater value than the tangible assets, yet these assets are often overlooked or their value destroyed under a business disruption. And, unlike the company, the lender may have no way to capitalize on these assets.

The costs of liquidation must also be considered. Auction and attorneys' fees and many other expenses can significantly reduce the net proceeds available on a forced liquidation.

Each of these variables means there can be a substantial spread between what the lender sees as a recovery from the collateral and what the company may foresee.

Lenders often try to optimize the value of the collateral by forcing the sale of the troubled company as a going business. The one danger in a delayed settlement is that it gives the lender time to find a buyer who will pay appreciably more for the business than its liquidation price. This lender strategy is particularly common when the lender controls the lease or has a pledge of the corporate stock and is therefore in a position to control the sale of the business.

Lenders may resist compromising the loan balance for other reasons. For example, bank loans backed by the SBA or other strong guarantors can take a hard stand, relying on the guarantors more than the collateral. Sellers of a business who hold the buyer's note can easily walk back in and take over the business—an alternative available to few institutional lenders.

Lenders who hold low-interest loans also show little patience when the loan proceeds can be loaned out again at much higher rates. A lender, for example, looks more favorably on collecting $30,000 on a $50,000 note bearing 9 percent interest when the money can readily be loaned out again and earn 15 percent. Supply and demand for money is often a big factor in a lender's thinking.

Lenders will do almost anything to avoid a debt reduction. They prefer to extend payments as long as necessary to eventually obtain 100 percent of what is owed. That is reasonable—to the lender. Virtually any loan can be repaid if the borrower wants to spend the rest of his or her life in serfdom.

Lenders also know that with patience the business may some day grow to the point where the loan can and should be repaid in full. Provided the collateral remains intact, the lender has little to lose but much to gain by waiting. Conversely, the troubled company will do far worse in negotiating a debt reduction when the company is on an upturn.

The time to strike and force a compromise settlement is when the company has poverty on its side. The lender must believe the settlement is the far better alternative to an increasingly likely liquidation.

Although lenders may be coerced into settlements slightly better than could be realized through foreclosure, they will be more likely to accept the proposition when it is a cash settlement instead of a deferred payment settlement. Banks particularly want to be completely taken out of a bad loan. Considering the trouble the company will have in attracting replacement financing, this is not always possible but should always be explored.

Larger companies may also be able to bargain a conversion of debt to equity, with the lender converting significant debt in exchange for stock ownership in the company. The stock ownership may be structured with a "put" or "call" with the lender or company having the respective rights to sell or buy back the shares at a later date for a predetermined or formula value.

Debt restructured as equity provides the lender the right to share in any upside turn while the company goes forward with a manageable debt level, thereby offering the lender an alternative to an outright loss and the company the prospects of a forced liquidation.

Turning lenders into partners works especially well when the company should have relied more on equity financing rather than debt financing in the first place. For example, a highly leveraged New York bioengineering firm escaped the dilemma of finding cash to pay down its $1.5 million bank loan by having the lender convert 70 percent of the debt into a 35 percent ownership interest. It was a smart deal for both. The lender realized the firm could not repay the loan but that it was foolish to foreclose and end up with 20–30 cents on the dollar while killing a business with growth potential.

For the business with future promise, the conversion of debt to equity can not only release the pressures of overfinancing but help the company achieve additional financing as well. Recently, a small but fast-growing software company convinced a finance company to cancel $120,000 on its $200,000 loan and add another $50,000 in exchange for 40 percent of the company.

What the company will have to give up in stock in exchange for a release for all or part of the loan will depend on many variables: the collateral value, growth potential of the company, and the type of lender involved are the three primary factors.

The willingness of a lender to accept stock in a turnaround company also has symbolic importance. General creditors, employees, stockholders, and other groups see it as a signal of confidence and a show of future strength so often necessary to marshall the total support needed for a complete recovery.

12

Out From Under

AFTER secured loans are restructured, management must begin to reduce or defer payment on unsecured debts, trade payables, and tax obligations. This is the final phase toward cleaning up the balance sheet, but it can prove even more complicated and tiring than dealing with problem loans since the number of unsecured creditors will be overwhelmingly larger and less manageable than one or two secured lenders. Moreover, the relationship of the company with its creditors who may also be principal suppliers may require particularly tactful handling if the company is to have their continued cooperation.

The bright side is that, unlike secured lenders, unsecured creditors are relatively powerless compared with secured lenders, and are forced to accept what remains after banks and other secured creditors have been fully paid. It may be paradoxical, but the less money available for unsecured creditors the more strength companies have in dealing with them. Creditors soon lose interest in chasing an account where any meaningful recovery—whether with or without a bankruptcy—is unlikely. Every year creditors owed billions of dollars agree to accept pennies on the dollar, knowing that pennies are better than thin air. As Robert Sammarco, credit manager for New England Wholesale Drug Company, says, "What they owe is a statistic. What they can afford to pay or what you can actually squeeze out of them is reality. So we settle not on the basis of what ought to be—but 'what is.' "

Financially troubled companies understand the same realities and use their poverty as power to reduce overpowering debts and gain a fresh start.

Our firm, Galahow & Company, specializes in debt restructuring and it has no shortage of stories to prove the point, as revealed by several cases completed recently:

☐ A nursing home settled with its creditors for 15 cents on the dollar, payable over three years. Over $700,000 in debt shriveled to $100,000.

☐ Creditors of a discount clothing chain agreed to accept a 10-cents-on-the-dollar dividend and 20 percent of the company stock to forgive nearly $7 million in trade debt.

☐ A local hardware store negotiated $200,000 in trade debt down to a more manageable $24,000, payable over two years.

☐ A chain of pet shops convinced creditors to take $90,000 and cancel another $620,000 in trade obligations once they realized the inventory of Cocker Spaniels and guppies would bring far less at public auction.

These are not unusual examples, but typify settlements that are negotiated hundreds of times a day in every city.

While these examples may appear encouraging it is often extremely difficult to negotiate settlements with unsecured creditors because they are numerous, share different relationships with the debtor firm, and have different stakes in the outcome.

A debt restructuring case should begin by evaluating the politics of the situation. We must understand both the relationship between the troubled company and its creditors and the composition of the creditor's group itself, for a tactical approach to the workout to be effective:

☐ How many creditors does the company have?
☐ What is the breakdown of creditors by size of claim?
☐ What is the breakdown of creditors by account aging?
☐ Who are the largest creditors?

☐ How good are relationships between the debtor and the creditors?

☐ What interests would creditors have in the continuity of the business?

☐ Are particular business interrelationships among the creditors relevant in the workout?

☐ Are credit associations likely to be active in the workout process?

☐ Are creditors likely to be represented by one—or a small group —of law firms?

This information will typically indicate whether settlement negotiations will be cordial and cooperative or hostile. Moreover, it will show whether one or two creditors will dominate or control the outcome or whether there will be no likely leader within the creditor group to whom other trade creditors will look for influence and direction. Through this we attempt to gauge what a good settlement offer may be, the best approach for selling the settlement plan, and whether an out-of-court settlement is likely to be reached, bypassing the need for a Chapter 11 reorganization.

DESIGNING THE PLAN

Just as secured lenders must look to the liquidation value of the collateral as the threshold from which to negotiate a restructured debt, unsecured creditors cannot be expected to accept less than would become available through a forced liquidation of the company.

Therefore, the company must begin with the same liquidation analysis as used with secured creditors. However, here the focus will be on what will be available for unsecured creditors after payment of all secured debt, together with unpaid taxes, accrued wages, attorneys' fees, liquidation costs, and other priority claims.

For example, if the liquidation analysis shows the company assets will bring $300,000 at auction and secured debts and other priority claims and costs approximate $200,000, then $100,000 would be available for creditors upon liquidation. Should the company owe $1 million to general creditors, then the liquidation analysis would disclose the expectancy of a 10 percent dividend under bankruptcy and an obvious need for the debtor company to offer somewhat more than 10 percent to avoid bank-ruptcy.

The question then becomes how much more should be offered. At what point would a settlement be so excessive that it no longer makes sense? How should the plan be structured?

The best strategy is to begin negotiations by offering creditors about 5 percent more on their claims than would be available through liquidation. For example, in the prior case where creditors would share a $100,000 dividend upon liquidation (10 percent of the $1 million owed), a reasonable offer may be $150,000 or a 15 percent dividend. The reasoning is that to offer only that which is available through liquidation might encourage creditors to force a liquidation for the sheer satisfaction of putting the hapless debtor out of business. To begin with more is a needlessly generous first move in the negotiation process.

More difficult is defining the upper limits of an acceptable settle-ment. A good yardstick for owners to follow is to ask how many years they are willing to work for the creditors, and then base a plan on the commitment of all profits for those years. For example, if an owner is agreeable to a three-year payback period, and the company has a net available cash of $50,000 a year projected, then this, of course, means that the settlement plan cannot exceed $150,000. It is generally unrealistic to commit more than three or four years' future profits to retire the debts of the past. It simply makes no sense to mortgage the corporate future for a longer period and it is usually better to start over again. And, of course, the company cannot very well pay more than the projected cash available, as the company will not survive with a negative cash flow.

While creditors may agree that these are the logical parameters for structuring a settlement, there can be considerable disagreement on fu-ture profits and therefore the amount that can be available to creditors. The argument typically centers on two points:

First, creditors, like lenders, may also ask the owners to invest ad-ditional capital to subsidize creditor dividends. This, of course, should be resisted unless the business becomes fully stabilized and the risk proportionate to the long-term profitability.

Then, creditors may question the profit projections and argue for a reduction of expenses—usually management salaries, fringe benefits, and other perks—that creditors eliminate to paint a far more rosy picture for the company. Management may back itself into the same corner by painting its own rosy picture and delude both itself and the creditors into a settlement plan that cannot be funded, or by paying far more than was necessary had negotiations had been predicated on less optimistic projections.

More often than not the slowness of implementing a financial restructuring renders underlying cash flow assumptions incorrect and obsolete before the final plan is even approved. We are often negotiating a revised plan two or three months after the original plan was agreed to. A more memorable case called for a 50 percent dividend to creditors over three years. Gradually the plan was reduced to 30 percent, then 20 percent, and finally 10 percent once it became increasingly clear the company was continuing its downward slide. Creditors will probably never see a dime from this company yet the case is a valuable reminder that projections are only predictions and predictions seldom come true.

Admittedly, it is difficult to project what a company will earn—and what it can therefore pay—and this is particularly true with a turnaround company whose future may be considerably brighter than its past. There are many cases where creditors projected future earnings two or even three times greater than those projected by management, leaving the parties too far apart for settlement.

The concept of offering general creditors a stock dividend in addition to a cash dividend can resolve this problem as the creditors as stockholders then become beneficiaries of the firm's future fortunes. Creditors frequently accept a 20–40 percent ownership interest if the company is large enough and its future bright enough to give the stock a marketable value. In return the creditors may cancel 70–80 percent of the debt owed. Further, an issue of at least 15–20 percent of the stock to creditors will allow the company to preserve its tax loss carryforward without deduction of the canceled debt, offering significant tax advantages.

It is also possible to base a plan on a formula approach guaranteeing creditors a minimum dividend coupled with bonus dividends based on corporate performance—typically tied to sales as a benchmark. Although a plan based on formula appears equitable, it can produce problems: the formula may prove to be an unrealistic yardstick for measuring cash availability, management may intentionally avoid or defer actions that would result in higher creditor dividends, or difficulties in drafting, interpreting or enforcing the formula may result.

Creditors may also demand the sale of specific assets—or even entire divisions or subsidiaries—if they believe them to be nonessential to the company's future, and more profitable as cash producers to pay creditors. Here too there can be considerable room for debate as creditors with their eye toward immediate cash do not necessarily share management's enthusiasm for marshaling assets as a foundation for long-term profits. Creditors see few sacred cows. Chrysler was nearly forced to sell its profitable tank division before creditors relented. Braniff had to give up many of its best air routes to raise cash for creditors. The previously mentioned 20-store discount clothing chain was forced to sell its three most valuable leases to generate an additional $250,000 for creditors. Lesser but no less notable luxuries such as fancy company cars, little-used computer systems, and other reminders of corporate flab are always obvious targets to alert creditors, anxious to wring even more money from its debtor.

There are always lesser points to negotiate on a settlement plan with creditors. If payments are to be extended over time, the creditors may want interest, which, of course, is only a higher dividend in disguise. Interest at the prime lending rate is reasonable; however, management may also want to remind creditors that if the business does go bankrupt they will have to wait two or three years for payment and the bankruptcy court does not pay interest.

Realizing a promise is not necessarily a payment, creditors may bargain for a mortgage or security interest on business assets, which is certainly a reasonable way to give present creditors both priority over future creditors and security to enforce the payment plan. Similarly, creditors may ask for personal guarantees to insure payment; however, this should normally be avoided as the future survival of the business may be far too speculative to incur personal exposure.

The most typical general creditor workout consists of a combination of extension and composition. The debtor company is given an extended time to pay a percentage of the total indebtedness with interest reduced or waived altogether. Equality of treatment is essential; however, creditors may be allowed to elect alternative plans. For example, a plan may allow a creditor the choice of a 10 percent cash dividend or a 15 percent dividend payable in three semiannual installments. Smaller creditors are usually offered full payment as their large numbers may make the settlement process too cumbersome, and small creditors with little at stake are less inclined to accept a settlement and thus play spoiler to a successful workout effort. In fact, larger creditors routinely buy the claims of small creditors, recognizing small creditors may obstruct an orderly workout plan.

Compositions or informal out-of-court settlement workouts are generally conditional on acceptance by creditors holding a stated percentage of outstanding claims. Required acceptance by 85–90 percent is common, as fewer acceptances leave the debtor with too many unresolved claims for a successful debt restructuring. The few holdouts that inevitably occur even under a successful plan either have their claims vigorously defended against or, as with the claims of small creditors, their claims are acquired by other creditors to avoid threat to the company and the plan. When the company can reach agreement with a significant percentage of its creditors, but too many holdouts remain, the company may require a Chapter 11 proceeding to force the plan on the few dissenting creditors.

When the overall debt level is not excessive, but the company is simply unable to pay its creditors when due, the settlement will call for 100 percent payment either on a stand-by or extension basis.

Simply stated, the stand-by means creditors agree to take no action for a specified time period. The stand-by is a meaningful strategy when time alone is the problem, such as when property is to be sold to pay down the debt. A temporary stand-by is an agreement by creditors to grant the company a moratorium period within which creditors will not press their claims until long-range financial decisions (the settlement plan) are formulated.

NEGOTIATING THE SETTLEMENT

Once the need for a workout is recognized, the company and its creditors must establish open lines of communication and organize manageable procedures for negotiating the settlement plan.

When the company is small and when the settlement is informal, the company may simply send its creditors a letter outlining its financial problem and including a proposed composition agreement (the plan) to accept and return. This very informal approach is indicated when the number of creditors and aggregate claims are sufficiently small so creditors will have little interest in spending time pursuing formal proceedings.

When the stakes are higher, direct negotiations with creditors may be required. It may be impractical to establish a working group of all creditors when the number is large. It may not even be practical to expect a moderate-sized group to work together efficiently. A manageable creditor body will typically include between three and 12 principal creditors —depending on the size and complexity of the workout.

The creditor workout committee (steering committee as it is sometimes called) accepts specific tasks on behalf of the entire creditor committee:

1. To review and evaluate the company's financial condition.

2. To audit the company for fraud, embezzlement, or other dishonesty that would justify bankruptcy proceedings.

3. To review the company's cash flow and profit projections on which the settlement plan is based.

4. To consider legal problems under alternate scenarios—such as a possible bankruptcy or sale of the company.

5. To evaluate any special problems or cash-raising opportunities.

6. To negotiate the final settlement plan with the debtor company.

7. To recommend acceptance of the negotiated settlement to other creditors.

8. To continue to monitor the progress of the company and enforce compliance with the plan.

To make the setup work effectively, the company must communicate exclusively through the steering committee. The steering committee should, in turn, continuously communicate to the creditor body and thereby free the company from the pressure of creditor contact. Most creditors are prepared to be patient while awaiting the final outcome, provided they are kept abreast of events.

No matter how the creditors may be organized, settlement negotiations are usually a long, tedious, and frustrating process. Numbers can be convincing, but creditors bring more to the bargaining table than a calculator. They often show up with anger, suspicion, irrationality, doubt, desire for vengeance, and the full array of human emotions.

A debtor facing 20 creditors deals with 20 different people, each with a different perspective on the situation. Over on the right hand side of the table sits the cynic, who thinks the company is headed by crooks who pillaged, plundered, and raped the business to bring it to its knees. Many creditors will think the worst until proven differently.

Management must therefore be prepared to tell creditors how the business got into trouble, pointing out the problems that caused losses.

Creditors should be invited to go over the books to defuse their suspicions. Once offered, creditors will usually decline, but offered resistance, they will go to any lengths to find out what is being hidden.

Next to the cynic sits the moralist. His attitude is common. "You owe him $1000, he wants $1000. Anything less is immoral, unconscionable and un-American." He listens only to "what ought to be," never "what is." All you can do with this character is slowly present the facts until they sink in. After all, you are moral too, but at least you know you cannot get blood from a stone.

Sitting over at the end of the table is the avenger. While he is upset over the $50,000 he may lose, he wants vengeance for the $500 in bad checks or is angry over the $5000 order shipped 10 days before the financial problems surfaced. Often debtors have to make "adjustments" on the small items before they can get down to business on the big points.

Next to the avenger squirms the credit manager whose only concern is how he will explain the $12,000 loss his company faces. Perhaps he even welcomes the loss if it reflects adversely on someone else within his organization.

Is there a lawyer in the crowd? He may harbor his own secret thoughts of how he might come out far richer under a bankruptcy—particularly if he can become counsel for the creditors' committee in a bankruptcy and thus earn a considerably higher fee than he could collecting a small dividend for a creditor-client.

There are, of course, other stereotypical characters that find their way into every creditors' committee. A guiding light in negotiating with creditors is to remember the famous line of Don Corleone in *The Godfather*: "Never get angry. Never make a threat. Reason with people."

Looking over scores of successful cases we can define six essential strategies for negotiating with creditors.

1. Play for time. Creditors are like fish; they must tire before they can be easily reeled in. Bear in mind that anger and emotion run high at the beginning. Months—or even years later—creditors are on to new problems and will be more anxious to settle on favorable terms. In larger cases wait at least several months before making an initial settlement offer and then try to wear creditors down over the next year or two. Persevere. It takes time for creditors to cool down from the maddening thought that they are about to lose money.

2. Meet individually or collectively with several friendlier and more influential creditors. Use them as a "nucleus" of support to inject the right positive tone into the meeting, neutralize opposition, and win converts.

3. Meet with holdouts individually. Find out specifically why there is opposition to a proposed plan. "Eyeball-to-eyeball" discussions may produce results not obtainable at a steering committee meeting.

4. Do not let a middle management executive or credit manager block the road. Remember, they work within their own bureaucracy and have someone else to answer to. While we all dislike jumping over someone's head, we must also realize that less-seasoned people who typically represent their companies at these meetings can be unreasonable, and therefore a fair resolution can only come from someone higher within the creditor organization.

5. Use your own professionals. While a debtor may not see eye to eye with a creditor, his lawyer may have better luck with the creditor's attorney. When negotiations strike out at one level, it makes sense to switch to another level.

6. Use persuasive arguments. Be prepared to convince creditors why the plan is fair and more generous than one available through bankruptcy. Show how the company will be able to pay the offered dividends. But go beyond these basic points and also use powerful motivators— the future profits creditors will earn by continued dealings with the firm. Always stress this point. In a recent case, for example, an uncooperative creditor quickly softened his position once he was reminded that my client purchased over $3 million a year from him, and, in fact, had paid him over $42 million since they began to do business together. Suddenly the loss on the $600,000 overdue debt was viewed from a new perspective.

Not infrequently creditors will reject even the most generous settlement plan because they simply do not trust or like the owner or top management. Creditors are generally cooperative with troubled business owners who fall on hard times despite their good efforts. Yet there are ample cases where distrust or resentment of top management forced liquidation of the business.

There is no end to the things managers may do to antagonize or alienate creditors. Before the workout period the company may have issued bad checks, given misleading financial statements, or otherwise conned credit long after it was obvious the bills could not be paid. Creditors may believe the owners "milked" the business or were too casual in their concern for its creditors.

There is also ample opportunity for relationships between creditors and the debtor to break down during the workout period. The most certain trouble spot is when the company switches its business to new suppliers. Then, too, creditors may not see an equality of sacrifice if owners and key managers continue to earn their same high salaries. Sometimes it is the small things that rankle creditors, as when a client of mine showed up at a creditors' committee meeting driving a new Jaguar automobile. The fact that the car was owned personally and not by the business did little to appease creditors who were being asked to sacrifice the bulk of their claims amidst all the symbols of wealth.

A more substantive reason for declining a settlement offer is the lack of confidence in management. Management may show a total inability to straighten out its problems, as exemplified by a lack of a logical turnaround plan, the constant disappointment with projections that never come true, or the continued losses that cannot be stemmed. Under each of these circumstances the creditors may believe they will gain more through immediate liquidation than will be available through continued operation.

Larger companies often have to bring in a new chief executive or financial officer to bring a fresh perspective, credibility, and vigor to the restructuring effort. A new person who can say, "I did not create this mess but I am here to help clean it up," can have a very different relationship with creditors than can the people who were part of the past.

TACKLING THE ONE LARGE CREDITOR

Perhaps the company does not have its debt scattered among many creditors but is primarily indebted to one—or perhaps a very few creditors.

When the target in only one creditor the company can use more imaginative solutions than when dealing with an entire pack, as it is no longer bound by a deal that requires the constraints of "equality."

Certainly, many of the same issues and negotiating points apply to "one-on-one" negotiations as apply to "all creditor composition." The one major difference is that the previous relationship between debtor and creditor may play a more acute role in the outcome.

There are many companies that owe substantial sums to one general creditor, and the survival of the company is based on its ability to reach an accord for restructuring the debt.

Texaco finds itself in exactly this predicament with Pennzoil. As I write this, Texaco remains in Chapter 11 proceedings as it appeals the $10 billion Pennzoil judgment through the Texas court system. But assuming the judgment is upheld, Texaco will find it must still come to terms with Pennzoil as its one big creditor. Texaco and Pennzoil are a classic study in creditor-debtor relations if only because they are in the limelight as a David-and-Goliath situation. No matter how the ultimate settlement is structured, it will probably include "nonmonetary" compensation such as oil lease and drilling rights through which the management of both companies can proclaim victory in what has become a face-saving contest. Psychology and appearances can often be considerations as important as money in a workout.

One-creditor settlements are frequently complex. For example, we recently worked out a settlement with a major creditor for a large fabric store that owed a whopping $115,000 to its principal supplier, a Danish textile manufacturer.

The liquidation analysis showed the creditor would obtain about $23,000, or a 20-percent dividend should liquidation occur. After months of hard bargaining we finally settled for $50,000, paying $10,000 immediately, $35,000 over two years, and returning $5000 in excess inventory for credit. The debt cancelation was further conditional on the company buying and paying COD on at least $250,000 a year in new purchases with penalties for purchases beneath the agreed quota.

While this settlement satisfied both the debtor and creditor, such an arrangement obviously could not be structured among a group of creditors. During initial restructuring efforts the parties may look to plans that stress simplicity, but eventually they discover the many variables that can bridge the gap, offering both debtor and creditor an even more beneficial arrangement.

COMBATING TAX PROBLEMS

A surprising number of distressed companies owe sizable tax claims to both the Internal Revenue Service and state taxing authorities. This is particularly true with smaller companies operating with few controls, less discipline, and the apparent ability to avoid early detection by the tax people.

Caught in a cash squeeze, the company uses withholding tax and sales tax funds to cover operating expenses. It is not uncommon to find financially troubled companies owing hundreds of thousands of dollars in tax obligations before the taxing authorities come breathing down their necks.

Considering the many laws and regulations that give taxing agencies nearly unlimited power in collecting overdue taxes, it is not surprising that so many businesses only accept the crisis as reality when the IRS padlocks their doors or seizes their bank accounts.

Dealing with the IRS can be tricky, and even insolvency lawyers frequently turn to tax lawyers in resolving tax claims against tax-delinquent companies. I highly recommend *Protecting Your Business From The IRS* by Robert Shriebman (Dow Jones-Irwin, 1987) as an essential guide for any businessperson with tax problems, and it certainly adds much to what I say here.

Perhaps the first objective in dealing with the IRS is to forestall the filing of a federal tax lien which disturbs the continued first priority position of a secured lender, forcing it to call its loan and cease making further advances.

The troubled company must then move to protect its cash balances from attachment or levy. With predictable regulatory the IRS levies recalcitrant accounts, creating the need to constantly open new and not so easily reached bank accounts. There are more than a few companies managing to stay one brief step ahead of an IRS levy, constantly opening new accounts as soon as the IRS discovers their prior accounts.

Eventually the company tires of playing musical chairs with local banks and must come face-to-face with its tax problems.

Companies can work their way out of tax problems provided certain conditions are met, not the least of which is a lenient revenue agent.

Most important is the assurance that the company will not fall further behind in its tax payments. Taxing authorities have absolutely no patience when the pattern of delinquency is continuing. Next, back taxes must be paid in full over a reasonable time. While the IRS has discretion to determine an acceptable repayment schedule, one or two years seems to be the maximum, provided the company has no clear opportunity for faster repayment. State taxing authorities may be more or less lenient, depending on their own administrative procedures and policies.

For the company burdened with extensive tax obligations, it generally does little good to seek out-of-court accommodations from secured lenders and general creditors while ignoring the tax problems, as a less resilient IRS will inevitably drive the company into forced liquidation or to seek protection under Chapter 11.

State taxes can be as troublesome as federal. Often the tax problems stem from sales and use taxes, leaving the company to collection policies of the state tax authorities. Massachusetts, for example, currently has an overly aggressive tax collection program underway and scores of businesses have been seized and closed. Even when the IRS agrees to a reasonable payback period, Massachusetts demands immediate or accelerated repayment, leaving a workout with other creditor group impracticable.

The attitude of the taxing authority is also governed to a large extent by its own ability to collect from the troubled company. While the IRS may stand behind secured creditors and obtain nothing from a forced liquidation, it may nevertheless seize the business with the hope it will encourage creditor groups or the principals to pay the taxes, thereby saving the company for rehabilitation. But sometimes a seizure is not the result of such tactical brilliance but only a tired tax agent who wants to stop chasing and close a file.

There is an unconfirmed rumor that the IRS shows greater tolerance toward businesses funded by SBA or other governmental loans, or involved in federal projects or contracts. Politically sensitive, high-visibility companies, and companies that are major employers, may also fare better in dealing with the tax agencies. Yet even these companies may fail to win the support of the taxing authorities and the company must then consider its other options.

13

Bankruptcy: Court of Last Resort

EVEN with the heroic efforts of management the troubled company may be unable to resolve its problems without the broad protection of the bankruptcy court and the far-reaching rehabilitative powers of a Chapter 11 reorganization.

Chapter 11 ("reorganizations" as they are commonly called) allows a company that cannot meet its debts to put itself under the jurisdiction of the bankruptcy court while it tries to straighten out its affairs and arrange a reorganization or financial restructuring plan with its creditors. Alternatively the company will move into an orderly liquidation under a straight Chapter 7 bankruptcy proceeding if attempts to rescue the company under Chapter 11 prove unsuccessful.

Reorganizations have become an enormously popular weapon in the distressed company's arsenal. The litany of corporate giants which have sought refuge under the protective arm of the bankruptcy courts are endless. Braniff, Interstate Stores, Penn Central, and Massey-Ferguson are stories of the past while Texaco and even Jim and Tammy Bakker's PTL Heritage Church are more recent if no less humble entries. Reorganizations have, in fact, become so popular that they have almost become fashionable, much like the corporate jet or limousine. The number of companies seeking relief in Chapter 11 is rising so rapidly that managers no longer wonder whether their company will need help from the bankruptcy court but when.

STRONG MEDICINE FOR THE SICK BUSINESS

Why is it that so many companies in trouble look to the bankruptcy courts to straighten out their messes?

The major reason is that it is often too difficult or even impossible to work out an acceptable settlement or debt restructuring plan with creditors on an out-of-court basis. There may be too many creditors to cope with, or, as is more often the case, creditors are too hostile and unmanageable to work with collectively as each tries to jump ahead of the others in picking the company clean. If a company has 10 or 12 creditors—and a reasonably good relationship with each—there is a good chance the company can put together a reasonable debt restructuring plan with its creditors without the long, complex, and costly hassle of a reorganization. However, when the company has numerous creditors, or the debt structure is complex with various classes of creditors, a successful workout typically requires the orderly process of a Chapter 11. A company often can reach a favorable out-of-court settlement with the majority of its creditors, but too many holdouts may remain. Under a Chapter 11, an approved plan (requiring a majority vote by creditors) becomes binding on all creditors, including the more stubborn holdouts.

"Sometimes the real purpose of a Chapter 11 is to give the creditors time to cool off and accept the reality they'll never be fully repaid," says Bill Weisman, a Fort Lauderdale bankruptcy specialist. "The Chapter 11 only buys the time to take away the emotion and bring order from chaos."

Companies that attempt an out-of-court workout usually do it against the backdrop of a Chapter 11. Once creditors are made aware of the company's plight they can be expected to react, and unless a rapid and controlled workout is achieved the company will have little choice but to resort to bankruptcy. More times than not the mere threat of a reorganization is enough to bring the creditors to the bargaining table, but it is dangerous to bluff unless a company prepared to follow through.

The ability of a Chapter 11 to tame creditors was seen in the fall of 1983, when a veteran of the successful reorganization of Penn Central, Victor Palmieri, was brought into the deeply troubled financial conglomerate, Baldwin-United, to try to stabilize its uncertain situation and to achieve an out-of-court restructuring. Very soon he had to contend with major creditors of the subsidiaries, who had very different interpretations of their vital interests and of what should be done to protect them. Palmieri threatened bankruptcy early on if the creditors could not achieve a working accord. In fact, the efforts failed and the company declared Chapter 11 bankruptcy. Through the reorganization Baldwin-United was able to fairly and equitably deal with the concerns of these creditors and eventually worked out a very favorable reorganization plan that again transformed Baldwin-United into a healthy company.

Other creditor groups can also precipitate a Chapter 11. Secured lenders threatening foreclosure of their collateral or seizing cash deposits or receivables may prompt the debtor company to forestall through reorganization the rights of its secured creditors to take over their collateral. Just as unsecured creditors cannot proceed against a company in Chapter 11, secured creditors are also enjoined from foreclosing without court approval, and the court will continue to protect the company from lender action for so long as the court believes the lender has adequate collateral to protect its position.

The secured lender faces even greater obstacles, as a debtor company may attempt to "cramdown" or reduce the amount of the secured debt to the value of the collateral. Therefore, a Chapter 11 can effectively restructure secured debt as well as unsecured debt.

Similarly, threatened tax seizures are also responsible for a large number of Chapter 11s. A company that cannot pay its delinquent tax obligations to the satisfaction of taxing authorities will have no choice but to either face seizure or go for bankruptcy protection. Under reorganization the company can structure the plan to pay taxes over six years from the date of assessment, and while the company is under Chapter 11 the taxing authorities, like other creditors, are prevented from taking action against the company. The mere filing of a tax lien may force the reorganization as secured lenders may lose the rights to their collateral to the IRS after 45 days unless the company files for reorganization. Even with an otherwise cooperative tax agent and lender, the mere existence of the lien alters their respective positions to the point that the lender must insist on Chapter 11 or liquidation, if it is to maintain its priority rights to the pledged collateral.

The threat of a Chapter 11 may be the only meaningful weapon a financially troubled company has in dealing with an impatient tax collector. Nothing less has the power to stop the tax collector from shutting down the business.

Chapter 11 also provides for the selective renunciation of burdensome executory contracts and leases. Many of the fast-growth discount chains of the 1960s sought protection under bankruptcy to shed their bad locations. Mammoth Mart, for example, was able to shrink in size, shedding scores of unprofitable leases under its reorganization. We recently marshaled a paper manufacturer through Chapter 11 so it could extricate itself from an unprofitable $250,000-a-year supply contract. In another case, a small typesetting firm was able to cancel an oppressive $60,000 lease agreement on typesetting equipment that no longer served its purposes and was only causing the company continuing losses. Companies that want to shed burdensome contracts and leases may have no option but to cancel these agreements under Chapter 11.

Although it appears to be a paradox, a Chapter 11 may actually allow a company to obtain additional credit or further financing, and it is this need for fresh credit and financing that may prompt the Chapter 11 filing. For example, suppliers hesitant to extend credit to the shaky business are in a far stronger position extending credit to the company in Chapter 11 because debts incurred after the filing have priority in payment over prepetition debts and are not subject to compromise under the Chapter 11 reorganization. It was this need for additional trade credit that prompted W.T. Grant to go into Chapter 11. Grant approaching the Christmas season and, unable to obtain credit from its suppliers, filed Chapter 11 allowing, its suppliers to open credit lines confident their postpetition debts would be fully paid.

The Chapter 11 company has many opportunities for creative financing arrangements. Principals of the debtor company can safely lend to their own company with court approval, new lenders are more easily attracted, and assets of affiliated companies may be pledged to secure new financing—options unavailable without bankruptcy. An interesting feature of a Chapter 11 is that it allows the troubled business to issue new stock to raise capital, bypassing most of the SEC registration requirements.

If Chapter 11 can be strong medicine for the sick business it is medicine that can also be administered by the creditors who may look upon Chapter 11 as their own bargaining weapon: Creditors can petition troubled companies into Chapter 11. Typically this occurs when creditors believe other creditors are receiving preferential payments or security subject to being set aside in bankruptcy, or that there may be fraud or embezzlement involved, requiring the broad investigatory powers of the bankruptcy court. Although less than 10 percent of all Chapter 11 cases are initiated by creditors, many of the filings come from creditors who are simply frustrated in dealing with distressed companies that never seem to move off dead center in resolving their problems. Robert Braunstein, a Cape Cod bankruptcy lawyer, sums it up: "A Chapter 11 can force management to come to terms with its problems, and one way or another creditors can put an end to the difficulties in working with the company."

Notwithstanding all the benefits and protection a Chapter 11 has to offer, the troubled company may resort to bankruptcy too quickly and without careful consideration as to whether an out-of-court workout could be successfully achieved. It may be that the company simply has no confidence that its creditors will be cooperative unless harnessed by the restraints of bankruptcy—a perception that is often correct. More often management does not try an informal workout because it does not know or understand the alternatives. For this attorneys and accountants are frequently to blame. The bankruptcy bar has long encouraged reorganizations over less formal workout proceedings to the point where an out-of-court restructuring is seldom attempted. This is a decided disservice in even those few cases where a reorganization might be avoided. One seasoned practitioner of the New York bankruptcy bar admits:

> Walk into any bankruptcy lawyer's office and you walk out a Chapter 11 case. Half the lawyers want the enormous fees they produce, and the other half simply doesn't know what else to do. The sad fact is that most of the companies in bankruptcy court don't belong there.

THE DARK HALLS OF BANKRUPTCY

Resort to bankruptcy as a means of bringing order and discipline into a deteriorating situation where the debtor company and its creditors are at odds often has considerable disadvantages; this is the downside that must be evaluated.

First, the bankruptcy may well have an adverse impact on the company's dealers, customers, and suppliers, who see reorganization as a threat to the company and therefore a threat to their own long-term interests. This was particularly true for companies like International-

Harvester that make complex, long-lived products that are highly dependent on continued warranties, guarantees, and replacement parts. No one wants to buy a potentially orphaned product. And no one wants to deal with a potentially dead company. For example, consider the plight of a Michigan machine shop that manufactures one small component part for a major automaker. Unquestionably the automaker will switch suppliers at the first hint of bankruptcy—forcing the company to stress an out-of-court workout. The impact of Chapter 11 on customers can be a primary issue. The company, of course, may have no realistic alternative but to go into Chapter 11, but even then the company must couple it with strategies to reduce customer concern and build confidence in its long-term survival.

Second, management may lose control of the process even if it is designated "debtor in possession" and left to run the company under the supervision of the creditors' committee and the courts. Thus, in the case of W.T. Grant, a banker-dominated creditors' committee decided that creditors would recover more through liquidation than through continued operation under Chapter 11 and potential reorganization. The decision to liquidate was made shortly after Christmas when the retailer's inventories were low and cash was high. In fact, the post-liquidation payout to creditors proved substantial and, in the view of many informed observers, the liquidation alternative did indeed maximize the lenders' recovery. In the case of most large concerns, reorganization promises higher values than liquidation, but success in reorganizing is by no means assured. Companies in Chapter 11 may also fall victim to creditors forcing a sale of the business to a third party if such a strategy will generate greater dividends than could be paid by the company, or the creditors may even propose their own plan of reorganization, restructuring the company along lines more advantageous to themselves than to the principals of the company.

A third constraint on resort to bankruptcy is particularly relevant to multinational concerns with operations and corporate entities in a number of countries. If there are important intercompany transactions among the subsidiaries domiciled in various jurisdictions, resort to Chapter 11 in the United States may trigger bankruptcy of the subsidiaries around the world. The relevant bankruptcy laws and procedures of most foreign countries are oriented more toward liquidation than reorganization; few countries have legislation and procedures as conducive to reorganization as those of Chapter 11. Attorneys for both lenders and for

Massey-Ferguson and International Harvester, considering the feasibility of reorganization under the diverse, often obscure, bankruptcy laws and procedures of many competing jurisdictions, reportedly concluded that reorganization in bankruptcy under these circumstances was simply not a feasible alternative. Even liquidation in bankruptcy in many disparate jurisdictions promises at best to be a long, expensive, cumbersome process.

Finally, the "orderly process" afforded by bankruptcy can prove to be anything but that. Indeed, it can become a forum for legal maneuvers, ploys, and counterploys by the lawyers for the various interest groups, which make the process more involved, expensive, and slower than a less legalistic, out-of-court effort. Owners and managers of a company immersed in Chapter 11 can soon become exasperated over the "red tape" and roadblocks to efficient, flexible management. A reorganization also can take several years (one to two years is average) and many managers frustrated by the process simply find it easier to move on to another company operating free of tiring restraints. It is these same complexities and bureaucratic inefficiencies that create the high legal fees that place reorganization beyond the reach of all but the larger companies with the money to pay for it and the organizational stamina to put up with it.

A TALE OF TWO COMPANIES

What is life really like in the throes of bankruptcy?

A closer look at the reorganization process can be seen by comparing the events of W.T. Grant and Interstate Stores, two firms selected for closer examination because both operated in the larger discount store chain industry and both declared Chapter 11 bankruptcy in the mid-1970s. Interstate Stores successfully reorganized and emerged from bankruptcy as Toys 'R' Us, while W.T. Grant was forced to liquidate its assets shortly after filing bankruptcy.

W.T. Grant filed for bankruptcy in October 1975. In February 1976, just four months later, a U.S. Bankruptcy Court judge ordered Grant to liquidate its assets. Although the downfall of Grant appears to have occurred suddenly, the failure process began as early as a decade before its widely publicized demise. This section describes nine failure events both before and after bankruptcy which comprised Grant's "failure process."

The first signal of financial problems for Grant was the firm's inability to generate cash from internal operations in the 1966–1975 period. While

Grant reported a steady net income and working capital from operations during this time, Grant's continuing operations provided positive cash flows in only 1968 and 1969. Hence, operations required more cash than it could generate in the next eight years. Grant first reported a net loss for the quarter ended April 30, 1972. Quarterly losses again were recorded by Grant in 1973, but it was not until 1974 that a significant decline in reported annual net income occurred.

The next failure event for Grant occurred in December 1973 when Standard & Poor's acknowledged Grant's mushrooming financial problems by downgrading its rating of Grant's debt instruments. In the first quarter of 1974, Grant's continuing financial deterioration prompted the firm to reduce its quarterly dividend by $15; two quarters later, the dividend was totally eliminated.

Two additional prebankruptcy events, which occurred in 1974 and early 1975, showed the seriousness of Grant's financial woes. First, it sought and was awarded a debt accommodation from a group of banks. The debt accommodation involved a time extension on a $40 million debt installment due in December 1974. A number of similar debt accommodations followed in 1975. Second, in 1974, Grant began a succession of changes in top-level management personnel and attempted to restructure its operations. The pre-bankruptcy reorganization attempts continued until Grant filed for bankruptcy in October 1975.

Following Grant's filing for bankruptcy, the firm made a number of futile efforts to reorganize its operations and thus avoid liquidation. These post-bankruptcy reorganization attempts involved closing hundreds of retail stores across the country, appealing to suppliers and other creditors for further debt accommodations, and paring its corporate headquarters staff. However, even these measures were too feeble to save Grant from liquidation. By then, Grant's creditors were reluctant to extend further concessions to the firm. Suppliers were demanding cash payments before shipping merchandise, which Grant desperately needed for the oncoming Christmas season. In February 1976, the bankruptcy court ordered Grant to liquidate its assets.

Interstate Stores, a major chain store operator, filed for protection under Chapter 11 in May 1974. Unlike Grant, Interstate successfully reorganized and emerged from bankruptcy in April 1978 with its name changed to Toys 'R' Us (after Interstate's one profitable division). Although Interstate's financial troubles received far less media attention than those of Grant, similar symptoms of decline can be identified for Interstate.

Perhaps the earliest symptom of its growing financial problems was in 1970 with a gradual decline of the firm's reported income from continuing operations. In response to this steadily falling profitability, Interstate reduced its quarterly dividends from $60 to $45 in 1971; in 1972, the firm discontinued all dividends.

In 1973, three significant failure events occurred for Interstate. First, the firm suffered its first operating loss. Second, in July, the firm obtained debt accommodations from its traditional lenders. These debt concessions included time extensions on debt repayment, pledging of stock to lenders, and agreements by Interstate to maintain certain financial ratios. Finally, Interstate attempted a (prebankruptcy) workout of its operations by discontinuing a major chain of retail stores and by disposing of a significant portion of its fixed assets and inventories.

When Interstate's prebankruptcy workout attempts failed in 1974, the firm filed for bankruptcy, allowing it to continue operations while formulating a reorganization plan. The firm's plan of reorganization involved focusing on its one profitable subsidiary, Toys 'R' Us, further closings of retail stores, restructuring of debt, and arrangements for additional financing.

In 1978, the firm emerged from bankruptcy as Toys 'R' Us. It has continuously posted profits since 1978 and today is the leading toy-specialty chain in the nation.

THE SUCCESSFUL REORGANIZATION

Chapter 11 can be strong medicine for the sick business but many patients do not survive even with strong medicine. Less than one-third of the companies going into Chapter 11 come out strong enough to be in operation two years later. And they succumb for a variety of reasons.

Perhaps the major reason is that companies cannot finance themselves through a Chapter 11. Although a reorganization can help cash flow by encouraging creditors to ship on credit terms, or create new opportunities for financing, the acute cash shortages may nevertheless prevail. Inadequate working capital probably accounts for 50 percent of the reorganizational failures. A company going into Chapter 11 has to do so with a clear understanding of how it will stay afloat, particularly if secured lenders resist the use of accounts receivable or cash collateral in the continued operation of the business.

Then companies often flee into Chapter 11 to prevent foreclosure by lenders, which protection may be short-lived if the lender can convince the court there is inadequate collateral to protect its interests. Survival of the overencumbered business typically depends on continued lender cooperation throughout the Chapter 11, and too few managers take the steps to win that cooperation.

Creditors may also bring about the demise of the business as a potentially profitable enterprise as creditors often force management to sell its winners or profit makers in order to satisfy creditor claims. Sometimes it takes a very strong turnaround leader to stand up to creditors in their attempt to shape the company for their own short-term gains instead of the long-term objectives essential to the company. This was the experience of Andrew Losyniak, Chief Executive of Dynamics Corporation, who fought to keep its one profit maker—the sizable Waring Division—despite the demands of creditors that it be sold.

Yet these reasons for failure are secondary to the one underlying reason for most reorganizational failure—the inability of management to achieve a strategic turnaround and make the company profitable. To a large extent a Chapter 11 must be looked upon as a safe harbor within which the company is given the opportunity to rebuild. But even then many companies do not use the opportunity wisely, as they think of the Chapter 11 only as a way to rid themselves of excess debts without curing the root causes of the insolvency. The big danger of the Chapter 11 is that by taking the pressure off the company, the company is lulled into believing its problems are over.

A pattern then emerges of five characteristics of the companies that successfully come through Chapter 11:

1. They enter the Chapter 11 with sufficient assets and a viable core of business activity.

2. They enjoy creditor cooperation and creditor support—particularly in obtaining new credit and bridge financing.

3. They maintain a positive cash flow throughout the reorganization process.

4. They address—and cure—the underlying problems, becoming revitalized with a strategic plan for profitability and new growth.

5. They restructure their debt to conform to the repayment capabilities of the company.

In the absence of these key elements for reorganizational success, a Chapter 11 is highly risky. However, this does not mean the Chapter 11 should not be attempted, because ingredients for a successful outcome may only come about after the company goes into reorganization.

Time and again in reorganizational success we hear the phrase "going back to basics," meaning that the company will again emphasize the keys to its earlier victories. The company will be forced to redefine its purpose and its values and define the business it should be in. Frequently the company is only reversing the actions that got it into trouble in the first place.

14

Buy-Outs and Buy-Backs

FEW companies go through the turnaround process without their owners or managers wondering whether a sale of the company would be a smarter decision than the decision to rehabilitate. Creditors may share the same thoughts.

THE DECISION TO SELL

The decision to sell the company may come at the threshold of the turnaround, when the company is in full crisis. The owner may decide he or she does not have the managerial skills, energy, or financial resources to achieve a successful turnaround. The alternatives then are narrowed to either selling or liquidating the business. Unfortunately, the decision may be made at the worst possible moment when the owners or managers are demoralized, often emotionally beaten, and mentally tired after months of wrestling with the pressures and problems of the failing company. Under these circumstances the owner may decide to sell as an act of desperation and despair rather than through an objective evaluation of the situation and what can realistically be accomplished.

The owner may also be guided by his or her own career goals, which often change under these circumstances, and therefore decides that even if the company can be rehabilitated, the preference is to follow a different career path, necessitating a sale.

While thoughts of selling are inescapable during every stage of the workout, it may come most strongly to the forefront only when the company is in the throes of the turnaround. Pressures to sell may be asserted by lenders or creditor groups, or the owner may only then be forced to accept the reality that while the company can be saved, it is beyond his or her power to save it.

For the owner unable to achieve a turnaround, a sale of all or part of the company should be certainly considered before the decision is made to liquidate. A forced liquidation will usually bring the least recovery to creditors, and although a sale of the business may not fully repay creditors, it will invariably earn creditors greater repayment, not to mention providing management a more graceful, face-saving exit. There are countless cases where owners and managers have earned the deserved respect of creditors, customers, employees, and suppliers because they rode with the company until the company could be advantageously sold rather than walked away from the company and those who relied on its continuity.

The decision to sell, however, may also be motivated by unrealistic expectations of what benefits the owner may derive personally from the sale. The owner may set an unrealistic price for the business, hoping to clear enough after full payment to creditors to put money in his or her own pocket. For example, the business worth $100,000 free of debt may be foolishly priced at $200,000 simply because the business has $150,000 in debts and the owner wants to clear $50,000 from the sale. Marlene Rosen, President of the Boston-based United Business Brokers, comments:

> We have countless listings of near-bankrupt companies that are priced backwards by sellers who mistakenly believe buyers will pay for their mistakes rather than pay what the business is actually worth. Oftentimes the owner can be motivated to sell when offered more readily obtainable benefits such as employment with the acquired company, a management consulting agreement or compensation in the form of a covenant not to compete with the acquiring company. The owner, however, must have a clear idea of what he wants from a sale of the troubled business—and whether he is likely to get it—before the decision to sell can be made or the business can intelligently be put on the market.

Conflicts within the organization may also cloud the decision or be destructive to an advantageous sale. Partners embroiled in battle may have caused the decline of the company, and they are less likely to see eye-to-eye on what should be done with the company once the problems become critical. The family-owned business presents its own brand of conflict. Even when one family member owns the business, the pressure to sell—or not to sell—asserted by other family members can be considerable, with husbands and wives frequently disagreeing on objectives.

Creditors may also encourage or discourage a sale, and to the extent they must compromise their claims to allow the sale their interests must be considered. However, convincing creditors to go along with a sale usually becomes easier when liquidation is seen as the only alternative.

HIDDEN CHARMS

"Owners of the small firm are champions of the 'do or die' philosophy, often futilely fighting for survival by plundering their resources when a marriage to another firm would make considerably more sense," says New York's Bernie Kopel, who calls himself a matchmaker for the troubled firm. He is always on the lookout for firms interested in marrying a sick business. As Bernie puts it, "They often produce profitable offspring."

Bernie recounts a few happy corporate weddings:

☐ Garden Chevrolet to Dwight Motor Leasing: Bernie calls it his "marriage made in heaven." The Chevrolet dealership could not move enough cars to stay alive, while Dwight was buying 200–250 cars annually to nourish its expanding fleet. So Dwight purchased a 50 percent interest in Garden Chevrolet, picking up its cars at slightly over dealer's cost while providing Garden Chevrolet the volume needed to win better prices from General Motors.

☐ Canterbury Cards and Gifts to Hutton Paper Corporation: Canterbury, a six-store Delaware chain, lay gasping in Chapter 11 without the funds to survive. But it did enjoy six valuable store leases. Hutton, always on the prowl for high-traffic locations, wasted no time becoming the anxious suitor. Hutton acquired controlling interest in Canterbury, bailed it out of Chapter 11, and added six more winning locations to its fast-growing chain.

☐ Economy Wallpaper and Capital Paint made another stunning couple. Economy sat idly on one end of a busy shopping center in the outskirts of Chicago while Capital, with its dismal sales and exorbitant overhead, languished only a few stores away. The romance was inevitable. Joining forces, they found a new location on a busy thoroughfare and proudly announced the birth of Capital Paint and Wallpaper Co.

Bernie Kopel keeps busy as corporate matchmaker. He explains: "There are thousands of small firms that can't make it on their own. My job is to discover what charms they can offer to another company. If I find those hidden charms, I don't have to sell, it's love at first sight."

Why would another company be interested in buying a troubled company? There are many reasons. Hidden under the mountain of debts lie assets that can be valuable to a buyer: leases, customers, franchise and distributorship rights, channels of distribution, and tax losses.

Leases

The troubled company may hold valuable leases to motivate another company to write out healthy checks.

Consider Canterbury Cards and Gifts. When Canterbury filed for Chapter 11, it had inventory and fixtures valued at $300,000. Liabilities, however, exceeded $800,000. Canterbury's owners did not think their debt-ridden company would be worth much to someone else, and they certainly could not finance the reorganization, but they were sitting on a hidden gold mine. Canterbury was paying annual rents averaging only $10,000 per location. Today, the landlords would demand over $25,000 for each of the same locations. Each lease represented a savings of $15,000 per year, and rent savings for the duration of the six leases created a whopping $850,000 bargaining chip.

Hutton Paper Corporation, anxious for bargain leases, agreed to purchase Canterbury shares for $400,000. Hutton then took over Canterbury and helped it through its Chapter 11, agreeing to pay creditors $250,000 to settle $800,000 in claims, and proceeded to build a healthy company. For Hutton it was a wise acquisition, as they purchased $300,000 in tangible assets and leases worth another $850,000 for a total price of only $650,000.

In another example, Homan's Candy Shops used their lease to a $168,000 advantage. Homan's held a valuable lease on a retail store in one of Boston's high-traffic waterfront malls. Homan's was not insolvent, but neither was it profitable, forcing it to pull out, liquidate its fixtures, and call it quits. However, one of Boston's busiest restaurants stood adjacent to Homan's, so it was correctly calculated that the restaurant would pay handsomely to take over Homan's lease in order to expand. Armed for negotiation, Bill Homan approached the restaurant owner and told him Homan's was about to sell out to another candy chain but wanted to give the restaurant first crack at the space. The restaurant owner jumped at it, agreeing to pay Homan's $168,000 in four annual installments. The restaurant, of course, could have declined the deal, waited three weeks for Homan's to move out, and then picked up Homan's space by simply writing a new lease with the landlord, but how could it know Homan's did not have a buyer in the wings?

Whenever Bill Homan thinks about the deal he pulled off, he says, "I can never understand why owners close up shop and abandon valuable locations without first trying to parlay those leases into cash."

Customers

Customers always have value, and may be channeled to another company in exchange for an interesting proposition.

When Chilton Meat Supply, a Midwest meat packer, began to fail due to undercapitalization and poor sales, it was decided to liquidate by throwing the company into bankruptcy. But why let competitors grab 400 retail accounts for nothing? Its owner approached Puritan Food, one of its larger competitors, and negotiated a deal to help turn his customers into Puritan customers, provided Puritan paid him a 3 percent commission on sales to his former accounts. Last year's sales to his prior customers amounted to $2 million, earning the feisty owner-turned-salesman $60,000 in commissions.

Many owners of troubled companies parlay their relationship with customers into profitable employment or consulting arrangements, and leave the tangible assets of their company behind for creditor liquidation. As is often the case, the owner of the troubled business may be its one most valuable asset.

Franchise and Distributorship Rights

These rights can also attract money-rich companies like magnets. A valuable distributorship certainly drew cash to Richmond Wholesalers, a growing baby goods wholesaler whose mainstay was its valuable Johnson & Johnson distributorship, granting Richmond exclusive sales rights to sell Johnson & Johnson products to department and discount outlets. When Richmond's owners, who built the firm into a profitable enterprise, ran into serious cash flow problems, they turned to the banks—but the banks would not consider further loans. Monarch Merchandising then rushed to the rescue. Well-entrenched in the discount trade as children's wear wholesalers, Monarch could see instant value in Richmond's customer base and its exclusive Johnson & Johnson products line. For Monarch, the acquisition was a perfect way to expand.

Monarch initially bargained for a total takeover. However, Richmond's management shunned a complete sale and instead negotiated to sell a 49-percent interest in their struggling company. The marriage worked. In 1986 Richmond's sales doubled to over $3 million and is expected to double sales again in the next two years. Jim Clancy, Richmond's Vice-President, says:

> When we sold a 49 percent interest in Richmond, we were able to demand top price and a commitment from Monarch to provide future expansion capital. Our Johnson products distributorship sealed the deal. Without it, we would be just another starving wholesaler, forced to give the company away for a few dollars.

Channels of Distribution.

Like franchises and distributorships, channels of distribution can attract interest. Many firms want to acquire or develop business-saving relationships with companies that can increase sales for their own products:

☐ Putnam Mills, for example, constantly searches for floundering retail men's clothing outlets, looking for stores that can feature its lines and effectively operate on a low-overhead discount basis. Putnam finances the turnaround, inventories the store on consignment, and even provides management assistance. In return, Putnam demands token ownership in the retailer and 10 percent of sales. But what it is really interested in is an opportunity to sell its goods. Some of its affiliated stores have quadrupled their former sales and many unprofitable retailers have begun to show a 10–15 percent profit operating under Putnam's umbrella.

☐ Similarly, a drug wholesaler recently acquired a 70-percent interest in a small drug chain, injecting a survival dose of inventory and cash. The wholesaler expects the chain to produce a profit, but the wholesaler also expects to sell its new subsidiary over $3 million in wholesale drug products this year.

☐ Reston Stereo, a seven-store stereo discounter, on the financial ropes with $300,000 in debt, could not raise the capital to pacify creditors or remerchandise the business. Eventually, a forward-thinking Hong Kong stereo manufacturer agreed to invest $500,000 in the struggling chain—$300,000 in the form of long-term debt and $200,000 for 40 percent of the shares. The manufacturer expects Reston to retail over $2 million worth of its stereo equipment annually.

Bernie Kopel loves to match the business that can provide sales to the business that needs a sales vehicle. Counsels Bernie:

Don't make a mistake. When you reach out in desperation for a marriage partner, don't just look horizontally to others in your business. Sure, they're your best bet, but companies that can flow their merchandise through your business can work wonders, too.

Tax Losses

Tax losses can offer tax savings for a profitable company that can apply a company's prior tax loss against their future taxable profits. A $200,000 tax loss may mean $70,000 in tax savings to the acquiring company with profits to shield.

Recent tax changes, however, have made the tax-loss carryforward a less attractive feature than in the past. Complicated limitations control the tax benefits of a net operating loss (NOL), and the IRS prescribes a long list of regulations one must follow to take advantage of tax-loss benefits. Although an accountant or tax counsel can analyze the situation, it must be remembered that companies seldom buy or merge with another company on the strength of the tax benefits alone. The successful marriage depends on more than wedding gifts from Uncle Sam.

A deal may come together for many other reasons. If management has special expertise, it may represent a valuable asset. Some buyers look to buy management, and the only way they can get it is to buy the company in the process.

The business name and its goodwill may also attract buyers. For example, a large mail order firm acquired a financially distressed small promotional outfit on the strength of its solid reputation. The promotional outfit had operated for years, and its name enjoys widespread recognition which proved highly valuable to the buyers.

The basic economics of the situation must also be considered. Many buyers will agree to a deal if they can acquire tangible assets at considerably less than their fair market or replacement value. In itself, this will not motivate buyers, but it certainly becomes a strong inducement when the buyer planned to acquire such assets elsewhere.

Highland Supermarket, a $6-million New Jersey food retailer, presents a perfect example. Highland amassed a $200,000 inventory and fixtures one could not replace for less than $50,000. Unfortunately, debts exceeded $300,000. Highland's owner did not welcome the hassle of revitalizing Highland, as Highland had not shown a profit for years, and its owner had no blueprint to create future profits. But why throw Highland into a liquidating bankruptcy? That certainly would not benefit its owners. Did the business own something that would entice a buyer? Could it design a deal to attract a buyer?

A small supermarket chain showed mild interest in Highland. It saw Highland as a borderline situation. Perhaps it could make Highland profitable. The solution was to give them a "no-risk" proposition along these lines:

Highland's owners would turn ownership of Highland over to the chain on a "no-cash-down" basis. Under the chain's ownership, Highland would file for a Chapter 11 reorganization to reduce the $300,000 debt. The chain agreed that Highland's assets had a fair market value of $250,000. The proposition was simple. Highland's owners would get 25 percent of every dollar by which Highland reduced its debts below $250,000. What could the chain lose? In the worst case, the reorganization would fail. The chain could walk away and lose only time and effort. Fortunately, the Chapter 11 worked. The creditors, convinced that the assets would bring only $100,000 at auction, agreed to settle all claims for $120,000. With assets having a replacement value of $250,000, Highland had an immediate "paper" gain of $130,000. Highland's prior owners picked up $32,500, or 25 percent of that gain. It was better than throwing the keys to the creditors. As it turned out, Highland did not prove to be a moneymaker for the chain either. However, the chain simply trucked Highland's inventory and fixtures to its other stores. As the acquiring chain figured it, it acquired $250,000 in assets for only $152,000, so it remained an attractive deal.

The opportunity to acquire assets at far below replacement cost can be attractive to a buyer. When coupled with a "no-risk" proposition, it becomes a powerful motivator. This double feature has loads of charm! Perhaps the more important lesson is that buying and selling a troubled business seldom follows the conventional rules of acquiring solvent, stable firms. Deals may end up a crazy patchwork of terms, but whatever form they take they must satisfy both the buyer and seller.

TWO'S COMPANY

In some cases, owners choose to hunt for a mate, even though they could muster the resources to save the company themselves. "Survival doesn't prompt every marriage," insists Bernie Kopel. "Some owners decide that an affiliation with a stronger company can offer even greater profit opportunities." Several of my own cases have proven that he is right.

For instance, K & C Printing, a New Hampshire offset firm, crept along for years with profitless sales and excess debt it needed to compromise. After a successful creditor workout, the continuing lack of profitability made the owners think of the future of the firm. So they decided to merge with another small printer, consolidating overhead and turning a small loss into a sizable profit. The stories continue:

"Selling out was the smartest decision of my life," reports Marilyn Pollack, an entrepreneurial maverick who started Computer Design on a shoestring. "We were undercapitalized from the first day. We had a growing company, but we couldn't finance its growth. So I sold to a publicly traded corporation and received 10,000 of their shares worth $150,000. They had the money to exploit our ideas." Today, Computer Design enjoys $12 million in annual sales. Hampered by Marilyn's limited capital, the company would remain nothing but undeveloped potential.

Harold Mendez simply ran out of steam:

> For 36 years, I worked day and night running Fairfax Creamery and earned a good living. But when my employees unionized and called a labor strike, I decided to turn the company over to some "bigger boys." Douglas Dairies straightened out the mess, offered an attractive buy-out arrangement and kept me on as corporate Vice-President. More than their cash, I needed their management. At that time in my life, I wanted more time with my family.

Academy Printers, a Madison, Wisconsin outfit, ran into trouble shortly after starting its business. Saddled with $50,000 in new equipment, Academy failed to generate the volume needed to meet its stiff monthly obligations. Academy found the perfect marriage partner, a local newspaper publisher who could not get the service it needed from other local printers. By joining forces with Academy, the newspaper could rely on in-house production. Academy, in turn, could keep its press constantly humming printing newspapers. After reviewing the economics, the printer and publisher decided to merge so the two equally matched firms could capitalize on each other's needs.

Carillon Sales discovered a well-orchestrated solution to a bad problem. Carillon, a large Pennsylvania-based houseware distributor, trembled when its major customer, Discount Kitchen & Appliance, filed for Chapter 11. Norman Carillon recalls the event:

> The discount chain owed us $470,000, and we realized we would have to write it off. To make matters worse, the chain represented 68 percent of our business. We worried about our own survival. It was a potential "domino effect," so we filed our own Chapter 11 to buy time to decide how to save our company as we were steadily losing money and couldn't cover current expenses. Creditors were screaming to have us liquidated before all our assets disappeared. Solutions? We knew we couldn't effectively reorganize the company, but we wondered whether our company might not seem valuable to someone. After all, we still had a warehouse full of inventory and several strong accounts. And that's what attracted Hillsboro Housewares, our oldest and most formidable competitor. They offered to buy 60 percent of Carillon's shares. Adding Carillon's sales to their own, they built on a profitable sales base, and by reducing our debt to 10 cents on the dollar, they picked up our inventory at bargain-basement prices. The sale to Hillsboro turned out to be our only alternative. Though we lost controlling interest in Carillon, our shares are now worth good money. Carillon, under Highland's control, will hit $7,000,000 this year. I stayed on to help manage Carillon for a $50,000 salary. Believe me, that's a lot better than watching Carillon liquidated and ending up with nothing but an unemployment check.

It happens every day: Owners struggling to survive but never quite making it. When the business is finally liquidated, they lose everything. If only they had turned to pros like Bernie Kopel, saying, "Okay, I can't save the business, but the business must be worth something to some-body. Can you help me cut a deal that will save something for me?"

Prentice Drug, a Cape Cod pharmacy, shared a similar experience. Prentice Drug was limping along on $240,000 sales and losing $10–12,000 annually. It could easily clear up its debts, but that would not give Prentice the long-term profitability it needed. Prentice would continue to suffer from a fatal combination of poor sales and excessive overhead. Checking further, it was discovered that Prentice had only one other competitor in town, Harbor Pharmacy, which also struggled to stay afloat. It appeared their competition would include a race to the bankruptcy court. Here were two small stores trying to divide a pie only big enough to satisfy one hungry appetite. Cleaning up the creditors of both stores, they com-bined the assets of Prentice and Harbor, making them equal partners in a new operation relocated to a dynamite location—a nearby shopping center recently vacated by a small supermarket. In three months, it all came together with the birth of Banner Pharmacy, grossing $800,000 an-nually with profits over $50,000. As Prentice's Sharon Thackheymer boasts:

> The merger allowed us to eliminate duplicate overhead, payroll, rents, and utilities. By combining our inventories, we had more to work with and could strengthen our buying and merchandising. The best part? Banner could set higher prices because it was the only pharmacy around.

Common sense? Of course. Yet that is what makes all minimergers work. They are seldom a matter of high finance and such exploits seldom make headlines within business journals, but they do save troubled businesses.

PUTTING THE DEAL TOGETHER

How can a troubled company join forces with another to achieve its owners' objectives? Unfortunately, no simple formula exists. Some buy-outs and mergers are extremely simple, others highly complex. Every successful marriage, however, demands a formula that satisfies everyone's objectives and fits economic realities.

The Outright Takeover

Over 60 percent of the smaller companies follow this route. The outright sale is simple, and it is considerably easier to find a buyer to take over completely rather than bargain for a more complex partnership arrangement. When a large corporation acquires a smaller one, it will commonly refuse anything less than a total takeover. To do otherwise would violate its own corporate structure.

Owners of the troubled company sometimes make the mistake of wanting to retain some ownership interest in the business, but they frequently come out ahead by agreeing to a complete sale rather than a minority ownership interest, even when it is available.

When Canterbury Cards and Gifts began its search for a cash-rich company, its owners wanted to retain at least a 50-percent ownership in the company, but it was not in the cards. Hutton Paper Corporation, a family-owned corporation, wanted complete ownership of its new subsidiaries. There was no room for partners.

However, Canterbury's owners wanted to continue in the card and gift business. If they could not do it through a partnership interest in Canterbury, at least they could get $400,000 from the sale of Canterbury and strike out again on their own, and today they own two healthy gift shops, made possible by turning over the keys to Canterbury before it was too late.

Partnerships

Countless combinations exist. In many cases, the acquiring company will agree to invest the necessary funds to keep the business afloat in return for an ownership interest in the business. But what ownership split is fair? Investing companies usually bargain for a majority interest and control. Ending up a minority stockholder in your own corporation may be slightly better than nothing, but as Harold Mendez of Fairfax Creamery explains it, it is not the perfect solution: "To bring in the turnaround financing, I had to sell out 80 percent of the company. As a 20-percent stockholder, I had little say in management issues. I was only one notch higher than an employee."

Sellers, however, should usually try to avoid the deal that provides only a minority stock interest. It is usually preferable to sell out completely for whatever cash can be obtained and then start over on a smaller scale with total ownership, if going back into business is the objective.

In the big-league mergers and takeovers, stock swaps provide the foundation for the takeover. The acquiring company pays for the takeover by issuing some of its own shares to stockholders of the acquired company, following the formula for the sale of Computer Design.

Employee stock ownership plans (ESOPs) are increasingly being used to buy out companies, and there has been a significant rise in the number of troubled companies that have been acquired by their employees under ESOP arrangements. Under an ESOP, the employees gradually assume ownership of the firm funded through the payments from the plan.

Stock/loan combinations are also popular. Here the acquiring company capitalizes the turnaround by loaning the troubled company a specified amount of cash plus investing for an ownership interest.

Most "partnership" transactions with larger troubled companies involve a combination of equity and debt. From the seller's viewpoint, it is far better to retain a controlling stock interest coupled with a loan, than to insist on a straight partnership deal where control may be sacrificed.

Of course, faced with a stock/debt deal, owners bargain to sell as little stock as possible and allocate as much as possible to the loan. But they often overlook the ability of the company to handle the resultant debt. Agreeing to an unrealistic debt level can be self-defeating. One beleaguered company obtained $200,000 in needed capital by agreeing to a $180,000, three-year secured loan, with the remaining $20,000 for 30-percent ownership in the company. Two months later, the loan went into default. The investor–lender simply foreclosed on its mortgage and conveniently picked up the entire company.

But there are ways in which nearly equal sized companies can adjust for their differences. For instance, when Prentice Drug and Harbor Pharmacy joined forces, their owners each ended up with 50 percent ownership in the successor Banner Drug. Although Prentice and Harbor were nearly equal in value, Harbor had more assets and fewer liabilities. The parties agreed that Harbor was worth about $30,000 more than Prentice, so Banner equalized the contributions with notes for $30,000.

Joint Ventures

Often the troubled company can affiliate with another firm which provides the tools to revitalize the company without either a sale or partnership arrangement. The present owners retain full ownership of the company and enter into a functional alliance or affiliation with another firm on a joint-venture basis.

This works best with companies that can offer distribution opportunities to another firm. Remember Putnam Mills? Two other companies joined forces to sell only Putnam's lines. Putnam gave them survival strength through strong merchandising, promotional "know-how," and managerial assistance. Nor did Putnam demand an ownership interest. Putnam was happy to move its lines through the stores, collecting an additional 10 percent override on sales.

The well-designed joint venture takes on some of the characteristics of a franchise. It can provide the distressed company the best of both worlds—the strength and support of a large, strong company coupled with the motivation and benefits of running your own show.

NEGOTIATING THE DEAL

Textbook formulas that suggest valuations formulas work poorly with troubled companies. Buyers well understand that the sale is an attempted last-ditch effort to save something from the rubble and the "deal" inevitably forces its owner to face the dismal reality that sellers in distress have little bargaining power.

Having put together deals for over 600 troubled companies, we always were inevitably forced to accept the best deal we could get. Sometimes it was far better than we hoped, in other instances it was far worse, but that alone is the measure of what a financially distressed business is worth.

However, in every case, the strategy was to beat the bushes for every possible buyer to be found, present our case, listen to the best offers, and try to boost the price through last-minute negotiations. When the final offers lay on the table, we simply had to accept the offer that best satisfied the owner's objectives. Very often there were few deals from which to choose, so the selection process was remarkably easy.

As dismal as this may sound, it does not mean the troubled company is at the total mercy of the buyer. After all, every company has something of value and if it has value to one buyer it is likely to be perceived as having value to another.

However, the bleak fact of life is that many prospective buyers have no inclination to cut a fair deal, but instead play "vulture," hovering around to see what they can pick up once the business goes under.

These "buyers" may be after the location, customers, employees, or whatever other benefit they can derive by staying close to the scene, merely pretending to be interested in buying. Competitors, of course, are always likely suspects, for they are in the best position to exploit a bankruptcy.

The "vulture" is not always easy to spot, but there are some telltale signs. Watch for the buyer who seems overly preoccupied with only one phase of operations. Delayed, protracted negotiations are another clue. Often these buyers will keep lulling the owner with increasingly better offers, hoping he will turn his back on sincere buyers and extend himself beyond the point of no return, when they can watch the business crumble and pick it up for pennies. It is a common ploy, but owners should not fall victim to it. The only defense is to watch the cutoff date for negotiations and cement the deal within a reasonable time thereafter. If the buyer stalls or refuses to close the deal within a reasonable time and after a reasonable opportunity to negotiate, he or she probably is not negotiating in good faith.

Sellers can equally delude themselves. Every owner thinks he or she will find a better deal the next week or the next month. Why not? If the company is worth so much to Company X, then who is to say there is not a Company Y lurking around the corner that will offer more? There may be, but from my experiences, it is not probable.

What routinely happens is that these owners take their search beyond the point of no return only to find they have lost any solid deal they had and that other birds in the bush were only a mirage.

Once a serious and qualified buyer is found, the approaches to valuation can be as varied as the type of transactions. No one valuation method is suitable for every type of acquisition. Special situations require their own unique approach. More than a few insolvent businesses are acquired under bankruptcy, receivership, or foreclosure proceedings for purposes of rehabilitation for continued operation. Although the buyer may view the profit or turnaround potential as the motivation for the acquisition, the future profitability is not the criteria for determining value. Instead, the buyer will approach valuations from the perspective of its liquidation value at auction, which is generally the apparent alternative. Where other interested buyers are bidding for the business, the competition may influence the price upward; however, each will nevertheless commence negotiations with liquidation value in their sights.

If the troubled business is to be dismantled and functionally merged into the buyer's business, the buyer may base value by translating the economic benefit of the merger on its own income statement. This requires the buyer to carefully analyze each of the operational changes resulting from the merger and to carefully reconstruct the buyer's profit and loss statement.

The functional merger may produce a synergistic effect on the buyer's profits, producing combined profits greater then the profits of the two separate organizations.

From the seller's viewpoint, a merger may justify a higher value then would be justified by operating the acquired company separately; however, this subtle benefit to the buyer rarely enters into the negotiation, unless stressed by the seller.

There are countless strategies and tricks of the trade for successfully selling the troubled enterprise, but a "baker's dozen" of the most important include these points:

1. Define objectives. Does the company need an outside firm to help achieve profitability, solvency, or both? This will help define the companies which can fulfill those needs and should be solicited as buyers.

2. Resolve any creditor problems before placing the business on the market. A seller will be in a much stronger bargaining position with a financially sound business with low debt and there will be no creditor interference.

3. Start early. If the business is slipping into insolvency and needs another company to help bail it out, considerably more can be obtained, for the company during the initial stages of a downturn than in the terminal stage of insolvency, when buyers develop the killer instinct.

4. Add up the selling points. What does the company have to offer? Translate it into terms a buyer can appreciate. Be prepared to convince the buyer it can make money with the business, and show the buyer how.

5. Know your objectives. Do you prefer a complete sale or do you want to remain affiliated with the company as a partner or employee? Match your objectives to the reality of the situation and the companies you are seeking out.

6. Solicit proposals aggressively. Contact every company which possibly might be interested in your firm and satisfy your objectives. In many cases, sellers must contact hundreds of firms before reaching a "no-nonsense" deal. Sellers do not have time to play the field but need as many offers as can be obtained in a hurry.

7. Stay flexible. The deal a seller thinks he or she wants may be entirely different from the deal offered. And what is offered may be the better deal. Listen to the buyer's ideas. They may be a more exciting proposition.

8. Do not fall for "pie-in-the-sky" deals. Sellers are usually better off with hard cash than soft promises. Many troubled firms are handed over on the basis of "future profits" and "earnout" or other speculative contingency. This usually is a mistake.

9. If you are to retain an interest in the company, then define the buyer's expectations for the company. It is the same as any other partnership. Seller and buyer must share objectives for the firm and define how the buyer expects to reach those objectives.

10. Watch for the "bailout." Many firms will invest in a troubled company and then liquidate or pull out of the business when the business fails to achieve expectations. The buyer's commitment to give the business a reasonable chance is an important ingredient in the transaction.

11. Consider personalities as much as finances. Most business marriages end in divorce, not due to business reasons but because of personality clashes. To rebuild the company, the seller needs a solid working relationship with his or her new partners. Once conflict occurs, the seller will probably fall victim to the acquiring company, which may have the upper hand legally and financially.

12. Look like a survivor. The buyer knows the seller is in trouble, but do not let him or her think time is running out. If the buyer believes the seller can survive without him or her, the seller can bargain at his or her level, and will not have to listen to any last minute "take-it-or-leave-it" ultimatums.

13. Use some "phantom" buyers. Do not let the buyer think he or she is the only interested buyer, even if he or she is. The buyer needs competition if you are to get a reasonable deal, and that can happen only when the buyer is forced to "outbid" other prospects.

Bernie Kopel adds this final point:

You can tell when the deal is right. The two companies can immediately see how they can fulfill each others' needs. The real key in making it work is the attitude. The parties have to see this not as an opportunity to exploit, or even as a marriage of convenience. It has to be a marriage of opportunity.

BUY-BACKS: THE ART OF REACQUIRING YOUR OWN COMPANY

Every year, thousands upon thousands of beleagured owners buy back their own companies.

To many owners, Chapter 11s, creditor workouts, and other internal reorganizations spell "death on the installment plan." For a new lease on life, many of these same owners avoid needless complications by simply starting over, reacquiring the assets of their business at auction prices, free of creditor claims.

Under the buy-back, the owner simply sets up a new corporation and it then bids to buy the assets of the defunct company. The end result? The owner continues to operate the same business at the same location with the same assets, but without the debt that caused sleepless nights.

Large corporations, due to their complexity, diverse stockholder interest, and visibility, are usually limited to solving their financial problems through Chapter 11. However, the small enterprise, particularly the sole proprietorship or the closely held corporation, may find starting over a more practical solution to more complex workout arrangements with creditors.

For instance, a discount health and beauty aid store was about to go "belly-up" with over $150,000 in unsecured debt. Under Chapter 11 it might have been able to reduce the debt to $40,000. However, it estimated that the same assets would bring only $15–20,000 under auction. Clearly, the smarter move was to have the owner let the assets go to auction and invest $20,000 to reacquire the assets free of creditor claims rather than spend $40,000 later, after tiring creditor negotiations.

Financing a distressed business buy-back seldom requires the resources needed to buy a viable company. "After all," as one auctioneer aptly states it, "you're only paying about a dime on the dollar for the assets."

A buy-back can be the only practical solution for the smaller company with pressing obligations. Its simplicity and practicality can be seen with one of my earliest cases involving a small health club that owned $10–15,000 worth of equipment on which it owed $6000 to a leasing company. In addition to its other small creditors, it was being sued for $100,000 by an old landlord who claimed the health club had breached its lease when it moved out. My client claimed the landlord had not maintained or properly repaired the premises, but I thought the landlord had the stronger case and would eventually win. Regardless of who was right, it would cost my client $10–15,000 to fight the case. The legal fees alone could ruin the company. The practical solution? Liquidate the health club. The leasing company holding a mortgage on the assets sent the equipment to auction. After my client set up a new corporation, he entered the highest bid at $6000, exactly what he owed the leasing company, and the leasing company readily agreed to finance the $6000 purchase price. In reality, the leasing company only swapped the debt from the old corporation to the new corporation. Then my client signed a new lease with his present landlord and was back in business, missing hardly a beat. Total cost—$500 in auction costs and $300 in legal fees. His old landlord eventually won a default judgment against the original corporation, but he could more easily have squeezed blood out of a stone than money out of a corporation with no assets.

Under a Chapter 11, my client would have had to litigate the landlord's claim. If the landlord won, he would have had to negotiate a settlement under Chapter 11. Legal fees of $10–20,000 coupled with perhaps a 10-percent settlement on the $100,000 would have cost my client $20–30,000, a clearly unreasonable expenditure for a business with assets of only $15,000.

An insolvent company can, of course, be liquidated in several different ways. The company may allow a bank or other secured party to foreclose on the assets. Creditors may petition the company into bankruptcy where a trustee will be appointed, or a state court may appoint a liquidating receiver. In many states the distressed company may make an assignment for the benefit of creditors with the assignee liquidating the business. Regardless of the type of proceeding, the objective of the liquidation is to sell the assets at the best price readily available.

A fair idea of what the assets will bring at auction can be obtained by inviting a business auctioneer to provide an estimate. Experienced auctioneers can predict auction values with reasonable accuracy. By obtaining a liquidation appraisal, the owners can determine what it will take to buy back the assets.

The assets may even be reacquired free and clear of liabilities, without a public auction. A liquidator can sell the assets at private sale if the price is fair to the creditors—a fair price being anything more than the creditors would receive if the assets were auctioned.

Our firm liquidates many insolvent businesses. Once the business is turned over to us, we call in an auctioneer to appraise its auction value. Often a buyer will show up before the auction and offer more than the appraised auction value, and we willingly sell, confident it is the best price available and in the best interests of creditors.

Suppose a retail business faces liquidation under an insolvency proceeding, and an auctioneer predicts its assets will bring $20,000 under the hammer. Along comes Buyer B, offering $24,000 under a private sale without an auctioneer. Are the creditors cheated? Of course not. The private sale will net them $4000 more. In fact, they may come out $7–8000 ahead because auction fees may run $3–4000. Knowledgeable liquidators understand that rationale.

To avoid even the hint of impropriety, some liquidators will refuse to sell privately to a new corporation owned by the principal of the distressed business. That position is understandable. But many conclude that they have one obligation—to convert the assets into as much money as possible. If the prior owner has the deepest pocket, why shouldn't he be allowed to buy them back?

The same people who criticize the "dump-buy-back" would not hesitate to attend the auction of their own house if the price was right. Why not? Distressed assets should go to the highest bidder. The identity of the buyer is not important. Even bankruptcy courts typically allow the original owners to reacquire their business assets provided they offer the highest bid.

Liquidators can also finance the purchase. There is no law to prevent it. A liquidator, for example, may find that the assets will bring $30,000 on a cash basis. But what if he was offered a premium price to finance it?

More often than not, liquidators will go along with a sensible financing arrangement, if convinced the creditors will come out ahead.

Existing mortgage holders often agree to finance the repurchase of a troubled business. It is frequently only good business. Mortgage holders know that the liquidation of the troubled business may not cover what is owed. By rewriting the mortgage to the new corporation, they at least have a fighting chance to collect more if they limit the debt to what the business can realistically pay. It makes no sense to rewrite a $100,000 loan on assets worth $30,000.

Orchestrated properly, the buy-back can be as fair to creditors as it is practical for the debtor company. We routinely handles liquidations for creditor groups and we often encourage owners of the defunct company to consider reacquiring the assets so they can begin again with a fresh start. It is not philanthropy, but simply the way to get the best price for the assets. But for the owners of the troubled business, buying back their own business can be like the rise of the Phoenix from its own ashes, or as one veteran of the "dump-buy-back" puts it, "If it's not a resurrection, it's certainly a reincarnation."

15

Bailing Out for a Soft Landing

A TURNAROUND requires bifocal planning: not only must owners look at the company's future, they must also consider their own. All too often owners and managers face devastating personal losses and liabilities in the wake of corporate collapse. The central concern of many owners, in fact, is not the fate of their business but their own personal exposure arising from business failure. It is one thing to lose a business, but quite another to lose a home, savings, and other personal assets because of business failure.

Thousands of distressed businesspeople express the same concern. Owners of the failing firm frequently look to diminish their personal losses and protect their assets from business creditors.

Everyone wants to bail out for a soft landing. So a personal loss-prevention program becomes an important part of the turnaround process. As consultants we often measure our success not by the business that may have been saved but by the personal wealth that may have been saved.

While executives of large corporations seldom suffer consequences greater than a lost job and bruised ego when their corporations fail, the owner of the small business typically has the business finances intertwined with his or her own finances. It is the excessive dependence by

198

the company on its owner's personal resources that causes so many personal bankruptcies to accompany corporate bankruptcies.

Fortunately, in most cases the personal losses are avoidable. Although it is not always possible to totally escape personal liability when a small business fails, careful planning can substantially reduce entrepreneurial risk.

The problem is, of course, that few small business owners adequately protect themselves. They incur needless financial risks when starting their business and incur still other risks once in operation. Once the company goes into a tailspin the owner may dig a deeper personal hole in an attempt to save the business. Inevitably it becomes too late to help either the business or its owner.

THE ROSE-COLORED GLASSES SYNDROME

Every new venture is started by an entrepreneur fueled by a healthy dose of optimism. Positive thinking does build empires, but full-time dreamers only see one side of the equation, never the "downside risk." They ignore the possibility of failure and the precautionary steps necessary to protect themselves against a less than prosperous future.

Realists, on the other hand, do not fall victim to the "rose-colored glasses syndrome." Instead, they do everything possible to reduce their risks. Realists understand and prepare for possible defeat.

Consider the dreamer who with boundless enthusiasm over plans to buy or start a business. He or she will spend hours figuring out the millions he or she is about to make but will not be sidetracked by asking, "What if I fail? What can I do *now* to reduce or eliminate my personal exposure? How can I start smart and best protect myself by hoping for the best but preparing for the worst?"

Recently, I supervised the liquidation of a large stereo shop. I had handled routine legal matters for the client and repeatedly pointed out several areas of personal vulnerability. I advised him to incorporate, substitute trade credit for some of his own investment, reduce his obligations on personally guaranteed debt, and pay delinquent taxes. But like most dreamers who only see the upside of business, he would only shrug and say, "What for? I've been in business nine years and business has never been better!" Unfortunately, about a year ago a large discount stereo chain moved nearby, destroyed his business overnight, and caused him to lose over $280,000 in personal assets. Had he taken the suggested steps to protect himself, he could have avoided personal bankruptcy and certainly would not have lost the many assets he worked many long, hard years accumulating.

My client's personal losses were predictable because I see the same mistakes made by businesspeople time and again.

REMOVING THE ROSE-COLORED GLASSES

The following sections describe the predictable pitfalls to avoid and the strategies to adopt when bailing out carries with it the hope for a soft landing.

Why a Corporation is a Must

"Starting smart" means choosing the correct form of business organization, and the corporation remains the greatest risk reducer of all as it protects its owners from the debts of the business. To go into business without the vital protection of a corporation is to needlessly gamble personal assets on the success of the business—a gamble based on very poor odds.

As basic as this may seem, the sad truth is that there are over 3 million businesses in America today that are not incorporated, and if the statistics of the past hold true nearly 2.5 million of these firms will fail within the next five years, jeopardizing the financial security of their owners.

Many businesses remain unincorporated because the owners, unsophisticated in the ways of business, simply do not understand the benefits of a corporation. Others rely on the advice of lawyers who are equally naive and do not fully appreciate the hazards of business. Still others are small service businesses whose owners cannot foresee liability problems and hence the need for corporate protection. But considering the many ways a business can create liability, size of the business or simplicity of operation provides few guarantees against lawsuits.

Still, a good number of unincorporated businesses are not of the kitchen-table variety but full-blown companies. Within the past year my law firm represented two failed hardware stores, one pharmacy, and several restaurants, none of which was incorporated. The pharmacy was a classic example of what commonly happens when the failed business is unincorporated, as creditors who were owed over $250,000 in unpaid bills in quick succession attached the owner's fully paid home, leaving him to ponder in his third-floor walkup apartment the most expensive legal advice he ever had—"Why incorporate?"

Swayed by over 20 years in the insolvency field, I believe lawyers who counsel businesspeople against incorporating do their clients a great disservice. Too many business books do an equal disservice by suggesting the small organizational expense or added paperwork of incorporating are disadvantages that might outweigh the advantages of the limited liability protection it affords. Incorporation should be looked at as just another form of insurance. It may cost $300–400 to initially incorporate and another $300 a year to keep records, but when those modest premiums protect personal assets it is unquestionably the best insurance available today.

Even if the business is presently unincorporated, it may not be too late to incorporate and gain its essential protection. I recently observed a skillful play of a nonincorporated owner of a hardware store who was in trouble with over $50,000 in bills. His attorney incorporated the business, transferring all the assets to the corporation, subject to its debt. Those debts that were personally incurred by the owner were, of course, paid first and when the business recently failed the only existing debts were those incurred by the corporation and for which the owner had no personal liability. His advice? "If you are not incorporated, run, don't walk to your lawyer. Everything you own may depend upon it."

Never Put All Your Eggs in One Basket

If one corporation is good, two can be better. If multiple businesses are involved, each business may be set up as a separate corporation so the failure of one will not threaten the others.

Many companies fail because they put all their eggs in one corporate basket. For example, a company may start out with one retail store and grow to three successful units. But its fourth store may turn out to be a failure, bringing down with it the prosperous units. Since the laws of probability hold that the expanding company will eventually take on a loser, it makes considerable sense to isolate it from the present winners.

I am now struggling to save a small corporation that owns two moderately successful restaurants. Unfortunately, it opened a third restaurant which was forced to close, leaving the company with a $90,000-a-year lease liability. Whether the company can absorb this loss is uncertain, but had there been foresight in planning, the restaurants would have been separately incorporated, and my clients could have mailed the landlord the keys to the $90,000-a-year location without further concern.

When planning the organizational structure, too much attention is often paid to the tax aspects and too little to the question of burdensome liabilities, the mistakes that are an inevitable part of growth, and the use of separate corporations to segregate the problems from the profit makers.

There are also too many cases where the operating company owns—and therefore places at risk—assets that are best owned by other entities and leased back to the operating company.

Real estate offers a common example. Recently one of the choicest parcels of Cape Cod property was auctioned off with the other assets of a defunct restaurant. The restaurant itself had liabilities of $200,000 against equipment worth no more than $30,000. However, the owner had made a serious mistake. When he purchased the real estate he had the restaurant corporation take title to it. There sat a beautiful waterfront building with a value of $250,000 and a low mortgage of $60,000, ready to satisfy creditor claims.

"Starting smart" in this case would have the real estate owned personally by the principals or perhaps through a separate real estate trust or corporation. The real estate could then be leased to the restaurant corporation, thereby protecting it from the business creditors.

We frequently redeploy assets for corporate clients. For example, one of our clients was ready to start a printing plant by investing $60,000 for a high-speed press. Rather than have the corporation own the equipment, we recommended the owner put it in his own name and lease it back to the corporation. Five years later the printing plant folded with debts in excess of $100,000. All our client had to do was go in and repossess his equipment, which he now leases to another printing plant for $15,000 a year.

Personal ownership and leasebacks can create tax advantages when structured properly, but the protection this technique provides can be far more significant.

If a corporation owns real estate, high-cost equipment, or perhaps even intangible assets such as a patent or trademark, then "starting smart" may mean personal, not corporate, ownership of these valuable assets.

Small Investments Mean Small Losses

The third most common error occurs when owners invest too much of their own capital in the business. Capital invested, is, of course, capital at risk; therefore, "starting smart" means investing as little as possible and constantly measuring the risk/benefit ratio to justify further investments.

Many people argue against "starving the business," claiming undercapitalization is a primary reason for business failure. I also refer to the problems of undercapitalization throughout this book, but in reality undercapitalization is simply a catch-all term that means the business fails to generate sufficient profits and cash flow to cover its debt. This can be corrected in many ways other than adding more capital, as we see in the number of successful leveraged buyouts and start-ups that have become so popular in the past decade.

By the same token, an excessive investment in an unproven or faltering business does nothing but buy more time before the continuing losses consume the investment. As I also warn throughout this book, too many owners make the recurring mistake of throwing more and more money at their problems and then end up wondering why they lost so much money.

There are countless ways to reduce investment, hundreds of which appear in my book *Starting on a Shoestring* (Wiley, 1984). There is one important message in that book worth repeating here: "It's easy to add cash to a business if it is doing well, but it's nearly impossible to get the cash back out if it isn't."

Protect Your Investment

Why are so many small businesses improperly financed?

Typically an owner invests a sum of money to buy or start the business, characterizing the investment as either equity (for the corporate shares) or debt (a loan to the corporation). In either case the failure of the business may mean a total loss of investment as creditors must be fully paid before the owner can recoup his or her investment.

However, owners can better protect their investment by lending the corporation most of the money and having it secured by a mortgage on company assets. A smaller amount can be allocated to the purchase of shares, which would remain capital at risk. For example, assume an owner decides to capitalize the business for $100,000. The owner may use $20,000 to buy the shares and structure the $80,000 as a loan. The $80,000 may be pledged to a bank to back up its loan to the company for the same $80,000, with the bank holding the mortgage on the assets as primary collateral. If the business turns sour the bank would be entitled to the proceeds from liquidating its assets, and, of course, once the bank is repaid the bank will release your $80,000 held, as additional collateral. The bottom line is that the owner's $80,000 has the optimum protection possible because it is first in line—not last in line—to be satisfied from business assets.

It is not advisable, however, for owners to make a direct loan to their corporation because bankruptcy courts may nullify a loan made by stockholders to instead protect "arms'-length" creditors who are entitled to priority. For that reason it is more sound to have a bank or other intermediary act as the actual lender.

The stockholder-financed loan not only helps protect the investment but gives the stockholder a measure of control over the corporation to the extent he or she can influence the lender. A bank, for example, may be quite receptive to taking direction from a stockholder of the business when the loan is backed up by the stockholder's savings passbook.

There is, of course, nothing wrong in a stockholder structuring his or her investment in such a way that his or her economic interests are best safeguarded, even when at the expense of general creditors. There are many variations on this same theme used each and every day by sophisticated business people who realize they must properly structure their investment in the company if it is to be adequately protected.

SIDESTEPPING COSTLY GUARANTEES

Personal guarantees for corporate obligations are another major trouble spot.

Owners of small businesses are constantly asked to personally guarantee corporate obligations. The extent to which they do it reduces the usefulness of the corporation as an insulator of personal liability. Frequently the owner cannot avoid extensive personal liability—or even bankruptcy—because so many corporate obligations are personally guaranteed.

Reducing entrepreneurial risk requires a two-pronged approach to guarantees: (1) using strategies to avoid guarantees, and (2) knowing how to escape liability on the few guarantees that may be inevitable. Personal liability on guarantees may be kept to the absolute minimum with caution and common sense. First, remember that just because one prospective supplier demands a guarantee does not mean they all will. A guarantee is only a bargaining point when considering a new supplier, and most suppliers will extend some credit to the corporation even when the guarantee is refused. If the supplier insists on a guarantee, shop around for a supplier with a more lenient credit policy. Understand the creditor's position and work with it to reduce its risk so it will be willing to forego the guarantee. Without a personal guarantee the supplier may be un-willing to ship a $20,000 order but may risk a $10,000 order. Alternatively, offer to secure the credit with a mortgage on business assets. If you must supply a guarantee, negotiate a partial or limited guarantee instead of a full guarantee. Further, avoid a guarantee on past indebtedness when a guarantee of only future credit is acceptable, and always limit the amount of the guarantee to an amount that represents an acceptable risk. Make it an unshakable policy never to guarantee an existing corporate debt. There is nothing to be gained. If the account goes into arrears or the business show signs of decline, credit managers will plead, promise, threaten, and cajole for guarantees. But do not risk personal assets to back up now questionable debts. Do not be victimized by the mistaken belief the business will make good on the obligations. Once a company runs into serious financial difficulty it seldom revives itself to the point that creditors are fully paid.

Banks and other institutional lenders rarely lend to small businesses without personal guarantees from the principals, so it cannot be avoided if bank financing is needed. But it can be done the correct way. First, make certain the bank is collateralized with business assets to reduce personal liability only to the deficiency rather than the full amount of the loan. Second, make certain the liquidation value of the assets is sufficient to cover the loan, thereby avoiding a deficiency and personal liability.

If there are partners in the venture make certain they also become bound on any guarantee. They enjoy the benefits of the business so why not the risk? I recount the sad story of a 25-percent owner of a restaurant who guaranteed $86,000 in bills without "bothering" his other three part-ners, leaving him to satisfy the debt as the partners safely walked away from the defunct business. Select partners also on their financial strength and ability to satisfy their share of the guarantee obligations. A creditor will most actively chase the guarantors with the "deepest pockets," and it can be a pleasant feeling to know a partner's pockets are as deep as your own.

When I was in law school I had a cantankerous but wise professor. He always defined a guarantor as an "idiot with a fountain pen." Twenty-five years and 2000 cases later, I must confess that more times than not his definition fits.

Although there are undoubtedly countless businesses built on the strength of their owners' guarantees, these are not the owners we usually see. More often our clients spend sleepless nights wondering how to extricate themselves from their guarantees before the business collapses. There are several important steps to be taken. Begin by verifying which obligations are guaranteed. Many people never realized they signed a guarantee with their original order form or credit application. A sound policy is to seek confirmation from each creditor that no guarantees exist, requesting copies of any that do. Guarantees can always be terminated as to future credit, and all such guarantees should be revoked to prevent further liability once the condition of the company falters.

Start an active paydown program on the debts that are personally guaranteed. The objective, of course, is to have these debts fully satisfied before the company folds. We will often keep a business operating for months only to apply all available cash flow toward the reduction of guaranteed debt. The owner's cooperation in working down the debt can have enormous benefit to a creditor and it may justify negotiating a release of any remaining liability in exchange for that cooperation. For example, one of our clients is now working to convert over $200,000 in raw material into finished furniture which can then be sold for over $800,000, to help satisfy the bank's $1.5 million loan. In return for my client's cooperation in increasing the value of the collateral, the bank agreed to release him from his guarantee, which, backed by modest personal assets, had far lesser value to the bank.

This is a most important point to remember. Secured lenders typically need an owner's cooperation if they are to realize as much as they can from the collateral, and that cooperation must always be coupled with concessions to reduce personal exposure. But this must be negotiated in advance when the creditor most needs the owner's assistance.

If a creditor or lender is unwilling to grant guarantee concessions for cooperation, it conversely may be more responsive to an action that can threaten to reduce the collateral value. For example, a threatened Chapter 11 filing, which to the lender means certain delay in foreclosure and the possibility of diminished collateral, is always a bargaining chip. Quite often lenders decide that their immediate ability to retake the collateral has a greater value than does the illusive guarantee.

Many other concessions can be granted a creditor in return for tearing up a guarantee. A mortgage on business assets may easily have greater value. Will the creditor accept returned goods? Will the creditor settle for immediate payment of a far smaller amount? The time to negotiate these alternatives is, of course, when there is still a business ready to provide the bargaining chips.

AVOIDING TAX TROUBLES

Possibly the most serious consequences of the failed business are the tax liabilities for which the officers of the corporation become personally liable.

Unpaid taxes and the bankrupt business commonly go hand-in-hand as the cash-hungry business uses withholding taxes, sales and use tax, and other collected "trust" taxes for operating expenses.

The stories are legion of business owners who have spent years paying the tax obligations of their defunct business. One of my less fortunate clients was the treasurer of a large shoe manufacturing firm that closed owing the IRS over $300,000 in unpaid withholding taxes. This came much to my client's surprise as he primarily worked the sales end of the business. Nevertheless we are still uncertain how successful we will be in saving his expensive home from the tax collector.

Corporate officers (the president and treasurer) are automatically responsible for unpaid "trust" taxes—withholding taxes deducted from the employees' gross pay. There is no personal responsibility for the nontrust portion—the taxes contributed by the business as the employer. There may also be corresponding liability for state withholding taxes, sales, meals, and similar taxes, which should be checked with local counsel.

It goes without question that an ounce of prevention is worth a pound of cure, and the troubled business is well advised to give tax payments priority over every other type of obligation. The tax collector is less forgiving, and has considerably greater power than does any other creditor. The important rule then is to stay current on all taxes and avoid falling further behind on already delinquent taxes in order to obtain cooperation from the taxing agencies for extended payments on the arrears.

Determine with an accountant or attorney the specific taxes that impose personal liability ("trust taxes") and concentrate specifically on the "trust" taxes for repayment. This will require earmarking each payment so it is properly applied only to the "trust" taxes rather than the taxes for which there is no personal liability. Without specifying the allocation of payment, the IRS automatically applies it to nontrust taxes, so they can collect remaining taxes from the principals.

There can be corresponding liability on others within the organization who have the authority and responsibility to pay taxes. Comptrollers, bookkeepers, and others who sign checks are advised to withdraw from positions creating tax responsibility at the first sign of delinquency. Subordinates who issue checks on the authority of superiors should also obtain affidavits stating their limited authority.

In recent years the IRS has become far more aggressive in collecting delinquent trust taxes. Although the Internal Revenue Code provides that the IRS must first exhaust its ability to collect from the employer before it can proceed to collect from the officers, the IRS now moves against the officers with little delay and far more aggressiveness.

Moreover, the IRS has apparently expanded its interpretation of who can be liable for unpaid taxes. There is a case of a consultant to a company who was held liable for the client's overdue taxes in excess of $70,000. The IRS argued the consultant was a co-signer on the checking account (although he never signed a check nor had any real authority to), which was sufficient to create tax liability. The case is now on appeal.

While technically the failure to pay over collected taxes is a criminal violation, the IRS seldom prosecutes. However, this is not always the case at the state level. Massachusetts, for example, does prosecute larger or more chronically delinquent cases. Unpaid employment compensation taxes automatically subject the officers to criminal prosecution in Massachusetts, for example, highlighting the need to know the specific penalties that may be imposed on each type of tax and therefore the priority that each tax may deserve.

MORE HIDDEN LIABILITIES TO WATCH FOR

There are an endless number of claims that can follow principals of the troubled company home long after the business closes its doors. While we have mentioned the most obvious problems, and can never hope to cover the many other pitfalls, there are nevertheless other sources of liability that frequently occur.

Bad Checks

Most states impose civil or criminal penalties on the maker of a bad check. Therefore, all outstanding checks should be paid before the business is terminated and this is particularly important on checks issued for COD purchases as these transactions are specifically protected by the bad check laws in virtually every state.

Unpaid Wages

The failure to pay all wages due can also subject officers to civil or criminal liabilities depending on state law. There may even be a duty to pay for severence pay, accrued vacation, and other "earned" time. Check with your attorney to determine the specific obligations and penalties.

Fraud Claims

There are two common situations where fraud claims arise. The first is the claim of creditors that they relied on fraudulent financial statements to extend credit to the defunct company. Even when the statements were reasonably accurate, the creditor may press the claim as the only hope for any recovery. But often financial statements or credit information given to creditors are not accurate. The owner may simply guess or wildly approximate what the right numbers should be, thereby creating something bright from a bleak situation.

Since the accuracy of a financial statement is neither easily challenged nor easily proven, it is best avoided altogether. For that reason it is unwise to issue financial statements if there can be any doubts as to the ability of the company to pay its bills.

The second frequent claim is that the owners diverted, concealed, or misappropriated business assets. This, of course, can be a serious charge and can also give rise to criminal prosecution under the bankruptcy laws.

Creditors often question the honesty of management when goods are transferred from the debtor company to other entities. The owner of a small retail chain may, for example, redistribute merchandise between stores. Creditors are certainly justified in their concern when the stores are separately incorporated and one store fails after relieving itself of a quantity of inventory, recently shipped to another store against which the creditors have no recourse. Because creditors can misinterpret even the most innocent business transaction it is best to curtail intercompany shipments or any transfers that may kindle their curiosity.

Insider Preferences

It is hardly surprising that when a business turns bad, its owners' thoughts may turn to recouping as much as possible on investments or to seeking repayment on loans or wages due from the company.

Much of this activity, while illegal, is done through "skimming" receipts that never show up on the books, thereby avoiding easy detection. In other cases the owner may keep accurate records of withdrawals or repayment that may bring claims for restitution or reimbursement after the business fails and is taken over by a bankruptcy trustee.

Repayment on loans or advances to principals within one year of a business bankruptcy, for example, can be set aside and recovered by creditors as an insider preference. One of our clients, for example, repaid himself $140,000 on a loan to his struggling business, prompting us to keep it out of bankruptcy slightly longer than a year so that it would be safe from recovery.

Grossly excessive wages may be viewed as a fraudulent transfer and a misappropriation of funds, as may compensation paid to relatives whose value to the troubled company may become questionable. Conversely, the company may disclose on its books loans or advances owed to it by officers or stockholders. It is quite easy to forget a $20,000 loan from the corporation made years earlier, but to the extent it is carried on the books the bankruptcy trustee will have little choice but to pursue collection. Principals, however, may be able to set off the loan against certain obligations the corporation may owe them, which should be attended to by the accountant well in advance of liquidation so that the books accurately reflect that no monies are, in fact, owed to the corporation.

THE DANGER OF DEEP POCKETS

No amount of caution can prevent at least the threat of personal liability or lawsuits stemming from the failed business.

Smart entrepreneurs, of course, go into business mindful of its risk and carefully deploy their personal assets to reduce exposure or to even become totally judgment-proof, frustrating the efforts of creditors to reach assets safely held beyond their grasp.

We can only wonder how business owners become so oblivious to their problems when we hear stories of how a bank attached a home or the IRS seized a personal savings account. Recently our law firm began representing a new client whose bankrupt business brought him a $80,000 tax lien and $200,000 in creditor attachments on his home and several parcels of income property which foolishly remained in his name long after it was obvious the business was in a downturn and personal liability was likely. Looking back, it was clear he could have easily protected these assets from his creditors through careful planning with a qualified attorney.

There is no shortage of devices used to shield personally owned property. A financial protection plan may include the use of family trusts, corporations, or transferring property to a spouse or other relative. My client, for example, could have effectively protected his home by use of the homestead laws available in his state, had he considered it in time.

The techniques for "judgment-proofing" are beyond the scope of this book, except to say the most important factor is the need for timely action. Owners cannot expect to incur substantial debts and then protect their property two days before the sheriff arrives. Every state has fraudulent transfer statutes allowing creditors to set aside transfers undertaken with the intent to place assets out of creditors reach. While the courts will consider who the property was transferred to and the consideration paid, they will even more closely look at *when* the transfer occurred. Therefore, transfers *before* the debt was incurred will be much safer than those attempted later.

Many people, however, do transfer property from their names in the face of imminent liability. Without doubt, many of these transfers effectively shield the property from less zealous creditors. For example, the IRS with all its enormous collection powers, seems slow to chase recently conveyed property. Creditors holding smaller claims may not consider the effort worthwhile. Arguably, there is nothing to lose by a late transfer, mindful that at worst the property will be ordered reconveyed, creating a "nothing to lose and much to gain" situation.

The far safer approach, however, is to intelligently plan how to protect your assets before going into business. Perhaps it is then best remembered that to bail out for a soft landing you must first take your parachute.

16

The Business Doctor

THIS chapter answers the most common and important questions businesspeople ask concerning the management and revitalization of their financially troubled businesses.

Q. As with most turnaround companies we are caught up in a cash squeeze. How can we decide which assets should be sold to raise cash?

A. Part of the turnaround process is an evaluation of the effectiveness of each corporate asset in contributing to the company's earnings and growth. There have been numerous turnarounds where a company with low capital availability has recognized that certain assets did not ideally fit the company's long-term goals. In these situations management should sell assets that can be put to better use as a capital injection into either growth opportunities or stabilizing operations.

Q. Should a company in financial difficulty consider an acquisition? Can an acquisition help stabilize the company?

A. In turnaround situations an acquisition may help in several ways: (1) by providing immediate cash flow, (2) by providing diversification, new products, or new markets to rebuild profits, or (3) to help the company build a new image.

A turnaround company cannot, however, afford an acquisition that will add to its problems. Therefore, the acquisition should be able to stand on its own managerially and financially so as not to drain the company's resources for its own turnaround program. Finally, the acquired company must fit into the overall strategic plan or mission. Even when an acquisition can support a troubled company, it does not replace the need to turn around the troubled unit so it can stand on its own. Therefore, the acquired company should serve as a temporary support and not a permanent crutch.

Q. We operate a large company with several hundred employees. Our company has been in difficulty for several years and is now in Chapter 11. What is the best way for us to monitor employee morale?

A. There are a number of things that can be done. Assign someone in personnel the special responsibility for monitoring and stimulating morale and motivation, beginning with the recruiting effort. Employee opinion surveys and exit interviews are also useful monitoring techniques. The best monitoring procedure, however, is the direct observation of employee attitudes by supervisors and key managers who in turn should constantly communicate the pulse of the organization to top management.

Q. What is the one most important step in motivating employees in a turnaround situation?

A. More important than monetary compensation is the importance of job recognition. Like the stonemason who thought of himself not as a bricklayer but as a cathedral builder, people appreciate their own contributions more, and, as a result, perform better as their understanding of their roles in the turnaround process becomes clearer. Employees must know how their individual efforts contribute to the whole, and they must also know how appreciated those efforts are.

Q. Should the president or CEO of a troubled corporation be given greater authority than a CEO of a well-performing company?

A. The CEO of the turnaround company may not need more authority but he or she does need more flexibility to respond rapidly to fast-changing events. Turnarounds are not easily managed in bureaucratic-style organizations and most turnaround leaders of major corporations rightfully insist on a relatively free hand in nurturing the company back to health. Perhaps the most important authority is to hire the best top management team the company can afford.

Q. What is the most important financial control for small and mid-sized firms?

A. As basic as it sounds, the CEO should personally sign all checks. Only check-signing can give top management the absolute control it needs over expenditures. Further, check-signing can give top management a much clearer sense of what is happening throughout the organization than can abstract reports. Notwithstanding strict budgets and rules on spending, management never realizes how many wasteful expenditures are made until it takes the reigns on the checkbook.

Q. I have heard that mathematical forecasting is increasingly used to predict bankruptcy. How accurate are mathematical forecasts?

A. Mathematical forecasts are 70–95 percent accurate depending on the forecast used and when it was applied. Mathematical forecasts can be quite complicated and are generally used only with larger corporations. *Corporate Financial Distress* by Edward I. Altman (Wiley, 1983) is the leading reference work on the subject.

Q. We are uncertain how many job cuts will be necessary for our company. Should we cut in stages or terminate as many employees as we think will be necessary at one time?

A. If at all possible surgery should be done in one step. It is very traumatic on employees to cut in stages. It is also generally best to cut too much, rather than too little. Most importantly, let your employees know that no further layoffs are planned.

Q. How important is bridge financing to the larger corporation?

A. Seriously troubled large corporations may need bridge financing to cover cash flow deficits until they can liquidate assets. But unlike small companies, the larger corporation almost always has assets to liquidate.

Q. To what extent does rapid growth cause financial difficulty?

A. It is a major reason since many fast-growth companies outrun their cash-generating capabilities. Of equal importance, they may expand faster than they can build a management team or essential controls. The turnaround strategy, however, is usually either to slow the growth rate, working existing capital harder, or reverse the process and downsize the organization.

Q. What steps can I take to develop a more coordinated and effective turnaround team?

A. I suggest these steps:

1. Keep the turnaround team fully informed about the current business situation, concentrating on facts and figures.

2. Map out specific goals for each layer of management and convince them the goals are attainable.

3. Pinpoint responsibility to each key manager.

4. Provide daily, weekly, and monthly formats to the management team.

5. Motivate managers through incentive compensation, performance feedback, and instilling pride in accomplishment.

Q. Can we terminate a labor union collective bargaining agreement under a Chapter 11?

A. A Chapter 11 company can reject collective bargaining contracts only to the extent the contract is overly burdensome and will prevent the company from effectively reorganizing. Unlike other contracts, the right to reject collective bargaining agreements is not absolute.

Q. At what point would a small company be considered to be in serious financial difficulty and in need of professional help?

A. There cannot be any hard-and-fast rule considering the many factors. However, a company that has more than four times the debt in relation to owners' equity will be highly vulnerable, particularly if the company continues to lose money. Professional help should also be retained whenever the company is undergoing more than a cyclical downturn and management is unable to turn the company around on its own. Obviously, the sooner professional help is enlisted the greater the chances the company will have to survive.

Q. What factors will determine whether a creditor is likely to be co-operative or hostile in a workout?

A. A creditor's position depends on its basic relationship with the debtor company:

> **1.** Has the relationship been historically profitable for the creditor?
>
> **2.** Is the debtor company likely to continue its relationship with the creditor?
>
> **3.** What is the size of the debt and the reduction or settlement proposed?
>
> **4.** To what extent does the creditor depend on the debtor as a customer?

For some trade creditors, the continued viability of the debtor company may be the primary goal and payment of the outstanding debt may be secondary. This will be particularly true when the debtor company is a profitable account and the creditor has confidence in maintaining a profitable future relationship. In such a situation, the adjustment of outstanding indebtedness represents nothing more than a temporary price adjustment to the seller, and must often be put into that perspective for a more cooperative creditor attitude to develop.

Q. How flexible is the SBA on a loan workout situation?

A. I have found the SBA reasonable. However, when the SBA only guarantees the loan, as is typically the case, the lender bank actually administers the loan and therefore sets policy. Often the bank will collect on the guaranty and turn back the loan to the SBA for handling, which may be preferable to the borrower insofar as the SBA can be more flexible. On large loans the workout decisions will be made by both the bank and SBA as the bank does have exposure for 10 percent of the loan.

Q. How lenient are lessors of equipment in a workout program?

A. Like other creditors, the leasing company will adopt a posiiton based on its available options. Those who lease property to the debtor company generally emphasize the importance of current payments. However, an overriding consideration in modifying the lease agreement is whether the leased equipment can be re-leased at the existing rate or whether the value of the equipment has decreased to the extent it cannot be rented again at the existing rate. This should be determined before negotiating with the leasing company.

Q. At what point does a bank as a secured lender overstep its bounds in controlling a debtor company?

A. Overreaching by secured lenders is becoming an important new issue in debtor-creditor relationships. Dominance by a lender over the management of the debtor firm can expose the bank to extensive civil liability and cause the bank to lose its rights to priority of payment over unsecured creditors. This is particularly true when the lender dictates who will be paid and otherwise controls cash flow, making what are traditionally management decisions instead of merely asserting normal lender controls. Admittedly, it is a fine distinction; however, most banks are becoming extremely cautious in overly involving themselves in the affairs of their troubled accounts, and wisely taking a more distant approach in the workout process.

Q. What is an assignment for the benefit of creditors?

A. This is another form of liquidation under state law. The company transfers its property to an assignee appointed by the company. The assignee then liquidates the assets and pays creditors using the same disbursement formula as used in bankruptcy. Assignments are generally useful only in small or simple cases, because the cost and speed of administration is significantly less than for a bankruptcy. Creditors who want a broader investigation into the affairs of the debtor company or seek to recover or set aside preferences to other creditors may convert the case to bankruptcy proceedings, which occurs in the minority of cases.

Q. Can creditors in a Chapter 11 case compel the appointment of an operating trustee to oversee management of the troubled company?

A. Creditors can petition the bankruptcy court for the appointment of an operating trustee when there is evidence of fraud, gross mismanagement, or the trustee can in some other clear way protect the interests of creditors. It is not, however, easy to convince a court to appoint a trustee unless for a very good reason since a trustee can significantly add to the costs of administration.

Q. What are the major benefits of a Chapter 11 reorganization?

A. Among the factors that may make a filing under Chapter 11 desirable are the following:

1. Need to stop foreclosure or seizure by secured lenders or taxing authorities.

2. Existence of a large number of creditors making an out-of-court workout impractical.

3. Need to bind a dissenting minority of creditors or stockholders who refuse to accept the plan.

4. Need to reject executory leases and contracts.

5. Need to obtain credit or borrowing using bankruptcy powers.

6. Desirability of using Chapter 11 to set aside preferences.

Q. If a company is petitioned into a Chapter 7 bankruptcy can it convert to Chapter 11?

A. A debtor company has the absolute right to convert a liquidating Chapter 7 case to a Chapter 11 at any stage in the proceeding. Obviously, it makes little sense to convert after the assets have been liquidated. A debtor company can even convert to Chapter 11 when it originally filed for Chapter 7.

Q. Can creditors propose their own plan of reorganization in a Chapter 11 case?

A. A debtor has the exclusive right to propose a plan for the first 120 days (or such extended time as approved by the court) and thereafter either the debtor or creditors can file a proposed plan. There are, however, various obstacles to creditors proposing their own plan. The first is that creditors' interests may vary and therefore creditors may be as hostile to each other as they are to the debtor. More importantly, the debtor may oppose a creditor's plan on the basis that the company cannot realistically comply with its provisions. A creditor's plan has little value unless management shares the belief that the terms can be self-fulfilling.

Q. We understand that turnaround strategies normally center around three actions: cost-cutting, revenue-generating and asset-reduction. When should each be used?

A. The decision is often based on pro forma cash flow projections and cash flow break-even calculations.

If a company is relatively close to its break-even point (70–80 percent of break-even) and it has easily identified overhead flab or high fixed overhead, then cost-cutting strategies are usually selected. However, if the firm's sales are between 30–60 percent of its break-even point, then revenue-generating and asset-reduction strategies will be needed for a successful turnaround. At the extreme, if the company sales are less than 30 percent of break-even, the only workable survival strategy is to reduce assets and significantly reshape the organization.

Q. What factors should we consider in evaluating a poorly performing division that is seriously eroding overall profits?

A. In your situation the hard questions include:

1. To what extent is the division a drain on the company's cash? Will it be so in the future? How much cash will be involved? Can the company afford the cash drain?
2. How much capital does the segment of the business tie up that could be freed for other uses?
3. What is the future profit potential of the division?
4. What capital will be required to rehabilitate the failing division?

Q. To what extent can we realistically reduce payroll costs associated with customer service?

A. The importance of the service component will depend very much on the nature of the business; however, I have found that managers who run service-related departments tend to encourage demand for additional services and to perform most services to a level of quality out of proportion to the actual need. In several of the companies I have consulted to I observed service-related overhead cuts of more than 50 percent without customer complaint.

Q. What percentage of companies that go through Chapter 11 or an informal creditor workout actually survive more than two years?

A. I do not know of any reliable statistics; however, my belief is that less then 40 percent survive for more than two years.

The principal reasons for turnaround failure are that the company did not chop away enough of the debt and failed to regain profitability. Even when both these objectives are achieved the company may go forward with inadequate cash flow. A turnaround is never really successful unless the company has fully regained solvency, profitability, and liquidity.

Q. What percentage of major corporations call in turnaround specialists to take over from a CEO during a turnaround?

A. Approximately 20 percent of major corporate rescues are led by turnaround specialists, although there can be varying interpretations of who is a turnaround specialist rather than a new CEO who happens to be skilled in turnaround strategies. The number of CEOs who are replaced during a turnaround are, of course, considerable.

Q. How necessary is it for a turnaround leader to have experience within the company's industry?

A. Prior industry experience is, of course, valuable; however, many impressive turnarounds were led by people with absolutely no experience within the industry. In these situations the turnaround leader must rely on the organization's existing management staff for operational matters, as the leader applies the turnaround strategies which are largely the same in every type business.

Q. Our company emerged successfully from a Chapter 11 two years ago and now we want to expand. Are there any general guidelines to follow?

A. Avoid bold moves in areas of the business where you are weak. If it is a big change involving hard-to-measure risks, test it on a small scale before moving out on a broader front. The soundest growth is organic, that is, it evolves from the strengths of the organization.

Q. My company owes me $65,000 in loans I made to it over the past several years, and because the business is doing poorly I plan to liquidate it within the next year. How can I best repay myself the loan?

A. Assuming the business will be insolvent with remaining creditors when you liquidate, you require a two-fold strategy: (1) try to keep the business operating (and out of bankruptcy) for at least one year from date of repayment—this will prevent a trustee in bankruptcy from recovering the repayment as an insider preference; (2) if you must close the business within the year, use a nonbankruptcy proceeding such as an assignment for the benefit of creditors where the insider preference rule does not apply. Considering the complex legal issues, you should, of course, rely on the advice of your counsel.

Q. Can I safely lend money to my corporation in Chapter 11?

A. Yes, if the loan is approved by the bankruptcy court and the court allows you a lien against the assets as collateral. Even in these circumstances you will want to limit your loan to no more than the estimated liquidation value of the collateral.

Q. I am the president of our corporation and my partner is the treasurer. Our business recently failed and the IRS levied my personal savings for $57,000 to cover unpaid withholding taxes. Can I recover one-half this amount from my partner?

A. In the absence of an express agreement, your partner has no liability to you. Unlike guarantees where one guarantor has the right of contribution against other guarantors, no such right exists with taxes. Of course, the IRS could have proceeded against either you or your partner, or both, but of course satisfied itself from the easiest source.

Q. Our firm is in serious financial difficulty and we want to recruit a top-notch comptroller, but the better-qualified candidates are reluctant to leave a good job for a shaky company. How can we recruit good people under our present circumstances?

A. Recruiting top people for the troubled company is always a problem. And to do it you will need to offer a more attractive compensation package, strong financial incentives if the turnaround is successful (bonus, stock, etc.), and possibly greater responsibility and title than the job candidate presently has. The reporting relationship also carries much significance to the candidate. The most successful inducement, however, is to convince the candidate of the long-term prospects for the company.

Q. Our company is completing its forecast for next year as part of our turnaround plan. How can we tell whether our projections are accurate?

A.   You probably cannot. Even stable companies have difficulty with accurate projections, and projections in a more turbulent turnaround company will be even less accurate. The rule of thumb, however, is to underpromise and overachieve. By beating the plan you will inspire greater organizational confidence and enthusiasm than if you fall short of the mark.

Q.   How effective is zero-based budgeting in a cost-reduction program?

A.   I believe zero-based budgeting is critical because it starts with the assumption that no expense is justified unless it can be shown to be necessary and justifiable in the amount budgeted. The cost-benefit relationship, the comparison of a cost with an evaluation of the benefit derived therefrom, is a useful exercise at this stage of a turnaround.

Q.   To what extent should top management be replaced in a failing company? Is it generally a good idea to make a "clean sweep"?

A.   Drastic management changes usually are not desirable in the short term and thus are not part of most interim plans. One or two individuals whose performance has been particularly deficient may be replaced; however, more far-reaching changes are difficult to implement quickly and are best phased in over a period of time to insure some continuity in management essential to the stability of the organization.

Q.   At what point in the turnaround should we decide whether to terminate a line of business or product line?

A.   Major decisions such as you mention are irreversible. If possible they should be deferred until the business is stabilized and a comprehensive strategic plan to return the company to profitability is developed. While drastic measures may be required for survival, every effort should be made to insure that long-term options are not unnecessarily foreclosed by the interim plan.

Q.   Can a mediator play a useful role if a debtor company and its creditors appear deadlocked on a plan of arrangement?

A.   Mediators are often useful as they have not yet been involved in the case and may provide greater objectivity as to the reasonableness of a plan than can either the debtor or its creditors, who may continue to be too adversarial to reach agreement. Further, a mediator knowledgeable in workouts can often suggest alternatives that have been overlooked.

Q. A failing furniture store is for sale in my area. The business has sales of $640,000 with losses of $70,000. I think the business has some turnaround potential, but it will take a new merchandising and pricing strategy. How would you value the business?

A. I would be more concerned with the terms than with the price. The business may head into bankruptcy under your management or perhaps you will turn it around and achieve spectacular sales and profits.

You should bargain to take over the shares of stock with a very small down payment, and any further payment on the purchase price should be tied to future profits. Essentially you want to ask yourself these questions:

> **1.** What is the stock worth (net worth) based on the actual value of inventory and fixtures (there is no goodwill) less existing liabilities? If assets are $200,000, but liabilities equal $100,000, the net worth is $100,000.
>
> **2.** You may agree to pay the $100,000 for ownership interest based perhaps on a $10,000–15,000 down payment. The balance may be payable over 5–10 years. Your obligation for the balance of the purchase price should be paid only from profits, and if the business fails, or does not achieve profitability, you would have no further liability on the purchase price.

Risk assessment is the important item. What do you have to lose if the business does not make it? Aside from hard work, you may lose your down payment and any capital you invested in the company. Measure those dollars from a risk viewpoint.

Q. Our corporation borrowed $30,000 from a neighborhood bank, and after two years of prompt payment we fell behind by 60 days. The problem is that without notice to me they took over $23,000 that I had on deposit in my personal name to discharge the note balance. What can I do about it?

A. You have some investigating to do. Check the documents you signed with the bank. Banks often incorporate in their "fine print" that if you owe the bank any money in any capacity and if the obligation is in default, the bank can, without notice to you, apply your personal funds on deposit to pay the defaulted indebtedness. This is the "offset" provision. You may have signed such a provision when you first applied to the bank as a depositor or when you borrowed for the corporation.

On the assumption that you did sign an offset provision and personally guaranteed the corporate loan, the bank was within its rights if your loan was in default. Your business loan must, however, be in default to the point where the bank can "call the note" and accelerate all future payments due. Since you were 60 days in arrears, you most likely were in the default period.

If these assumptions are correct, then you might try to renegotiate your loan and have the bank reinstate it on the basis that it continues to hold your funds as collateral security for the loan. You will lose the use of your money, but the business will once again be obligated to pay the note.

Should the bank refuse, then ask the bank to sell you the note on a "nonrecourse" basis instead of canceling it. In that way the business will pay you the future installments, and you will be able to take the money out of the corporation as a nontaxable "repayment of a loan," except for the interest portion.

Using one bank is seldom good policy, as you have discovered. It is unwise to give a bank to which you owe money that convenient ability to offset by using it as a depository bank.

Q. Our corporation has had financial problems and needs about $300,000 in working capital to improve operations and pay some long-term debts. The Small Business Administration turned us down and so have several local banks. One firm advertising as a "money broker" indicated to us that it could find us either a lender or an investor. How do these money brokers work, and what should we pay them?

A. Move cautiously. Money brokers are no different from other professionals. Some are worth every penny you will pay them, and others are outright frauds living off hefty advance fees without finding their clients a dime. You can however protect yourself with these 11 tips:

   1. Avoid large advance fees. Never pay more than the out-of-pocket costs. Some money finders ask for a $2000–$5000 advance payable on a noncontingent basis. I do not recommend an advance in excess of $500, as you should not have to pay on a retainer basis but should pay only for results.

2. Watch for guarantees. Trustworthy money brokers never guarantee they will find you the funds, and you should not expect them to. Once you hear assurances of a loan be wary.

3. Check the firm thoroughly. How long has it been in business? Who are the principals, and what are their backgrounds? Are any complaints lodged against it with the Better Business Bureau or law enforcement agencies?

4. Check references. A reputable firm will give you a reference list of other clients and you should inquire about the firm's track record.

5. How does your money finder approach your problem? Professional firms are very selective in the clients they accept. They will want to know as much as possible about your company before they will accept the assignment to find you capital. After a thorough analysis they should report the likelihood of success and the type of loan and sources proposed. A willingness to accept you as a client without prior research is a highly questionable practice.

6. What will your money finder do for you? Some simply mail a proposal letter to several hundred capital sources. Others will work with you in developing a workable and comprehensive business plan and then present it to the few best sources for your situation. Discuss exactly how they will present your company and to what type of lender.

7. What type of loan can you expect? Money finders do not usually deal with conventional lenders. You may find that the only loans they can obtain require interest payments of 24–36 percent a year. Determine this in advance to avoid chasing loans that are unacceptable to you.

8. Are their fees reasonable? Most money finders work on a sliding scale percentage. A typical agreement may provide for a 5 percent commission on the first $100,000 scaled down to 0.5 percent on a $1 million loan. Money finders have no standard rate, but a commission of 2–3 percent is average.

9. Watch hidden costs. Will you be obligated to pay for development of the business plan, mailing costs, travel, computer time, or any other fees or expenses?

10. Your money finder may want an exclusive arrangement. An "exclusive agency" contract for 90 days is reasonable, but you should retain the right to obtain your own financing in competition with the money finder.

11. The contract should provide that you can reject any loan proposed and that you will not be liable for commissions until the proceeds of any accepted loan are received. Never pay on mere acceptance of the loan as many loans do not go through. When you receive the money, the broker will receive his or her agreed-upon fee.

Money brokers are particularly active in working with financially troubled businesses, and because these companies are most desperate for financing they are the firms most likely to fall victim to unscrupulous practices.

Q. Our printing plant is in financial difficulty and owes a local bank over $100,000, and we are delinquent by 3 months in our payments. The bank is threatening foreclosure on the chattel mortgage (security agreement). Does it have to go to court to foreclose, and what can be do to stop it?

A. In most states, a secured lender does not have to go to court to foreclose; however, the steps a lender must take include:

1. The lender must notify you of the intent to foreclose, the balance owed, why the loan is in default, and when the lender will take possession of the collateral. The notice must also tell you your rights to pay the note and stop the foreclosure.

2. The lender must then take physical possession of the collateral, and can take whatever steps are necessary to protect it, either removing it or padlocking the entire premises if the collateral consists of all business assets.

3. The next step is to advertise the collateral for sale. The lender must notify you of the day and place for any intended sale so that you can be present to protect your interests. The security agreement will often specify the amount of time that must transpire before the sale.

4. The collateral must be sold in a "commercially reasonable" manner. This means either a public auction conducted by a qualified auctioneer and reasonable advertising of the sale or a private sale without auction. If a private sale, the lender will establish by appraisal that the sale price is in excess of what could be obtained by public auction.

5. The foreclosure may be terminated any time prior to the sale by paying the loan in full, including costs and attorneys' fees. Upon sale, however, you lose the rights to the collateral.

6. Any sale surplus over the loan must be returned. However, if the collateral is sold for less, you will be liable for the deficiency.

Practical steps that may be successful in stopping the foreclosure include:

1. Negotiate with the lender. Foreclosure should only come about if you cannot pay the loan or when the lender will be jeopardized by delay in foreclosing on the collateral.

2. If negotiating a loan extension is unsuccessful, try to convince the lender to sell only part of the collateral, to the extent necessary to pay the loan. For example, it does not make sense to sink a business by foreclosing on $100,000 worth of collateral if the lender is owed $10,000. Why not isolate excess assets, receivables, or little-used equipment to satisfy the $10,000 and allow the business to survive?

3. There may be legal defenses to the foreclosure. If you can raise any legal defense to the loan or the loan balance (disagreement as to the balance owed, misrepresentation, breach of contract, etc.), your attorney may be able to restrain the foreclosure in court.

4. If other efforts fail, a Chapter 11 reorganization under the Bankruptcy Code will automatically stop the sale. If you file before the collateral is sold, the lender will have to stop its foreclosure proceedings and return the collateral. The lender can then petition the bankruptcy court for permission to foreclose, and the court's decision will then be based on whether the lender is adequately protected.

Many troubled companies are needlessly liquidated through secured lender foreclosure when various strategies are available to prevent foreclosure and create the opportunity for a more favorable loan workout.

Index